Paralegal Litigation:
Forms and Procedures
Third Edition

By Marcy Fawcett-Delesandri

Paralegal Litigation: Forms and Procedure, Third Edition contains everything a paralegal needs to successfully manage litigation. Written by veteran paralegal Marcy Fawcett-Delesandri, it includes model interrogatories, demand letters, sample motions, checklists and practice tips. This book supplies all the forms, pleadings, and instructions required for most types of litigation. In addition to the sample forms, there is comprehensive information on meeting with clients and witnesses, preparing exhibits, summarizing files and depositions, investigation, document control, and countless other time-consuming and crucial tasks. Wherever possible, this book includes information available on the Internet to make a paralegal's job faster and easier.

2004 Cumulative Supplement Highlights:

Newly added chapter containing discussion, forms, rules and agreements pertaining to *Alternative Dispute Resolution, Mediation and Arbitration,* such as sample:

- Agreement to Arbitrate—Contractual Issue
- Agreement to Arbitrate—Non-Contractual Issue
- Award by Arbitral Tribunal
- Form of Arbitration Clause
- Notice Regarding Alternative Dispute Resolution
- Order of Referral for Mediation
- Rules, Accident Claims Arbitration, and
- Rules, Mediation

and

D1227747

Newly added forms and checklists relating to *Initiation of the Suit* and *Trial Readiness and Settlement,* such as:

- Sample Civil Case Information Sheet
- Sample Notice of Disposition Deadline
- Sample Joint Case Questionnaire
- Sample Order Scheduling Conference
- Sample Pretrial Order
- Trial Book
- Trial Notebook Checklist

10/03

For questions concerning this shipment, billing or other customer service matters, call our Customer Service Department at 1-800-234-1660.

For toll-free ordering, please call 1-800-638-8437.

A WoltersKluwer Company

PARALEGAL LITIGATION
FORMS AND PROCEDURES

2004 Cumulative Supplement

PARALEGAL LITIGATION
FORMS AND PROCEDURES
THIRD EDITION

2004 Cumulative Supplement

MARCY FAWCETT-DELESANDRI

North Harris College

1185 Avenue of the Americas, New York, NY 10036
www.aspenpublishers.com

This publication is designed to provide accurate and authoritative information in regard to the subject matter covered. It is sold with the understanding that the publisher is not engaged in rendering legal, accounting, or other professional services. If legal advice or other professional advice is required, the services of a competent professional person should be sought.

—From a *Declaration of Principles* jointly adopted by
a Committee of the American Bar Association and a
Committee of Publishers and Associations.

© 2004 Aspen Publishers, Inc.
A Wolters Kluwer Company
www.aspenpublishers.com

ISBN 0-7355-4328-3

Printed in the United States of America

1 2 3 4 5 6 7 8 9 0

About Aspen Publishers

Aspen Publishers, headquartered in New York City, is a leading information provider for attorneys, business professionals, and law students. Written by preeminent authorities, our products consist of analytical and practical information covering both U.S. and international topics. We publish in the full range of formats, including updated manuals, books, periodicals, CDs, and online products.

Our proprietary content is complemented by 2,500 legal databases, containing over 11 million documents, available through our Loislaw division. Aspen Publishers also offers a wide range of topical legal and business databases linked to Loislaw's primary material. Our mission is to provide accurate, timely, and authoritative content in easily accessible formats, supported by unmatched customer care.

To order any Aspen Publishers title, go to *www.aspenpublishers.com* or call 1-800-638-8437.

To reinstate your manual update service, call 1-800-638-8437.

For more information on Loislaw products, go to *www.loislaw.com* or call 1-800-364-2512.

For Customer Care issues, e-mail *CustomerCare@aspenpublishers.com;* call 1-800-234-1660; or fax 1-800-901-9075.

Aspen Publishers
A Wolters Kluwer Company

SUBSCRIPTION NOTICE

This Aspen Publishers product is updated on a periodic basis with supplements to reflect important changes in the subject matter. If you purchased this product directly from Aspen Publishers, we have already recorded your subscription for the update service.

If, however, you purchased this product from a bookstore and wish to receive future updates and revised or related volumes billed separately with a 30-day examination review, please contact our Customer Service Department at 1-800-234-1660, or send your name, company name (if applicable), address, and the title of the product to:

Aspen Publishers
7201 McKinney Circle
Frederick, MD 21704

ABOUT THE AUTHOR

Marcy Fawcett-Delesandri received her B.A. in English from San Diego State University, and graduated with honors from the University of San Diego Lawyer's Assistant's Program. She began her legal career at the defense firm of Thorndal, Backus & Maupin in Las Vegas, Nevada in 1981 where she was intensely involved in the MGM Grand Fire Litigation for three years.

In 1984, Marcy and her family moved to Houston, Texas, and she applied her big case experience to the Continental Air Lines Bankruptcy case as a legal assistant for Dotson, Babcock & Scofield. As legal assistant to the firm's head litigation partner, she was active in assisting with the firm's move toward automation. She has worked extensively in personal injury, insurance defense, product liability, commercial litigation, and oil and gas litigation. Marcy has also been active in the Houston Legal Assistants Association, State Bar of Texas Legal Assistant Division, and the Legal Assistant Management Association.

In July 1988, Marcy left Dotson, Babcock & Scofield to accept a faculty position with the new legal assistant program at North Harris College in Houston, Texas. In addition to her teaching, she has been a frequent seminar speaker across the country. As an independent consultant to law firms and commercial entities, she has performed in-house training seminars and videos for their legal assistants and support staff.

Marcy makes her home in Clear Lake Shores, TX, with her family.

CONTENTS

Sections listed below appear only in the supplement and not in the main volume.

PREFACE

Paralegal Litigation: Forms and Procedure, Third Edition contains everything you need to manage your litigation successfully. Written by veteran paralegal Marcy Fawcett-Delesandri, it includes model interrogatories, demand letters, sample motions, and checklists and practice tips. This book picks up where your form file leaves off supplying all the forms, pleadings, and instructions needed for most types of litigation. In addition to the sample forms, there is information on meeting with clients and witnesses, preparing exhibits, summarizing files and depositions, investigation, document control, and countless other time-consuming and crucial tasks. Wherever possible, information available on the Internet is included to make your job easier and faster.

Clear Lake Shores, TX   MARCY FAWCETT-DELESANDRI

ACKNOWLEDGMENTS

Books are seldom written by the author alone. In this case, the actual writing of the book was secondary to the help and support that I received from the people who care about me. I want to thank both my family and my friends for encouraging me throughout my writing of this book and for their understanding during those times when my writing had to take precedence over my time with them. I want to thank Steve Scholl at Dotson, Babcock & Scofield, for his never-ending support and motivation of my professional development. I want to thank Brenda Turner, my secretary, without whose unselfish help, this book truly would never have been possible.

PARALEGAL LITIGATION
FORMS AND PROCEDURES

2004 Cumulative Supplement

CHAPTER 2

INITIATION OF THE SUIT

Page 42, add at the end of § 2.1:

FORM 2-2A
SAMPLE CIVIL CASE INFORMATION SHEET

Cause No. _____

_____ Plaintiff	IN THE DISTRICT COURT OF HARRIS COUNTY, TEXAS
_____ Defendant	_____ JUDICIAL DISTRICT

CIVIL CASE INFORMATION SHEET

This form must be completed and filled with every original petition, and a copy attached in every original petition served. The information should be the best available at the time of filing, understanding that such information may change before trial. <u>This information does not constitute a discovery request, response, or supplementation, and is not admissible at trial.</u>

Service must be obtained promptly. Notice is hereby given that, per Harris County Local Rule 3.6, any case in which no answer has been filed or default judgment signed FOUR (4) MONTHS from filing will be eligible for DISMISSAL FOR WANT OF PROSECUTION.

Type of action: ☐ Commercial ☐ Personal Injury ☐ Death ☐ Other

Check all claims pled:

☐ Account due	☐ Defamation	☐ Fraud	☐ Products liability
☐ Admiralty	☐ Disbarment	☐ Garnishment	☐ Post judgment
☐ Assault	☐ Discrimination	☐ Injunction/TRO	☐ Railroad
☐ Asbestosis	☐ Dram Shop	☐ Insurance bad faith	☐ Real estate
☐ Auto	☐ DTPA	☐ Malicious pros.	☐ Securities fraud
☐ Bill of review	☐ Employ. Disch.	☐ Legal Malpr.	☐ Sequestration
☐ Conspiracy	☐ Expunction	☐ Med. Malpr.	☐ Silicone Implant
☐ Contract	☐ False Imprison.	☐ Name Change	☐ Tortious Interfer.
☐ Deed Restriction	☐ Foreclosure	☐ Note	☐ Trespass
☐ Declaratory Judg.	☐ Forfeiture	☐ Premises Liability	☐ Workers comp.
☐ Other _____			

1

INITIATION OF THE SUIT

Has this dispute previously been in the Harris County courts?
☐ No   ☐ Yes, in the following court: _____

Monetary damages sought:
☐ less than $50,000   ☐ 50.001-$100,000   ☐ greater than $100.000
_____

Estimated time needed for discovery:
☐ 0-3 months   ☐ 4-6 months   ☐ 7-12 months   ☐ >1 year

Estimated time needed for trial:
☐ 1-2 days   ☐ 3-5 days   ☐ 6-10 days   ☐ >10 days
_____

Are you going to request Level 3 status?   ☐ Yes   ☐ No

If yes, please state your estimate for total hours of deposition per side: _____
and the number of interrogatories needed for each party to serve on any other
party: _____
_____

Name of party filing this cover sheet:

Signature of attorney or pro se filing cover sheet:

_____

Name printed: _____

Phone number:_____Bar No.:_____
_____

FOR COURT USE ONLY:

　　　Track assigned   ☐ Track 1   ☐ Track 2   ☐ Track 3

Court Coordinator _____ Date: _____

FORM 2-2B
SAMPLE NOTICE OF DISPOSITION DEADLINE

Cause No. _____

_____
　　　　Plaintiff

vs

_____
　　　Defendant

IN THE DISTRICT COURT OF
HARRIS COUNTY, TEXAS

_____ JUDICIAL DISTRICT

NOTICE OF DISPOSITION DEADLINE

To All Counsel and Pro Se Parties:
　Please be advised that the disposition deadline for this case is _____.
If you have not set and had this matter heard before the disposition deadline this
case will be DISMISSED FOR WANT OF PROSECUTION on that date without
further notice. Hearing dates may be obtained from the court (clerk/coordinator)
_____.

§ 2.1   INTRODUCTION

If you have any questions regarding this notice, please contact the court)clerk/co-ordinator) _____ at (   ) _____.
Thank you for your prompt attention to this matter.

_____

JUDGE

_____ District Court

FORM 2-2C
SAMPLE JOINT CASE QUESTIONNAIRE

Cause No. _____

_____ Plaintiff vs _____ Defendant	IN THE DISTRICT COURT OF HARRIS COUNTY, TEXAS _____ JUDICIAL DISTRICT

JOINT CASE QUESTIONNAIRE

This form must be completed and filed by plaintiff after conferring with all counsel and pro se parties. The completed questionnaire must be filed with the court by _____, or the case will be DISMISSED FOR WANT OF PROSECUTION. In the setting dates, the court will not consider the concerns of any party who fails to assist in completing this questionnaire. If you have any questions, contact the Court Coordinator, _____, (   ) _____. This form does not constitiute a discovery request, response, or supplementation and is not admissible at trial.

1. <u>Largest monetary claim by plaintiff(s) or counter claimant(s):</u>

   ☐ <$25,000   ☐ $25,000-$100,000   ☐ $100,000-$500,000   ☐ >$500,000

2. Are there any counterclaims?   ☐ Yes   ☐ No

3. Will addition parties be added?   ☐ Yes   ☐ No

4. Have all named defendants been served?   ☐ Yes   ☐ No

5. Will this case be tried non jury?   ☐ Yes   ☐ No

6. Estimated trial time: ☐ 1-2 days   ☐ 3-5 days   ☐ 6-10 days   ☐ > 10 days

   Parties disagree: Plaintiff _____ days
                        Defendant _____ days

7. Likelihood of experts other than treating physicians or experts on attorney's fees?
   ☐ Yes   ☐ No

INITIATION OF THE SUIT

8. Other information that may aid or affect the court in scheduling this case for trial:

_____

_____

_____

_____

9. NOTE: State and local guidelines call for trial settings in eighteen months or less.

(a) Suggested trial date: _____

(b) Suggestions for time needed for pretrial deadlines, if any:

   *joining new parties _____ months   *ADR _____ months

   *designating experts: *amending pleadings _____ months

   (a) plaintiff(s) expert(s) _____ months

   (b) defendants(s) experts(s) _____ months

   (c) Do the parties request a scheduling conference with the court?
      ☐ Yes   ☐ No

10. Name(s) of any attorney or pro se party failing to assist in completing questionnaire and reason for such failure

   :_____

   _____

   _____.

11. Date completed: _____

12. Signatures. Attach a sheet that includes the name, bar number, address, phone number and signature for each attorney or pro se assisting in completing this questionnaire.

_____

For court use only: Case type: _____ Track assignment: _____

FORM 2-2D
SAMPLE ORDER SCHEDULING CONFERENCE

Cause No. _____

_____	IN THE DISTRICT COURT OF
Plaintiff	HARRIS COUNTY, TEXAS
vs	
_____	_____ JUDICIAL DISTRICT
Defendant	

§ 2.1 INTRODUCTION

ORDER SCHEDULING CONFERENCE

To All Counsel and Pro Se Parties:

Pursuant to Rule 166, Texas Rules of Civil Procedure, you are ordered to appear at a Scheduling Conference in the (courtroom / court coordinator's office/ _____)

on _____ at _____ o'clock ___.m. Be prepared to discuss and set pretrial and trial dates.

If you do not appear, the Court will sign an order of DISMISSAL FOR WANT OF PROSECUTION or other appropriate order.

If you have any questions regarding this notice, please contact the court (clerk/coordinator). _____ at (   ) _____.

Signed _____, 20_____.

_____

JUDGE

_____ District Court

FORM 2-2E
SAMPLE ORDER SETTING STATUS CONFERENCE

Cause No. _____

_____	IN THE DISTRICT COURT OF
Plaintiff	HARRIS COUNTY, TEXAS
vs	
_____	_____ JUDICIAL DISTRICT
Defendant	

ORDER SETTING STATUS CONFERENCE

To All Counsel and Pro Se Parties:

Pursuant to Rule 166, Texas Rules of Civil Procedure, you are ordered to appear at a Scheduling Conference in the courtroom on _____ at _____ o'clock ____.m. If the attorney in charge does not attend, an attorney with authority to bind the client should appear. Be prepared to discuss all aspects of the case, including but not limited to, the following:

Service and addition of parties;

Discovery completed, discovery remaining, discovery issues or disputes;

Settlement and ADR;

Dispositive motions, pleas, special appearances, abatements, pending motions;

INITIATION OF THE SUIT

Any issue that may impact preparation or trial, such as health problems, vacations or religious holidays of counsel, witnesses and parties;

Other issues such as companion cases, bankruptcy or receiverships.

If you do not appear, the court will sign an order of DIAMISSAL FOR WANT OF PROSECTUION or other appropriate order.

If you have any questions regarding this notice, please contact the court (clerk/coordinator), _____ at ( ) _____.

Signed _____, 20_____.

_____
JUDGE

_____ District Court

Page 50, add at end of § 2.6:

FORM 2–6A
SAMPLE ORDER AUTHORIZING APPLICANT AS
A PRIVATE PROCESS SERVER (TEXAS)

IN RE: APPLICATION OF [name]	IN THE DISTRICT COURT OF [county] COUNTY, TEXAS [judicial district] JUDICIAL DISTRICT

ORDER UNDER T.R.C.P. RULE 103

On this day came to be heard the application of Applicant [applicants name] to be authorized as a private server of process issued from the _____ District Court of said County, Texas pursuant to the Texas Rules of Civil Procedure.

This Court has examined the application and affidavit of the said Applicant and finds that the said Applicant is competent to testify, is more than eighteen years of age, and will not serve any process in any suit in which Applicant is interested in the outcome of the suit or is a party. It is the judgment of this court that this application be approved in a manner consistent with the said Texas Rules of Civil Procedure.

It is therefore ordered that [name] is designated as an authorized person authorized to serve citation and other notices issued from the [judicial district] District Court of said County, Texas as described in Rule 103 T.R.C.P. The authority granted by this order is not delegable or assignable and expires December 31 of the year following the year in which the same was entered.

SIGNED this day [day], 20 [year].

_____
Judge Presiding

IN RE; Application of
[name]

AFFIDAVIT

BEFORE ME, the undersigned authority, on this day personally appeared, _____, the undersigned Affiant, being by me duly sworn on oath stated that the following facts are true and within his personal knowledge:

I, [affiants name], Affiant, being of sound mind, capable of making this affidavit and fully competent to testify to the matters stated herein, make the following representations to the Judge of the [judicial district] District Court to induce the Judge to enter an Order authorizing me to serve citations and/or notices issued from this Court pursuant to Rule 103 of the Texas Rules of Civil Procedure. I have personal knowledge of the facts and statements contained in this affidavit, and each is true and correct.

- I am not less than eighteen years of age
- I am an individual person
- I will not serve any process in any suit in which I am a party or in any suit in which I am interested in the outcome of the suit

I have not been convicted of any felony or misdemeanor involving moral turpitude in any jurisdiction.

_____
Affiant

SUBSCRIBED AND SWORN TO BEFORE ME by _____
on this the [date] day of [month], 20 [year], to certify which witness my hand and official seal of office.

_____
Notary Public

INITIATION OF THE SUIT

APPLICATION FOR AUTHORIZATION
AS A PRIVATE PROCESS SERVER IN THE
_____ DISTRICT COURT

NAME:_____

ADDRESS:_____

CITY:_____ ZIP_____

DRIVERS LIC. #_____ STATE _____
(ATTACH A COPY OF LICENSE)

SOC. SEC. #_____ DATE OF BIRTH:_____

PLACE OF BIRTH:_____

PHONE NO: WORK:_____ HOME:_____

FAX NO._____ EMAIL ADDRESS_____

EXPERIENCE AND EDUCATION IN CIVIL PROCESS:
_____
_____
_____
_____
_____

HAVE YOU EVER BEEN CONVICTED OF A FELONY OR MISDEMEANOR
INVOLVING MORAL TURPITUDE? YES____ NO____

IF YES,
EXPLAIN:_____
_____
_____

HAVE YOU EVER BEEN DENIED A LICENSE, PERMIT, OR OTHER
AUTHORIZATION TO DO BUSINESS: YES____ NO____

IF SO, STATE THE PLACE, DATE, CIRCUMSTANCES, NATURE OF THE
PERMIT OR LICENSE AND IDENTIFY THE AGENCY HAVING RECORDS
PERTAINING TO SAME:
_____
_____
_____

NAME, ADDRESS AND PHONE NUMBER OF A PERSON WITH
PERMANENT INFORMATION AS TO YOUR WHEREABOUTS AND
FUTURE LOCATION AND ADDRESS:

_____
_____
_____
_____

I, _____, having personally completed the foregoing application for authorization as a private process server, and do hereby swear, subject to the penalties of perjury, that the facts stated above are true and correct and of my own personal knowledge, and do further swear that I have read and am familiar with the provisions of the Texas Rules of Civil Procedure relating to the service of civil process, and am familiar generally with law relating to civil process. I do hereby swear to comport myself in all respects as an officer of the court in connection with the service of civil process, and to uphold the constitution and laws of the State of Texas in connection with my service in this capacity as a special officer of the Court.

_____
Signature of Applicant

SUBSCRIBED AND SWORN TO BEFORE ME this the [date] day of [month], 20 [year].

_____
Notary Public Signature

§ 2.12 Affidavits

Page 67, add after Form 2-16:

FORM 2–16A
SAMPLE TEMPORARY INJUNCTION

[PLAINTIFF(S) NAMES]	)	
Plaintiffs,	)	
	)	IN THE CHANCERY COURT FOR
	)	
v.	)	_____ COUNTY, [state]
	)	
[DEFENDANT(S) NAMES]	)	
Defendants	)	

MOTION FOR TEMPORARY INJUNCTION AND/OR
RESTRAINING ORDER

The [plaintiff], through the Division of Consumer Affairs of the Department of Commerce and Insurance and the Attorney General and Reporter, moves this Court, pur-

INITIATION OF THE SUIT

suant to Section [cite section] of the [cite statute] ("the Act"), for a statutory injunction temporarily enjoining the [defendant], its officers, directors, employees, agents, successors and assigns, and other persons in active concert or participation with the Defendant who receive actual notice of this temporary injunction, from engaging, directly or indirectly, in acts which are unfair or deceptive to consumers, including, but not limited to, the following:

(a)   Representing that goods or services have sponsorship, approval, characteristics, ingredients, uses, benefits or quantities that they do not have or that a person has a sponsorship approval, status, affiliation or connection that such person does not have [cite statute]; and

(b)   Engaging in other acts or practices which are deceptive to the consumer or to other persons [cite statute]. Specifically, the Court should order the following:

(1)   The Defendant shall not conduct the seminars scheduled for presentation at the [location] on [date], or any other seminars scheduled for locations within the [state] which were promoted using the same or similar advertisements as that which is attached as Exhibit B to the State's Complaint unless, prior to conducting such seminars, the Defendant provides reliable and competent medical and/or scientific evidence substantiating to this Honorable Court the following claims:

(A)   That a certain amount of weight loss can be expected by the individual consumer;

(B)   That the program is relatively or absolutely effective at reducing weight;

(C)   That the Defendant or any employee, agent and/or representative is a "certified hypnotherapist," given the [state] does not certify hypnotherapist.

(D)   That it is "safe" to lose a specified amount of weight using Defendant's weight loss program;

(E)   That supervision by a physician is not necessary for safe, fast weight loss of up to ninety pounds;

(F)   That weight loss is "guaranteed" as effective for each individual consumer in attendance at Defendant's hypnosis seminar;

(G)   That every individual is susceptible to hypnosis or that every individual will be hypnotized during Defendant's seminar;

(H)   That weight loss will not require calorie counting, starving, dieting, or result in cravings;

(I)   That weight loss will be "fast" or that weight loss will be attained faster or quicker than through other weight loss programs; and

(J)   That any consumers' damages are limited to attendance at an additional weight loss seminar.

Additionally, the Court should temporarily and permanently enjoin the Defendant from engaging in the following activities:

A.   Defendant shall not engage in any unfair or deceptive acts or practices in the conduct of its business and shall fully comply with all applicable provisions of the [cite statute].

B.   Defendant shall not conduct, participate, and/or promote any weight loss seminar in the [state] involving the use of hypnosis for the purpose of helping individuals lose and/or reduce weight unless Defendant, at the time of making any such representation, possesses and relies upon competent and reliable scientific and/or medical evidence substantiating that conducting such a seminar is in all respects safe.

C.   Defendant shall fully comply with all aspects of [cite statute] when offering a "bonus," prize, gift, award, incentive promotion or anything of value.

D.   Defendant shall not conduct any "bonus" drawing or offer any gift, prize or other item of value in a manner which would violate [state] law regarding lotteries.

E.   Defendant shall not directly or indirectly represent, state, solicit, promote and/or advertise that the effect of its hypnosis service is permanent, "forever," "once and for all," "keep it off for good," or term of similar import, unless Defendant possesses and relies upon competent and reliable scientific and/or medical evidence substantiating that the services do in fact result in permanent or lasting effects. If Defendant represents, directly or indirectly, that such results will be available to everyone, all, "you," or terms of similar import, the evidence must substantiate such claims for each individual.

F.   Defendant shall not directly or indirectly represent, state, solicit, promote and/or advertise that its hypnosis services are effective for everyone, all, "you," or terms of similar import, unless Defendant possesses and relies upon competent and reliable scientific and/or medical evidence substantiating that its services are effective for every person.

G.   Defendant shall not directly or indirectly, represent, state, solicit, promote, and/or advertise weight loss seminars by representing that the program is relatively or absolutely effective at reducing weight unless Defendant, at the time of making any such representation, possesses, and relies upon competent and reliable scientific and/or medical evidence substantiating the representation.

H.   Defendant shall not directly or indirectly, represent, state, solicit, promote, and/or advertise that it, any employee, agent and/or representative is a "certified hypnotherapist."

INITIATION OF THE SUIT

I.   Defendant shall not directly or indirectly, represent, state, solicit, promote, and/or advertise that it is "safe" to lose weight under Defendant's program unless, at the time of making any such representation or claim, Defendant possesses, and relies upon competent and reliable scientific and/or medical evidence substantiating the representation that the program is "safe" for each person.

J.   Defendant shall clearly and conspicuously disclose to consumers in the initial solicitation and again at the beginning of each weight loss seminar when representing, stating, soliciting, promoting and/or encouraging consumers to lose a specific amount of weight that they should be under the close supervision of a physician at all times.

K.   Defendant shall not directly or indirectly, state, represent, solicit, promote and/or advertise that weight loss is "guaranteed," unless at the time of making such representation, Defendant provides that the consumer's money will be refunded at any time or that the consumer may, at the consumer's election, choose to attend additional weight loss hypnosis seminars as many times as desired. The refund policy must be clearly and conspicuously disclosed in all solicitations, promotions and/or advertisements and at the actual seminars, and indicate that either option is fully available to all consumers without restriction.

L.   Defendant shall not directly or indirectly, represent, state, solicit, promote and/or advertise that everyone is capable and/or susceptible to hypnotism, or can be hypnotized, in any advertisement, solicitation, and/or promotional material, unless, at the time of making such representation, Defendant possesses and relies upon competent and reliable scientific and/or medical proof substantiating such claim.

M.   Defendant shall not directly or indirectly, represent, state, solicit, promote and/or advertise that weight loss will not require "dieting," "calorie counting," "cravings" or "starving" unless, at the time of making such representation, Defendant possesses and relies upon competent and reliable scientific and/or medical proof substantiating such claim. If Defendant represents, directly or indirectly that such claims will be available to everyone, all, "you," or terms of similar import, the evidence must substantiate such claims for each person.

N.   Defendant shall not directly or indirectly, represent, state, solicit, promote and/or advertise that its weight loss seminar will not require "dieting" and then promote dieting of any form in connection with the seminar.

O.   Defendant shall not directly or indirectly, represent, state, solicit, promote and/or advertise that weight loss will be "fast" or term of similar import, unless, at the time of making such representation, Defendant possesses and relies upon competent and reliable scientific and/or medical evidence substantiating such claim. If Defendant represents, directly or indirectly, that such results will be available to everyone, all, "you," or terms of similar import, the evidence must substantiate such claims for each individual.

P.   Defendant shall not limit or purport to limit any damages or recovery to which consumers may be entitled under [state] law. Defendant is specifically prohibited from restricting any refund or guarantee exclusively to attendance at another seminar.

The State's Motion should be granted because the Defendant has engaged in unfair and/or deceptive acts or practices in violation of the Act. In support of this Motion, the State relies upon the Complaint filed against the Defendant, the Memorandum in Support of Motion for Temporary Injunction and/or Temporary Restraining Order, and the exhibits filed simultaneously herewith.

THIS IS THE STATE'S FIRST REQUEST FOR EXTRAORDINARY RELIEF.

Page 70, add new § 2.12A:

§ 2.12A   Declaratory Judgment (New)

Occasionally, a plaintiff or a governmental entity will ask the court for an order clarifying or defining the rights of a party or parties in a document, contract, or imminent dispute. The case below is an example of a suite for declaratory judgment.

Universal Printing Co., Inc. v. Premier Victorian Homes, Inc.
2001 WL 170964 Tex. App.—Hous. (1 Dist.), 2001.

MIRABAL.

In this dispute over land access in the Houston Heights, a homebuilder sued neighboring landowners to prevent them from blocking an alley. The homebuilder prevailed in a bench trial. The homeowners appeal the trial court's judgment, awarding $10,000 in actual damages and $100,000 in attorney's fees. We affirm.

I. Case Background

The homebuilder, Premier Victorian Homes, Inc. ("Premier"), sued several individuals and a printing company (collectively, "the homeowners") to obtain and maintain access to land owned by Premier. Premier alleged the homeowners were intentionally cutting off access to three homes it was building. In an amended petition, Premier added the City of Houston as a defendant.

In its live pleading at the time of trial, Premier alleged civil conspiracy and common law nuisance claims and sought a declaratory judgment, permanent injunction, damages, and attorney's fees. The homeowners pursued a counterclaim against Premier and a cross-claim against Paul Gomberg, president of Premier, alleging trespass and seeking injunctive relief.

Following a five-day bench trial, the trial court entered the following findings of fact and conclusions of law:

INITIATION OF THE SUIT

FINDINGS OF FACT

1. Since January 30, 1998, Plaintiff has been the owner in fee simple of a parcel of real property and of all improvements on that property located in Harris County, Texas, more particularly described as follows:

   The North 25' of Lot 18 and Lot 19 of Block 303 Houston Heights Addition, Harris County, Texas (hereinafter the "Property").

2. Plaintiff purchased the Property for the purpose of constructing three (3) Victorian homes for resale to the public.

3. Plaintiff received building permits from the City of Houston to construct all three houses, allowing for alley access to rear-loading garages for each house.

4. All of the Defendants, other than the City, own property either on Cortlandt or Arlington that abuts the common 15' alley that runs behind the Property.

5. Plaintiff was prevented from gaining access to the alley by Defendants Universal Printing Company, Inc., Davis W. Claxton, Amy M. Ell, Matthew Kalisek, Alda Escobedo, as Independent Administratrix of the Estate of Reuben [sic] C. Martinez, Rabih S. Assaf, J. Linne Girouard, and Donald J. Pinckard (hereinafter collectively referred to as "Defendants") who had constructed fences in and/or maintained other obstructions such as automobiles and/or filed affidavits of adverse possession claiming ownership in a portion of the alley.

6. Because of the actions of Defendants, Plaintiff was unable to complete construction of one of the homes and thereby suffered permanent damages.

7. Because of the actions of Defendants, Plaintiff incurred attorney's fees in prosecuting its claim.

8. Plaintiff filed the above referenced cause seeking declaration of its rights in and to the alley as well as a permanent injunction, money damages, and attorney's fees.

9. The City of Houston was brought into the lawsuit as a necessary party to determine the respective rights of the parties *vis-à-vis* the alley.

   Should any of these findings of fact be deemed conclusions of law, then they shall be treated as such.

CONCLUSIONS OF LAW

1. Plaintiff's declaratory judgment action is maintainable.

2. It is declared that the alleys were publicly dedicated in 1892 pursuant to the map or plat thereof, and the alleys are public.

3. Defendants' properties are subject to the public dedication as stated in the original map or plat of the Houston Heights.

4. That ownership interest in the alley is subject to an individual's superior rights of ingress and egress in the alleys.

5. The Plaintiff has the private right of ingress and egress through the alley, including vehicular ingress and egress.

6. Defendants had a right to use the alley up until Plaintiff requested to exercise its superior rights to use the alley.

7. Defendants had no right to keep obstructions in the alleys after Plaintiff requested use of the alley.

8. Defendants' obstructions constituted a nuisance, particularly to Plaintiff.

9. There was a conspiracy among the Defendants to support each other to wrongfully maintain their fences in the alley.

10. Defendants entered into a conspiracy to keep Plaintiff from exercising its legal right to ingress and egress in the alleys.

11. Defendants' affidavits of adverse possession were perjured because when they filed the affidavits they did not know whether the affidavits were accurate or not; the affidavits were perjured because the Defendants did not have personal knowledge of the information contained therein; and the affidavits were erroneous and wrongful.

12. Defendants are jointly and severally liable to Plaintiff for damages in the amount of Ten Thousand and No/100 Dollars ($10,000.00).

13. The indebtedness of Defendants to Plaintiff for damages bears prejudgment interest at the rate of ten per cent (10%) per annum from March 19, 1998 until paid, and post-judgment interest at the rate of ten per cent (10%) per annum from November 13, 1998 until paid.

14. Defendants are jointly and severally liable to Plaintiff for costs of court.

15. The indebtedness of Defendants to Plaintiff for costs of court bears post-judgment interest on this sum at the rate of ten percent (10%) per annum from November 13, 1998 until paid.

16. At trial Plaintiff proved up reasonable attorney's fees.

17. Defendants are jointly and severally liable to Plaintiff for attorney's fees incurred by Plaintiff in the amount of One Hundred Thousand and No/100 Dollars ($100,000).

18. The indebtedness of Defendants to Plaintiff for attorney's fees bears post-judgment interest on this sum at the rate of ten percent (10%) per annum from November 13, 1998 until paid.

19. Plaintiff may put gravel or whatever material it chooses in the alley without following any particular City of Houston code or ordinance. No City of Houston code or ordinance requires any other material.

20. Should any of these conclusions of law be deemed findings of fact, then they shall be treated as such.

The homeowners bring five issues with multiple sub-parts, asserting the trial court erred by (1) denying them a jury trial; (2) denying a trial continuance; (3) awarding attorney's fees; (4) determining Premier has a choice in surface material for the alley; and (5) awarding damages.

II. Jury Demand

In issue one, the homeowners assert the trial court committed reversible error by denying them a jury trial. To make a proper jury request, a party must timely (1) make a written request for a jury trial, and (2) pay the jury fee. Tex. R. Civ. P. 216; *Huddle v. Huddle,* 696 S.W.2d 895 (Tex.1985). Here, the issue is whether the homeowners *timely* paid their jury fee.

INITIATION OF THE SUIT

On April 16, 1998, the homeowners demanded a jury trial in their first amended answer. Also on April 16, the homeowners tendered $105 to the court clerk (a $101 check and $4 cash). The court clerk did not credit any of the $105 sum to the jury fee. The case was set for trial on October 19, 1998. Counsel for the homeowners determined that, according to the district clerk's records, the jury fee had not been paid. Immediately after discovering that the clerk's records showed the jury fee was unpaid, the homeowners tendered a $30 jury fee. The next day, on October 20, 1998, the homeowners filed an emergency motion to place the case on the jury docket, which the trial court addressed at a hearing on October 23, 1998.

The reporter's record from the emergency hearing consists of extensive discussion by counsel and testimony by a deputy clerk. Counsel for the homeowners attributed all error, if any, for untimely payment to the court clerk's office. According to an attorney for the homeowners, he *believed and intended* that the $105 sum paid on April 16, 1998, included payment of a $30 jury fee. Although the face of the check did not contain a breakdown of the fees paid, counsel showed an annotation, made by the law firm, on the *check stub* (file-stamped by the clerk's office) that indicated payment of a $30 jury fee, as well as a $45 constable fee and $26 filing fee. Counsel asserted the check stub put the clerk on notice about the jury request and that the clerk's office was in error by failing to take affirmative action to correct any payment shortages with regard to the jury fee. Counsel also complained that the clerk's office had not mailed an itemized receipt to the law office, showing how the $105 had been assessed.

Before the deputy clerk entered the courtroom to testify, the trial court indicated it would not consider the non-payment of the jury fee to be clerk error if the homeowners did not pay enough money for a jury fee, as follows:

THE COURT: I'm not talking about the check stub. I'm talking about when you file a case, there's some fees that have to be paid and a jury fee is not one of them. So if you give them a check, they're going to allocate it to the fees that have to be paid.

THE COURT: Okay. I—I would not be impressed with an argument that movant didn't want to pay the fees they had to pay and intended to pay a jury fee instead. That—I wouldn't be [impressed] with that at all.

[COUNSEL FOR HOMEOWNERS]: I don't think there was any conscious decision making going on, Your Honor. That's what we're saying.

THE COURT: If the clerk assessed some fee that the clerk should not have assessed that would be enough to pay the jury fee, then I would say that then you've got a leg to stand on.

According to testimony by a deputy clerk, the $105 paid by the homeowners was inadequate to cover the jury fee after mandatory filing costs and constable fees were deducted. In fact, the $101 check issued by the law firm was inadequate for the mandatory fees, and that is why the person who filed the documents in-person had to pay $4 cash. The clerk also explained that its standard practice is to give receipts to people, rather than mailing them. Specifically, the testimony provided:

[CLERK]: It is required that they pay the filing fee for a cross-action and that's what we did in this instance here. If they had requested a jury fee and they filed a cross-action, a jury fee is considered a request. The cross-action is required to have a fee at the time of filing. So if we didn't do the jury fee, the money would have gone automatically to what is required to have a filing fee at the time of filing, which is the cross-action. So, if we didn't apply the money to the jury fee, it's because we had a cross-action that they filed and the money should have been for that. . . .

THE COURT: Tell me about those other charges.

[CLERK]: A cross-action is really $26. It's [sic] just breaks down the fee. The $45 is for citation, constable fee and the $8 is for citation. So the $15 and the $1 and the $10 fee is actually a total of $26, which is a filing fee for a cross-action. The $8 plus the $45 is $53, which went for the citations . . .

THE COURT: Okay. Mr. Grosz, did you guys file two cross-actions at that time?

[COUNSEL FOR HOMEOWNERS]: There was a—one cross claim and one counter-claim filed. . . .

THE COURT: So if they gave you enough money for filing the cross claim and filing the counterclaim, which would be $26 each for a total of $52 and they still had some money left over, how would you know to apply part of that to the constable fee? . . .

[CLERK]: The address and probably a service 29 form or a cover letter telling us they wanted that to go out and to be served upon that defendant. . . .

THE COURT: So you're saying the clerk should have chosen the jury fee and left out the constable fee and said, "Well, I know you wanted a jury so here, I'm going to do that"?

[COUNSEL FOR HOMEOWNERS]: We're just saying that that's how it was submitted and that was the intent. . . .

THE COURT: Well, the cover letter doesn't say anything about what you wanted. It says you're filing an original answer and counterclaim. . . .

[COUNSEL FOR PREMIER]: And in this case where the fee wasn't sufficient by the person—whoever came there in person and $4 was paid in cash so it appears that somebody was there knowing—I mean, they got a number of $4 from someplace and they paid [$4] instead of 34. Seems like they could have paid 34 and got the jury fee paid, too. . . .

[COUNSEL FOR PREMIER]: Does it appear that somebody paid in person here, that there was somebody standing there?

[CLERK]: No, it don't always tell if the person—if it's cash, it is in person. Okay.

[COUNSEL FOR PREMIER]: Does this show cash?

INITIATION OF THE SUIT

[CLERK]: It does.

[COUNSEL FOR PREMIER]: Does the person standing there need to ask for the receipt if they want a copy of the receipt?

[CLERK]: Right. Usually we ask them if they want to wait for their receipt and if they don't, we'll tell them they can pick it up in the case file or sometimes we mail it.

At the conclusion of the hearing, the trial court conditionally denied the emergency motion for jury trial as follows:

THE COURT: All right. What I think is that if the case goes to trial on this setting that it should not be a jury trial. So the motion is denied. However, if I do not reach this case on this setting, then I don't know if it will be reset for as much as thirty days or not but whether it is or not, I'll permit a jury on the next setting if we don't reach it on this setting and more than likely it will be thirty days anyway so that the jury fee would become good then. . . .

THE COURT: Yes, where is Premier in relation to the case we're trying right now?

[COURT COORDINATOR]: They are two out. The next case is the Foley's case, which is—they say they can get it tried in a day and a half.

THE COURT: Okay. So we have a case that we're finishing up for a day or two next week. Then we have another case that says a day and a half so figure at least two and you all might possibly be called to start on Thursday if everything goes as bad as I think it may.

On November 3, 1998 (15 days after the homeowners made the October 19 payment of $30), the matter proceeded to trial without a jury.

The homeowners first reurge the same argument they made before the trial court, that they timely paid the jury fee on April 14, 1998, more than six months before trial, and that any error should be attributed to the clerk's office. Although the trial court did not make express findings about these matters, in light of the court's ruling, we must presume the court concluded the homeowners did not pay any part of the jury fee until October 19 and that the clerk's office did not misapply the fees. *See Roberson v. Robinson,* 768 S.W.2d 280, 281 (Tex. 1989); *Wadsworth Prop. v. ITT Employment & Training Sys., Inc.,* 816 S.W.2d 819, 822 (Tex. App.—Houston [1st Dist.] 1991, writ denied). There is ample testimony by the clerk, as well as an indirect admission by counsel, to support these implied findings. See *Roberson,* 768 S.W.2d at 281; *Wadsworth,* 816 S.W.2d at 822.

Next, the homeowners urge the Court to apply a 10 day jury fee deadline under section 51.604 of the Texas Government Code, rather than a 30 day deadline under rule 216 of the Texas Rules of Civil Procedure. Thus, the homeowners assert, they were entitled to a jury because the trial began more than 10 days after October 19, the day they paid the jury fee.

The statute relied on by the homeowners provides:

18

Jury Fee

(a) The district clerk shall collect a $30 jury fee for each civil case in which a person applies for a jury trial. The clerk of a county court or statutory county court shall collect a $22 jury fee for each civil case in which a person applies for a jury trial. The clerk shall note the payment of the fee on the court's docket.

(b) The fee required by this section must be paid by the person applying for a jury trial *not later than the 10th day before the jury trial is scheduled to begin.*

(c) *The fee required by this section includes the jury fee required by Rule 216, Texas Rules of Civil Procedure,* and any other jury fee allowed by law or rule.

Tex. Gov't Code Ann. § 51.604 (Vernon 1998) (italics added).

Premier, on the other hand, relying on rule 216 of the Texas Rules of Civil Procedure, asserts the jury fee is due 30 days before trial. Rule 216 provides:

Request and Fee for Jury Trial

a. **Request.** No jury trial shall be had in any civil suit, unless a written request for a jury trial is filed with the clerk of the court a reasonable time before the date set for trial of the cause on the non-jury docket, but *not less than thirty days in advance.*

b. **Jury Fee.** *Unless otherwise provided by law, a fee of ten dollars if in the district court* and five dollars if in the county court must be deposited with the clerk of the court *within the time for making a written request for a jury trial.* The clerk shall promptly enter a notation of the payment of such a fee upon the court's docket sheet.

Tex.R. Civ. P. 216 (italics added).

The homeowners assert section 51.604 and rule 216 conflict, and that a statute prevails over a rule. However, we conclude the statute and rule are not inconsistent; instead, they supplement one another. Based on a plain reading of the statute and rule, rule 216 requires that a $10 jury fee be paid "not less than thirty days in advance" before "the date set for trial." Section 51.604, on the other hand, addresses additional revenue-enhancing or administrative-type fees that a district clerk shall charge in relation to the jury fee, and states those additional fees must be paid "no later than the 10th day before the jury trial is scheduled to begin." Sub-section (c) specifically states that the $30 jury fee *includes the [$10] jury fee required by rule 216.* Section 51.604 increases revenue to the clerk's office, but does not supplant the 30-day deadline imposed by rule 216.

We note that the $30 fee provision of section 51.604, sub-section (a), is separate from the 10-day deadline provision, sub-section (b). Also, sub-section (c) harmonizes the statutory fee and rule 216 fee by prohibiting the clerk from charging a $30 section 51.604 fee *and* a $10 rule 216 fee. Thus, to ensure a jury here, the homeowners were required to pay as follows: at least $10 as the jury fee, no later than 30 days before trial was set (pursuant to rule 216); and the remaining $20, no later than 10 days before trial was scheduled (pursuant to section 51.604). Because, as the trial court implicitly found, the homeowners did not pay rule 216's $10 jury fee 30 days in advance of trial, they did not timely pay the jury fee.

Having concluded that section 51.604 does not conflict with rule 216, and that the homeowners did not establish timely payment, we next consider whether the trial court properly denied the jury request. When a party does not timely pay the jury fee, the decision to permit a jury trial is strictly within the trial court's discretion. *General Motors Corp. v. Gayle*, 951 S.W.2d 469, 476 (Tex. 1997) (orig.proceeding); *Dawson v. Jarvis*, 627 S.W.2d 444, 446-47 (Tex. App.—Houston [1st Dist.] 1981, writ ref'd n.r.e.). However, even where a party does not timely pay the jury fee, courts have held that a trial court should accord the right to a jury trial if it can be done without interfering with the orderly handling of the court's docket, delaying the trial, or injuring the opposite party. *General Motors*, 951 S.W.2d at 476; *Dawson*, 627 S.W.2d at 446-47.

We first examine whether granting a jury trial would have interfered with the orderly handling of the trial court's docket. *General Motors*, 951 S.W.2d at 476; *Dawson*, 627 S.W.2d at 446-47. At the emergency hearing, the trial court expressed genuine surprise regarding the jury request and court docketing concerns, as follows:

THE COURT: I don't care how counsel for defendants allocated their money.

[COUNSEL FOR HOMEOWNERS]: Well, I understand.

THE COURT: If you guys have made a mistake, that's tough.

[COUNSEL FOR HOMEOWNERS]: That's what we're—that's what I'm saying, Judge. We're not—we're not disputing that. It was an inadvertent mistake, Your Honor, and the point is—

THE COURT: Okay.

[COUNSEL FOR HOMEOWNERS]: —under these types of circumstances where we made a timely request for the jury but just due to inadvertence failed to timely get the fee in, and once we discovered it, paid the fees.
  The cases are replete, Your Honor. It would be an abuse of discretion to deny the jury trial.

THE COURT: If I grant a jury, the only thing I can do is also grant a continuance for two reasons. *One, because I have to give the plaintiffs time, since nobody has been planning on a jury trial in this case, and the other one is because the Court didn't plan on a jury trial in your case.*

[COUNSEL FOR HOMEOWNERS]: Understood.

THE COURT: *And I always count on nonjury cases—I do not have a separate nonjury and jury docket but I count on the nonjury cases allowing me to complete the docket.*

Since nonjury cases always take at least a day and probably two days longer than a nonjury trial for the same case, it prevents me from reaching at least one other case and in this case, it would prevent me from reaching this case as well.

We're already a week behind on our docket, which is not your fault, but it does mean that we have less time to play with and—
(Italics added.)

Contrary to the homeowners' assertions, we conclude the trial court's stated concerns about delaying the instant case, as well as at least one other case, are understandable and legitimate. We are unpersuaded by the homeowners' reliance on *Dawson,* where the trial court had expected a jury trial up to the morning of the trial. *Dawson,* 627 S.W.2d at 446-47. We also conclude *Hardy v. Port City Ford Truck Sales, Inc.,* 693 S.W.2d 578 (Tex. App.—Houston [14th Dist.] 1985, writ ref'd n.r.e.), is inapposite. In *Hardy,* the party timely paid the jury fee. *Id.* at 579.

The homeowners, relying on *General Motors,* also assert the trial court applied "sham" reasoning when it denied them a jury. 951 S.W.2d at 477. As stated by the Texas Supreme Court, *General Motors* arose under "particular and unusual circumstances." *Id.* In *General Motors,* the court began the trial 26 days after the jury fee was paid, and after acknowledging significant discovery issues would probably cause multiple interruptions to the trial, with no expectation of reaching the heart of the case for weeks or months. *Id.*

To support their sham argument here, the homeowners seek to refute the trial court's expression of surprise about the homeowner's desire for a jury trial by relying on the following events:

(1) Two filed documents that reference a jury:

(a) on August 31, 1998, the trial court signed its standard trial preparation order, which included the statement, "Bring trial preparation report including proposed jury questions, special instructions, and all of the above to docket call"; and

(b) on June 24, 1998, the trial court signed an order granting in part Premier's motion for severance or bifurcation, filed June 15, 1998, which referenced a jury (the motion included language, "will confuse the jury");

(2) The trial court's statement during the jury demand hearing, "If you guys have made a mistake, that's tough"; and

(3) The cause was tried 15 days after the denial of the motion for jury trial and, when it was tried, it was tried "seriatim" on November 3 (Tuesday), 4 (Wednesday), 5 (Thursday), 9 (Monday), and 13 (Friday).

We are unpersuaded by the homeowners' argument. In the context of the entire record, these three isolated matters are insufficient, either individually or collectively, to carry appellant's burden of showing the trial court was not surprised and gave a sham explanation. The two jury references are minor, pre-typed references in documents that were filed in a case involving a very large clerk's record, and that were filed two and four months before the trial court's hearing on the jury trial. Also, the trial court's "tough" statement was isolated and casual. Additionally, it is undisputed the trial court reached the case on its then-current docket setting. Also, it is not uncommon for a trial to be continued on non-consecutive days—particularly with an intervening weekend and holiday (Veteran's Day), as here. Moreover, these events are especially over-shadowed by the trial court's ruling that it would allow a jury if the case was not reached during its current docket.

We next examine whether granting a jury trial would have delayed the trial of the case. *General Motors,* 951 S.W.2d at 476; *Dawson,* 627 S.W.2d at 447. The trial court's statement, set forth above, indicates permitting a jury would have delayed the trial and, for reasons already discussed, we take this statement at face value. Also, the homeowners did not establish any evidence to the contrary. Accordingly, the homeowners have not met their burden to show a jury would not have delayed the trial of the case.

Finally, we consider whether granting a jury would have injured Premier. *General Motors,* 951 S.W.2d at 476; *Dawson,* 627 S.W.2d at 447. At the hearing, counsel for Premier very clearly stated she was surprised by the jury request and would be harmed if the court granted the request, as follows:

[COUNSEL FOR PREMIER]: That's not the situation here is what we're trying to point out. We never thought that there was going to be a jury. In fact—I mean, we obviously—we filed findings of fact and conclusions of law. We checked prior to—we checked the—you know, we have subscriber access. We checked that to make sure that there was no jury fee paid.
We never relied on that fact. We didn't prepare for a jury. We're not prepared to go before a jury. It's more—it's much more expensive to have a trial before a jury than before the bench and we're not prepared to do that and because—

[COUNSEL FOR HOMEOWNERS]: Your honor—excuse me.

[COUNSEL FOR PREMIER]: The issues are very complicated. Most of them are legal issues. There's—there's very few fact issues involved and we think it's more proper before the bench. . . .

[COUNSEL FOR HOMEOWNERS]: I don't have any—I mean, I understand the Court's position on what it will do to the Court's docket but for them to stand here and tell this Court they didn't know about a jury trial when it's been a demand in every pleading since April the 14th is not accurate. . . .

THE COURT: I'm sorry. You don't know about a jury trial until the jury fee has been paid and it's a jury trial on the court's docket.

To refute Premier's claim of surprise, the homeowners reurge the same points to this Court that they urged before the trial court: (1) Premier was aware of the jury demand included in the homeowner's amended answer, served April 14, 1998; (2) in Premier's motion for severance or bifurcation, it argued for separate trials or bifurcation because a single trial "will confuse the jury"; and (3) Premier filed a motion in limine that included, "Permitting interrogation of witnesses, comments to jurors, or prospective jurors, or offers of evidence concerning any of these matters would unfairly prejudice the jury." Premier explained the language was boilerplate, the motions in limine were filed in response to the trial preparation order, and the proposed findings of fact and conclusions of law was evidence that Premier anticipated a bench trial.

Again, although the trial court did not make express findings about injury to Premier, in light of the court's ruling, we must presume the court believed that Premier did not expect a jury. See *Roberson,* 768 S.W.2d at 281; *Wadsworth,* 816 S.W.2d at 822. The trial court, as the trier of fact at the jury demand hearing, is the sole judge of the credibility of the witnesses and the weight to be given their testimony. *Nordstrom v. Nordstrom,* 965 S.W.2d 575, 580 (Tex. App.—Houston [1st Dist.] 1997, writ denied).

There is sufficient testimony by counsel to support the implied finding.

We conclude the trial court did not abuse its discretion in denying the jury request. Accordingly, we overrule issue one.

III.   Continuance

In issue two, the homeowners alternatively assert the trial court abused its discretion when it denied their motion for continuance. The homeowners' motion to place the cause on the jury docket alternatively asked for a continuance. The homeowners reurge the same complaints raised in their first issue. For the same reasons discussed in the preceding section, we conclude the trial court did not abuse its discretion when it denied the continuance motion.

We overrule issue two.

IV.   Attorney's Fees

In issue three, the homeowners assert the trial court erred in awarding $100,000 in attorney's fees because the attorney's fees were improper under the Uniform Declaratory Judgments Act ("the Act"), Tex. Civ. Prac. & Rem. Code Ann. §§ 37.001-37.011 (Vernon 1997 & Supp. 2001), and because the fees were not properly segregated. The homeowners do not complain about the sufficiency of the evidence to support the $100,000 sum.

A.   Declaratory Judgment

The homeowners essentially complain that Premier brought a declaratory action solely for the purpose of obtaining attorney's fees. It is undisputed the trial court awarded the attorney's fees pursuant to the Act. Therefore, if an award of attorney's fees is improper under the Act, Premier cannot recover any attorney's fees.

Although a court may render a declaratory judgment "whether or not further relief is or could be claimed," the Act may not be relied on to convert all actions into declaratory judgment actions. Tex. Civ. Prac. & Rem. Code Ann. § 37.003 (Vernon 1997); *see, e.g., Hartford Cas. Ins. Co. v. Budget Rent-A-Car Sys., Inc.,* 796 S.W.2d 763, 772 (Tex. App.—Dallas 1990, writ denied) (holding a plea for declaratory relief may not be coupled to a damage action merely to pave the way to recover attorney's fees). The homeowners assert the attorney's fees were improper under the Act for two reasons: (1) Premier's cause of action duplicated its injunctive cause of action; and (2) the declarations sought were moot.

There is no basis for declaratory relief when a party is seeking in the same action a different, enforceable remedy, and a judicial declaration would add nothing to what would be implicit or express in a final judgment for the enforceable remedy. *See Kenneth Leventhal & Co. v. Reeves*, 978 S.W.2d 253, 258-59 (Tex. App.—Houston [14th Dist.] 1998, no pet.); *Barnett v. City of Colleyville*, 737 S.W.2d 603, 606-607 (Tex. App.—Fort Worth 1987, writ denied). The homeowners assert that Premier sought equitable title and injunctive relief, rather than declaratory relief. Specifically, the homeowners assert that all the findings requested in the declaratory judgment pleading hinge on a declaration that the alley is public, and that same finding that the alley was public—was also essential to grant injunctive relief.

In their live pleading, Premier sought the following declarations relevant to the homeowners:

a. A declaration that the 15′ strip of land that runs north/south in the middle of the block and the entire length of Block 303, Houston Heights Addition is dedicated to public use to the City of Houston and is accepted by the City of Houston for public use;

b. A declaration that the Plaintiff has unrestricted right of egress and ingress to the alley in question;

c. A declaration that the obstructions in the alleys erected or allowed to remain in place by Defendant Property Owners constitute a nuisance and/or a public nuisance and/or purprestures;

Following the trial, as set forth above in the conclusions of law, the trial court granted the declaratory relief. The homeowners do not dispute the merits of the trial court's declarations.

The homeowners primarily rely on *McRae Exploration & Prod., Inc. v. Reserve Petroleum Co.*, 962 S.W.2d 676, 684 (Tex. App.—Waco 1998, no pet.), to assert that equitable relief, rather than declaratory relief, was appropriate here. Premier, on the other hand, relies on *Viscardi v. Pajestka*, 576 S.W.2d 16 (Tex. 1978), to establish that declaratory relief was appropriate. Neither case is dispositive. The facts and issues in *McRae*, which involved ownership of mineral interests following competing fraudulent acquisitions, and the cases relied upon by the *McRae* court, are not sufficiently similar to the facts and issues here. In *Viscardi*, although the court affirmed a declaratory judgment action that resolved an individual's right to use an alley, it did not address the issue of whether another cause of action was appropriate.

After reviewing all authority and the record, we are persuaded by a significant matter here—the existence of the adverse possession affidavits (which were recorded in the public records)—that a declaratory action was appropriate. It is undisputed that some of the homeowners had filed affidavits of adverse possession in the public records during the dispute and they had not revoked the affidavits when the case proceeded to trial. Also, the individuals continued to testify at trial that they still owned the alley.

Although, as pointed out by the homeowners, the live pleading for the homeowners no longer asserted they owned the alley, we are not always bound by the status of the live pleadings with regard to attorney's fees. *See, e.g., City of Carrollton v. Duncan,* 742 S.W.2d 70, 79 (Tex.—App. Fort Worth 1987, no writ) (awarding attorney's fees despite disclaimer of title, due to long-asserted position to the contrary). From the inception of the dispute until very shortly before trial, the homeowners asserted the alley was not public, and, during trial, some homeowners testified they owned the alley.

The homeowners also assert the attorney's fees were improper because the relief sought was moot. *See Speer v. Presbyterian Children's Home & Serv. Agency,* 847 S.W.2d 227, 228-29 (Tex. 1993) (dismissing employment declaratory action as moot because service agency withdrew from offering adoption services and abolished position); *Kenneth Leventhal,* 978 S.W.2d at 259 (holding declaratory action was moot because accountant received everything he sought in a breach of contract claim). Generally, a case is considered moot if the issues are no longer "live" or the parties lack a legally cognizable interest in the outcome. *Camarena v. Texas Employment Comm'n,* 754 S.W.2d 149, 151 (Tex. 1988).

Again, due to the unrevoked affidavits in the deed records and the continued insistence of ownership, the declaratory relief was appropriate. We also find the homeowners' reliance on *Coombs v. City of Houston,* 35 S.W.2d 1066 (Tex. Civ. App. Galveston 1930, no writ), unconvincing. *Coombs,* addressing the streets and alleys in the Houston Heights, had long been published, as well as discussed by the parties, when the homeowners were pleading private ownership in the alley.

B. Segregation of Fees

Next, the homeowners complain Premier did not segregate its attorney's fees between claims and parties.

As a general rule, in a case involving multiple claims, the party seeking attorney's fees must present sufficient evidence of a reasonable fee for the legal services attributable specifically to the claims for which recovery of attorney's fees is authorized. *Stewart Title Guar. Co. v. Sterling,* 822 S.W.2d 1, 11 (Tex. 1991). An exception to this duty to segregate arises when the attorney's fees rendered are in connection with claims arising out of the same transaction and are so interrelated that their prosecution or defense entails proof or denial of the same facts. *Id.*

We conclude the facts relied on for each of Premier's claims and defenses were sufficiently interrelated to avail it of this exception. Premier had to prove the same allegations to establish its right to relief under each theory of recovery. Also, with regard to the issue of not segregating the fees for Amy Ell, the settling homeowner, Premier had to establish the same allegations of civil conspiracy and nuisance, which necessarily involved each homeowner. In any event, Premier's attorney testified in extreme detail about the attorney's fees for each day of her representation, including the fees specifically associated with Ell's settlement.

The homeowners assert that if we conclude, as we have, the facts relied on for each of Premier's claims and defenses were sufficiently interrelated so as to allow attorney's fees, it necessitates a holding that Premier cannot recover attorney's fees under the Act. We disagree. Just because the same facts are relied upon to establish different causes of action, does not mean that different types of relief are not appropriate. As discussed in the preceding section, the additional relief afforded by the Act was appropriate under the facts presented here.

We overrule issue three.

V. Alley Surface

In issue four, the homeowners assert the trial court erred as a matter of law in determining that Premier can surface the alley as it chooses. Specifically, the homeowners challenge the following conclusion of law:

Plaintiff may put gravel or whatever material it chooses in the alley without following any particular City of Houston code or ordinance. No City of Houston code or ordinance requires any other material.

It is clear from the record that, at the time of trial, there was no City of Houston code or ordinance requiring any particular type of material to be put on the alley surface. The homeowners' complaint has no merit.

We overrule issue four.

VI. Damages

In issue five, the homeowners assert the evidence is legally insufficient to support the award of $10,000 in actual damages.

Findings of fact entered in a case tried to the court have the same force as a jury's answer. *Catalina v. Blasdel*, 881 S.W.2d 295, 297 (Tex. 1994); *Bond v. Kagan Edelman Enters.*, 985 S.W.2d 253, 256 (Tex. App.—Houston [1st Dist.] 1999), *rev'd on other grounds*, 20 S.W.3d 706 (Tex. 2000). The trial court's findings of fact are reviewable for legal sufficiency of the evidence to support them by the same standards that are applied in reviewing the legal sufficiency of the evidence supporting a jury's answer to a jury question. *Catalina*, 881 S.W.2d at 297; *Bond*, 985 S.W.2d at 256.

Accordingly, when, as here, the party without the burden of proof challenges the legal sufficiency of the evidence, we consider all of the evidence in the light most favorable to the prevailing party, indulging every reasonable inference in that party's favor. *Associated Indem. Corp. v. CAT Contracting, Inc.*, 964 S.W.2d 276, 285-86 (Tex. 1998); *Ned v. E.J. Turner & Co., Inc.*, 11 S.W.3d 407, 408 (Tex. App.—Houston [1st Dist.] 2000, pet. denied). If there is more than a scintilla of evidence to support the finding, we must uphold it. *Associated Indemnity,* 964 S.W.2d at 285-86; *Ned,* 11 S.W.3d at 408.

The trial court's finding of fact six states: "Because of the actions of Defendants, plaintiff was unable to complete construction of one of the homes and thereby suffered permanent damages." Conclusion of law 12 states: "Defendants are jointly and severally liable to plaintiff for damages in the amount of . . . ($10,000.00)." The evidence at trial includes the following. Paul Gomberg, Premier's president, testified that, due to the alley dispute, he had to modify his plans from building three homes to building two homes. According to Gomberg, Premier suffered lost profits and increased land costs from the inability to sell a third home. He testified that he would have gotten better deals from subcontractors and real estate agents if he had built three houses rather than two, and that the costs increased $54,234 per house from his original plans. Premier had to construct a temporary culvert, and had to resurvey the property, allowing for two homes instead of three. In connection with the 428 Cortlandt home, which sold for $255,000, Premier had to pay a 5% broker's commission ($12,750), rather than a 4% commission ($10,200). Gomberg stated that Premier experienced substantial construction delays due to the alley dispute, and Premier lost other business. Premier's employees dropped from five to two because of the lawsuit. Premier had to extend its bank loans and change lenders. Jeffrey Schneider, President of Universal Printing Company, acknowledged during trial that in his deposition he had agreed that Premier's inability to continue constructing three homes cost Premier money.

We conclude the evidence supports the finding that Premier suffered actual damages of $10,000 as a result of Defendants' actions.

We overrule issue five.

We affirm the trial court's judgment.

Although Premier filed its own notice of appeal, it raises no points of error and does not seek reversal of any portion of the trial court's judgment. See Tex. R. App. P. 25.1(c). Accordingly, we dismiss Premier's appeal.

The homeowners' motion includes copies of the clerk's receipts, which the clerk examined as she testified, that show how the clerk's office applied the $105. Based on the cumulative testimony and the receipts, the clerk's office applied the $105 as follows: (purposely omitted)

Additionally, Premier sought, "A declaration that Article I, section 40.07 of the [City of Houston] Code of Ordinances applies to obstructions in the alleys in the Houston Heights," which relates to the City of Houston, rather than the homeowners. However, the parties agreed before trial that they were seeking no attorney's fees and no damages against the City.

The Act did not authorize attorney's fees for suits filed before September 1, 1981 and, thus, were not at issue in Viscardi. See Tex. Rev. Civ. Stat. Ann. 2524-1, § 10 (Vernon Supp. 2001).

As stated at the beginning of this opinion, Premier raises no points of error and does not seek reversal of any portion of the trial court's judgment. Therefore, we dismiss Premier's appeal.

§ 2.17 Necessary Elements for Selected Causes of Action

Page 81, add at end of section:

Bad Faith

1. The insurer unreasonably refuses to pay a claim.
2. The insurer does not make a good faith or reasonable investigation before denying a claim.
3. The insurer is guilty of unfair claims practices against claimant.

Page 81, add new § 2.17A:

§ 2.17A Special Types of Liability (New)

A. Vicarious Liability

Vicarious Liability is the doctrine under which a person, such as an employer, is liable for the injuries or damages caused by a person under his control but outside the scope of his employment as long as the employer knew or should have known that the employee was or could be reckless or harmful. If the negligence of an employee occurred within the course and scope of his employment, the liability is assigned to the employer under the doctrine of respondeat superior. An employer is not usually liable for the acts of an independent contractor unless the negligence falls under the realm of hazardous activity or materials. There is a common misconception among laymen that parents are responsible for the negligence of their children. Under vicarious liability, this is untrue, except of course, if the parents were aware of the child's negligent behavior and did nothing to stop it. Below is a case which represents the concept of vicarious liability.

Adams v. New York City Transit Authority
88 N.Y.2d 116 (N.Y. 1996)
Margaret Adams, Appellant,
v.
New York City Transit Authority, Respondent.
Court of Appeals of New York

In 1882, this Court held that a common carrier is liable to passengers for the torts of its employees regardless of whether those torts were committed within or outside the scope of their employment (*Stewart v. Brooklyn & Crosstown R. R. Co.,* 90 N.Y. 588). This appeal requires us to determine whether the New York City Transit Authority may be held liable under this holding for injuries sustained by a subway rider as a result of an unprovoked attack by a Transit Authority token booth clerk. Concluding that the liability rule enunciated in 1882 is no longer viable as a matter of law or policy, we hold that the token booth clerk's assaultive conduct, which was indisputably outside the scope of her employment, does not give rise to vicarious liability on the part of her employer.

According to the complaint allegations and deposition testimony, plaintiff Margaret Adams was waiting in line to purchase a subway token when she heard the clerk inside the token booth yelling at the man immediately in front of her. After the man walked away, plaintiff stepped up to the booth, slid her fare through the opening in the window and asked for directions to her destination. Inexplicably, the clerk responded with a barrage of verbal abuse.

Shocked by the clerk's reaction, plaintiff walked away from the booth, placed her token in the slot and attempted to proceed through the turnstile. Her movement was interrupted, however, when she was assaulted from behind by the token clerk, pushed to the ground and choked. The incident ended when plaintiff's companion, who had been waiting on line with her, called for help and obtained the assistance of a man who pulled the assailant away from plaintiff. According to plaintiff, she suffered physical and emotional injury as a result of the assault.

Plaintiff commenced the present action for damages against the Transit Authority, alleging several causes of action. On cross motions for summary judgment, plaintiff's claims based on negligent hiring, training and supervision and the Authority's alleged acquiescence in its employee's misconduct were dismissed for lack of factual or legal support. The Supreme Court concluded, however, that plaintiff had established entitlement to summary judgment on her cause of action that was based on defendant Authority's breach of its carrier's duty to provide its passengers with transportation " 'free from insults or assaults by [its employees]' " (quoting PJI 2:239).

On defendant Authority's appeal, the Appellate Division reversed this aspect of Supreme Court's ruling and modified its order accordingly by dismissing plaintiff's remaining cause of action. After reviewing the legal history of the special common-carrier rule of vicarious liability on which the Supreme Court relied, the Appellate Division concluded that the rule was no longer viable. This appeal, taken by permission of the Appellate Division, ensued. We now affirm.

As a general rule, employers are held vicariously liable for their employees' torts only to the extent that the underlying acts were within the scope of the employment (*see, e.g., Riviello v. Waldron,* 47 N.Y.2d 297; *Cornell v. State of New York,* 46 N.Y.2d 1032, 1033; *Sauter v. New York Tribune,* 305 N.Y. 442; *Higgins v. Watervliet Turnpike Co.,* 46 N.Y. 23). The scope-of-employment limitation on employers' vicarious liability is a logical consequence of the policies underlying the vicarious liability doctrine itself. The modern justification for the doctrine lies in the view that "[t]he losses caused by the torts of employees, which as a practical matter are sure to occur in the conduct of the employer's enterprise," are most fairly allocated to the employer "as a required cost of doing business" (Prosser and Keeton, Torts § 69, at 500 [5th ed]). It follows from this rationale that torts which are outside the scope of employment and are therefore not part of the "conduct of the employer's enterprise" should not be made the responsibility of the employer.

One particularly significant exception to the general rule is the expansive liability that has been imposed on common carriers for the torts of their employees. In *Stewart v. Brooklyn & Crosstown R.R. Co. (supra)*, this Court held that carriers are liable for their employees' torts regardless of whether those torts were committed within the scope of employment. The *Stewart* decision was premised principally on the carrier's implicit contract with its passengers, which was held, as a matter of law, to require the carrier to transport its passengers "'safely and properly, and to treat [them] respectfully'" (90 N.Y., at 591, quoting *Goddard v. Grand Trunk Ry.*, 57 Me. 202). An assault on a passenger by a carrier's employee constituted a breach of this contractual duty and, in the *Stewart* Court's view, should therefore be actionable without regard to the relationship between the employee's conduct and the master's business.

In subsequent cases applying the rule, the Court retained the breach of contract theory but also acknowledged the rule's equally important underpinnings in tort law (*Busch v. Interborough R. T. Co.*, 187 N.Y. 388; *Gillespie v. Brooklyn Hgts. R. R. Co.*, 178 N.Y. 347; *see also Dwinelle v. New York Cent. & Hudson Riv. R. R. Co.*, 120 N.Y. 117). Modern authorities have recognized that the special duty of a common carrier to its passengers is a tort-based duty rather than an obligation derived from an implied contract between the carrier and the passenger (Prosser and Keeton, *op. cit.*, § 12, at 57-58; see also *Webber v. Herkimer & Mohawk St. R. R. Co.*, 109 N.Y. 311; *Loeher v. East Side Omnibus Corp.*, 259 App. Div. 200, aff'd 287 N.Y. 670). As one court has noted in a somewhat different context, "'the tickets [issued by a carrier to a passenger] do no more than evidence a relation of common carrier and passenger for hire; it is the law of torts that imposes the standard of care and responsibility appropriate to the carrier-passenger relationship, but that standard, and any consequent liability, are not creatures of contract'" (*Gelfand v. Tanner Motor Tours*, 339 F.2d 317, 322). Accordingly, if the special rule adopted in *Stewart* is to retain its force in our contemporary body of law, it must find some justification in modern tort principles.

Consideration of the broad policies underlying the vicarious liability doctrine does not reveal such a justification. Where an unprovoked assault or other intentional tort committed by a carrier's employees is determined to be outside the scope of the actor's employment, it is, by definition, not of the kind of activity that is "as a practical matter . . . sure to occur in the conduct of the [carrier's] enterprise" (Prosser and Keeton, *op. cit.*, at 500). Thus, it makes no more sense to treat the cost of such misconduct as "a required cost" of the carrier's business (*see id.*) than it would to treat the same class of misconduct as a required cost of the business of a restaurateur, storekeeper or any other class of proprietor.

Since the general vicarious-liability principles that are applicable to all employers do not suggest a sound basis for the *Stewart* rule, its justification, if any, must be found in the special characteristics of common carriers. The lengthy history of the law's attempt to address common-carrier liability suggests several possibilities. However, as the Appellate Division correctly found, none of these furnishes a wholly satisfactory ground for applying the 100-year-old *Stewart* rule to contemporary controversies.

In the past, carriers were held subject to a higher duty of care, and terms like "absolute liability" and "duty of an absolute nature" were often used to explain why "the usual distinctions which attend the doctrine of respondeat superior cut little or no figure" in cases involving common-carrier liability (*Gillespie v. Brooklyn Hgts. R. R. Co., supra*, at 354 [emphasis in original], quoting Thompson, Negligence § 3186; see 3 Harper, James and Gray, Torts § 16.14 [2d ed]; Prosser and Keeton, *op. cit.*, §§ 56, 70, 92). However, the higher duty of care imposed on carriers has been subject to considerable criticism (*see McLean v. Triboro Coach Corp.*, 302 N.Y. 49; 3 Harper, James and Gray, *op. cit.*, § 16.14; Prosser and Keeton, *op. cit.*, § 56) and is no longer applied in many quarters (*see Lesser v Manhattan & Bronx Surface Tr. Operating Auth.*, 157 A.D.2d 352, 355, *aff'd* 79 N.Y.2d 1031; *Bracco v. Manhattan & Bronx Surface Tr. Operating Auth.*, 117 A.D.2d 273, 278; *Kermarec v. Compagnie Generale Transatlantique*, 358 U.S. 625; *Plagianos v. American Airlines*, 912 F.2d 57; *Rainey v. Pacquet Cruises*, 709 F.2d 169; PJI 2:161). Moreover, there is no real logical connection between a carrier's higher duty of care and the imposition of "absolute" liability for the unforeseeable acts of employees that are both beyond the employer's control and outside the reasonable scope of the employer's enterprise.

Further, the apparent historic underpinnings of the carrier's absolute liability for employee misconduct are of dubious validity under current social and legal conditions. Any analogy between the carrier's absolute responsibility as a bailee of inanimate goods and its responsibility to human passengers (*see Rabon v. Guardsmark, Inc.*, 571 F.2d 1277, 1281, n. 5) has long been discredited (*see* Kaczorowski, *The Common-Law Background of Nineteenth-Century Tort Law*, 51 Ohio St. L.J. 1127, 1157-1158; *see also Boyce v. Anderson*, 2 Pet [27 U.S.] 150). Similarly, although the special hazards once posed by rail travel have sometimes been cited as an important source of the absolute liability imposed on carriers (*see Philadelphia & Reading R. R. Co. v. Derby*, 14 How [55 U.S.] 468, 486-487; *Vanderhule v. Berinstein*, 285 App. Div. 290, 297), that rationale has long since become outdated as public conveyances like trains, planes and boats have become at least as safe as private modes of travel. Moreover, even if travel by common carrier could still fairly be regarded as an especially hazardous activity, that circumstance would not provide a persuasive explanation for the *Stewart* rule's retention, since the risks arising from the independent non-work-related tortious actions of an employee are unrelated to the hazards of travel and, in fact, are essentially the same regardless of whether the individual is hurtling through a subway tunnel or is instead leisurely sipping a cup of coffee in a quiet restaurant.

The status of passengers as helpless prisoners confined within the carriers' travel compartments is another factor that has been mentioned in support of the absolute liability rule (*see Lopez v. Southern Cal. R. T. Dist.*, 153 Cal. App. 3d 1135, 200 Cal. Rptr. 779, *rev'd on other grounds* 40 Cal. 3d 780, 710 P.2d 907; *Derwort v. Loomer*, 21 Conn. 245, 253, 254; *see generally* Wheat, *Liability of Carrier to Passengers for Injuries by Its Servants*, 14 Mich. L. Rev. 626, 642; Comment, *Strict Liability or Negligence: What Standard of Care Applies When Crew Members Assault Passengers on*

Cruise Ships, 19 Tul. Mar. L.J. 353). Like the ultrahazardous activity rationale, this theory proves too much. As one court has noted, the same factors that appear to enhance the risk of assault in public conveyances, i.e., the difficulty of escape and the involuntary exposure to many strangers, may actually operate as deterrents to would-be wrongdoers and thereby reduce the risk of harm from third-party attacks (*Jaffess v. Home Lines,* 1988 WL 42049 [S.D.N.Y.]). Furthermore, modern life includes a host of other situations in which a consumer of services, such as a hospital patient or movie theater patron, might be confined to a limited area or find his or her movements similarly curtailed. It is doubtful that a court today would hold the proprietor of these classes of enterprises absolutely liable for an employee's intentional torts solely because of the existence of those conditions (*see Cornell v. State of New York,* supra; *Moritz v. Pines Hotel,* 52 A.D.2d 1020; *Tobin v. Slutsky,* 506 F.2d 1097).

Finally, the former absolute duty of carriers to protect their passengers from criminal attacks by third parties is an unconvincing reason for imposing absolute liability for assaults by employees. Since this Court decided *Basso v. Miller* (40 N.Y.2d 233) in 1976, landowners have been absolved of the heightened duties of care that they previously owed their business invitees and guests. *Basso*'s holding undermines the basic notion that owners of particular businesses should be held to special or different duties of care that are determined solely by their relationship to or the status of the injured party. Moreover, where governmentally operated carriers like the Transit Authority are concerned, the premise that carriers should be liable at all for third-party criminal assaults has been drastically curtailed (*see Weiner v. Metropolitan Transp. Auth.,* 55 N.Y.2d 175). Thus, the theoretical predicate for the third-party liability rule has itself been substantially eroded.

Even more importantly, the *Stewart* Court's reasoning on the point is fundamentally flawed. The Court concluded in *Stewart* that carriers should be held liable for the irrational and gratuitous *intentional* misconduct of their employees, since it would be anomalous to deny liability in those circumstances while imposing liability when an employee *negligently* permits a passenger to be attacked by a stranger. First, this syllogism, if valid, is as pertinent to all other service enterprises as it is to common carriers and is therefore not a sound basis for a special rule for the common carriers. Second, the syllogism is logically defective because it overlooks that liability in situations involving employee negligence requires the existence of an analytically critical fact not present in cases involving gratuitous intentional employee misdeeds, i.e., employee misconduct occurring *within the scope* of employment. As previously noted, it is only that condition that justifies the imposition of vicarious liability on an otherwise faultless employer.

In this case, plaintiff's only cause of action against the Transit Authority that was not dismissed for want of proof is her claim based on the Authority's vicarious liability for the tortious acts of its employee. Plaintiff does not contend that those acts were within the scope of her assailant's employment and, accordingly, her claim depends wholly on the special rule of "absolute liability" that was previously applied to carriers under *Stewart v. Brooklyn & Crosstown R. R. Co.* (supra). Since that rule is no longer viable, we conclude that plaintiff's remaining cause of action was properly dismissed.

Accordingly, the order of the Appellate Division should be affirmed, with costs.

Chief Judge Kaye and Judges Simons, Bellacosa, Smith, Levine and Ciparick concur.

B. Strict Liability

Some torts do not require that you prove intent or negligence; only that the thing which caused the damages happened. These are called strict liability torts. They include defective products, animals, or any substance or thing that is inherently dangerous and is highly capable of causing harm, regardless of the degree of caution excercised by the claimaint. The case below is an example of a finding of strict liability.

Hall v. E. I. Du Pont De Nemours & Co., Inc.
345 F.Supp. 353 (D.C.N.Y., 1972)

These two cases arise out of eighteen separate accidents scattered across the nation in which children were injured by blasting caps. Damages are sought from manufacturers and their trade association, the Institute of Makers of Explosives (I.M.E.). The basic allegation is that the practice of the explosives industry during the 1950's—continuing until 1965—of not placing any warning upon individual blasting caps and of failing to take other safety measures created an unreasonable risk of harm resulting in plaintiffs' injuries.

In most instances the manufacturer of the cap is unknown. The question posed is whether a group of manufacturers and their trade association, comprising virtually the entire blasting cap industry of the United States, can be held jointly liable for injuries caused by their product. Our answer is that there are circumstances, illustrated by this litigation, in which an entire industry may be liable for harm caused by its operations. While the cases are closely linked in their litigation history and underlying legal theory, they differ in several crucial respects. *See Hall v. E. I. Du Pont De Nemours & Co.,* 312 F. Supp. 358 (E.D.N.Y. 1970) for an earlier phase of the litigation. In *Chance,* the name of the manufacturer who actually produced the cap causing a particular injury is apparently unknown. In *Hall* it is, plaintiffs allege, known. We turn to *Chance* first since it presents the more difficult legal problems.

I. THE CHANCE CASE
A. *Facts and Proceedings*

Thirteen children were allegedly injured by blasting caps in twelve unrelated accidents between 1955 and 1959. The injuries occurred in the states of Alabama, California, Maryland, Montana, Nevada, North Carolina, Tennessee, Texas, Washington and West Virginia. Plaintiffs are citizens of the states in which their injuries occurred. They are now claiming damages against six manufacturers of blasting caps and the I.M.E. on the grounds of negligence, common law conspiracy, assault, and strict liability in tort. In addition, two parents sue for medical expenses. Federal jurisdiction is based on diversity of citizenship. 28 U.S.C. § 1332.

While the plaintiffs' injuries occurred at widely varied times and places, the complaint alleges certain features common to them all. Each plaintiff, according to the complaint, "came into possession" of a dynamite blasting cap which was not labeled or marked with a warning of danger, and which could be easily detonated by a child. In each instance an injurious explosion occurred.

The complaint does not identify a particular manufacturer of the cap which caused a particular injury. It alleges that each cap in question was designed and manufactured jointly or severally by the six corporate defendants or by other unnamed manufacturers, and by their trade association, the I.M.E.

Plaintiffs' central contention is that injuries were caused by the defendants' failure to place a warning on the blasting caps, and to manufacture caps which would have been less easily detonated. This failure, according to the plaintiffs, was not the result of defendants' ignorance of the dangerousness of their product to children. The complaint states that the defendants had actual knowledge that children were frequently injured by blasting caps, and, through the trade association, kept statistics and other information regarding these accidents. Recognizing the dangerousness of their product to children, the defendants, through the trade association, used various means— such as placards and printed notices—to warn users of the caps and the general public. These measures were allegedly inadequate in light of the known risks of injury. Moreover, defendants are said to have jointly explicitly considered the possibility of labeling the caps, to have rejected this possibility, and to have engaged in lobbying activities against legislation which would have required such labeling. The long-standing industry practice of not placing a warning message on individual blasting caps was, it is urged, the result of a conscious agreement among the defendants, in the light of known dangers, with regard to this aspect of their product.

The six corporate defendants are: E. I. Du Pont De Nemours & Co., Inc. ("Du Pont"), Hercules Powder Co. ("Hercules"), and Atlas Powder Co. ("Atlas"), all citizens of and having their principal places of business in Delaware; American Cyanamid Co. ("Cyanamid"), a citizen of Maine with its principal place of business in New Jersey; Olin Mathieson Chemical Corp. ("Olin"), a citizen of Virginia with its principal place of business in Connecticut; and Austin Powder Co. ("Austin"), a citizen of and having its principal place of business in Ohio. The defendant I.M.E. is an unincorporated association with its principal place of business in New York.

Defendants move to dismiss on the grounds that the plaintiff-children do not state claims upon which relief can be granted. They also request dismissal of the parents' claims for medical expenses as barred by statutes of limitations. Finally, they seek a severance on the grounds of improper joinder and transfer of the severed claims or their outright dismissal on the ground of inconvenient forum. 28 U.S.C. § 1404(a).

B. *Issues Presented*

The issues common to products liability cases are well known: did the manufacturer (or other supplier) violate a duty of care to plaintiffs, and was the violation a legal or "proximate" cause of plaintiffs' injuries. 2 Harper & James, The Law of Torts §§ 28.1-.2 (1956). Moving to dismiss the complaint, defendants have the burden of showing "beyond doubt" that plaintiff "can prove no set of facts in support of his claim which would entitle him to relief." *Conley v. Gibson,* 355 U.S. 41, 45-46, 78 S. Ct. 99, 102, 2 L. Ed. 2d 80, 84 (1957).

A central question raised by defendants' motion is whether their parallel safety practices provide a basis for joint liability. Interlaced with the issues of duty to warn, proximate cause, and joint liability is a conflicts question of considerable complexity: what choice-of-law principles are to be applied in a case such as this one where planning, design, manufacture, and sale of a product occurred in different states, and injury in yet others?

Since, as indicated below, further briefs will be required on the choice-of-law problem, we have, for the purposes of this memorandum, assumed the existence of a national body of state tort law. A growing consensus on the substantive law in this country permits such a gross first approach to the preliminary motions before us since all we need to determine now is whether the plaintiffs might succeed on the law and facts. *See, e.g., Wright v. Carter Products,* 244 F.2d 53, 56-60 (2d Cir. 1956) (Massachusetts law applicable but general treatises, articles and case law of other states cited on motion to dismiss).

Under both negligence and strict liability standards manufacturers and other suppliers have a duty to users, consumers, and in some circumstances to the general public or portions of it, to produce products with appropriate warnings, instructions, and other safety features. *See, e.g.,* Noel, Manufacturer's Negligence of Design or Directions for Use of a Product, 71 Yale L.J. 816 (1962); Noel, Products Defective Because of Inadequate Directions or Warnings, 23 Sw.L.J. 256 (1969); Rest. 2d Torts § 388, comment e, § 402A, comments *j, l* (1965) (warnings under negligence and strict liability standards). Defendants' duty of care is basic to liability, and we turn first to that issue.

C.   *Duty to Warn and Standard of Care*
(1)   *Negligence*

A manufacturer's duty to produce a safe product, with appropriate warnings and instructions where necessary, rests initially on the responsibility each of us bears to exercise care to avoid unreasonable risks of harm to others. See, e.g., 2 Harper & James, The Law of Torts § 28.3 (1956). An "unreasonable risk" in any given situation depends on the balancing of probability and seriousness of harm if care is not exercised against the costs of taking precautions. *See, e.g., United States v. Carroll Towing Co.,* 159 F.2d 169, 173 (2d Cir. 1947); 2 Harper & James, *supra* §§ 16.9, 28.4; Rest. 2d Torts §§ 291-293, 298 (1965).

Activity involving a small likelihood of death or serious injury may require greater and more costly precautions than that involving a higher probability of lesser harm. *See, e.g., The Glendola,* 47 F.2d 206, 207 (2d Cir. 1931), *cert. denied,* 283 U.S. 857, 51 S. Ct. 650, 75 L. Ed. 1463 (1931); Rest. 2d Torts § 388, comment n at 309 (1965); 2 Harper & James, The Law of Torts § 16.9 at 931-32 (1956). Where an act involves a risk of death or serious bodily harm, and particularly if it is capable of causing such results to a number of persons, the highest attention and caution are required even if the act has a very considerable utility. Thus those who deal with firearms, explosives, poisonous drugs, or high tension electricity are required to exercise the closest attention and the most careful precautions, not only in preparing for their use but in using them. Rest. 2d Torts § 298, comment b at 69 (1965).

(a) *Standard of Care*

In most products liability cases the court does not have to make an explicit determination that the defendant owed the plaintiff a duty of reasonable care. The general scope of such a duty is well established: manufacturers must provide products that are reasonably safe for their foreseeable use. *See, e.g., MacPherson v. Buick Motor Co.,* 217 N.Y. 382, 111 N.E. 1050 (1916); Rest. 2d Torts § 395 (1965); 2 Harper & James, The Law of Torts §§ 28.3-.9 (1956).

In the explosives industry, producers have long been on notice that they have an obligation to users of their products to guard against defects (*Dement v. Olin-Mathieson Chemical Corp.,* 282 F.2d 76, 80 (5th Cir. 1960)) and "to adequately warn a foreseeable purchaser or user of foreseeable and latent dangers upon proper and intended use of [the] product." *Littlehale v. E. I. Du Pont De Nemours & Co.,* 268 F. Supp. 791, 798 (S.D.N.Y. 1966), *aff'd,* 380 F.2d 274 (2d Cir. 1967). Similarly, those who use or store explosives have been held to a high standard of care, commensurate with the obvious dangers, to maintain storage facilities that are secure against tampering by children. *See e.g., Lone Star Gas Co. v. Parsons,* 159 Okla. 52, 14 P.2d 369 (1932); Annot., 10 A.L.R.2d 22 (1950); 2 Harper & James, The Law of Torts § 20.5 at 1144, n. 34 (1956).

Defendants suggest, nevertheless, that because the plaintiff-children were neither purchasers nor intended users of the caps, their injuries were "unforeseeable" as a matter of law, and hence outside the scope of the duty of reasonable care. While cast in terms of foreseeability—a term of the experiential world-the issue is finally one of duty—a question of law and public policy. Green, The Causal Relation Issue in Negligence Law, 60 Mich. L. Rev. 543, 562-569 (1962). Because foreseeability is one of the vectors bearing on the finding of duty, we must analyze the meaning of the term in the context of this case.

(i) *Foreseeability*

"Foreseeability" at this stage of decision includes two related elements. The first is the likelihood or probability of harm if reasonable care is not exercised-"whether the harm threatened is likely to occur." Noel, Manufacturer's Negligence of Design or Directions for Use of a Product, 71 Yale L.J. 816, 830 (1962). The second element is the manufacturer's actual or constructive knowledge of the risk-"whether the manufacturer was in a position to foresee the likelihood of such harm." *Id.* at 847.

The probability of the known risk needed to trigger the duty of reasonable care cannot be expressed in a mathematical formula. Judge Cardozo suggested that "[t]here must be knowledge of a danger, not merely possible, but probable." *MacPherson v. Buick Motor Co.,* 217 N.Y. 382, 389, 111 N.E. 1050, 1053 (1916). Since "probabilities" are but quantifications of "possibilities," what is meant in *MacPherson* is apparently a probability so low that it can be ignored in our everyday world. Judge

Learned Hand, discussing foreseeability and scope of reasonable care in the context of proximate cause, utilized much the same formulation: "[The injurious result] has got to be one of those consequences which is not entirely outside the range of expectation or probability, as ordinary men view it." *The Mars,* 9 F.2d 183, 184 (S.D.N.Y. 1914). Judge Frank, adopting language of the New Hampshire Supreme Court, argued that the proper threshold test of the applicability of reasonable care "is not of the balance of probabilities, but of the existence of some probability of sufficient moment to induce action to avoid it on the part of a reasonable mind." *Tullgren v. Amoskeag Mfg. Co.,* 82 N.H. 268, 276, 133 A. 4, 8 (1926), cited with approval in *Hentschel v. Baby Bathinette Corp.,* 215 F.2d 102, 106 (2d Cir. 1954) (Frank, J., dissenting), *cert. denied,* 349 U.S. 923, 75 S. Ct. 663, 99 L. Ed. 1254 (1955), and in *Pease v. Sinclair Refining Co.,* 104 F.2d 183, 186 (2d Cir. 1939); cf. 2 Harper & James, The Law of Torts § 18.2 at 1018-1026, particularly at 1020 (1956).

Whatever the verbal formulation, the concept of "foreseeable risk" is universally taken to mean the foreseeability of a general kind or type of risk, rather than the foreseeability of the precise chain of events leading to the particular injury in question. *See, e. g., Pease v. Sinclair Refining Co.,* 104 F.2d 183, 186-87 (2d Cir. 1939); 2 Harper & James, The Law of Torts § 18.2 at 1026, § 20.5 at 1147-49 (1956).

The related issue of whether the manufacturer was in a position to foresee the risk turns on whether "the manufacturer knew, or through the exercise of reasonable care should have known, of the existence of the danger." Dillard & Hart, Products Liability: Directions for Use and the Duty to Warn, 41 Va. L. Rev. 145, 156-57 (1955). Plaintiffs must demonstrate actual notice to the manufacturer of particular kinds of risks (*see, e.g., Noel v. United Aircraft Corp.,* 219 F.Supp. 556, 568-69 (D. Del. 1963), *aff'd in pertinent part,* 342 F.2d 232 (3d Cir. 1965), or reasonable inferences from known characteristics of the product and its use. *See, e.g., Larsen v. General Motors Corp.,* 391 F.2d 495, 501-505 (8th Cir. 1968); *Simpson Timber Co. v. Parks,* 369 F.2d 324 (9th Cir. 1966) and 369 F.2d 324, 333-35 (9th Cir. 1966) (Browning, Hanley, Merrill, and Duniway, JJ., dissenting), *vacated sub nom. Parks v. Simpson Timber Co.,* 388 U.S. 459, 87 S. Ct. 2115, 18 L.Ed.2d 1319 (1967), discussed in Noel, Products Defective Because of Inadequate Directions or Warnings, 23 Sw. L.J. 256, 275-77 (1969); *see also* Noel, Manufacturer's Negligence of Design or Directions for Use of a Product, 71 Yale L.J. 816, 834-36, 856-66 (1962).

The plaintiffs' injuries in this case are within the range of reasonable expectation and probability. They are likely to occur in the absence of reasonable care. The manufacturer has capacity to foresee them. Plaintiffs allege that the manufacturers not only "had reason to know," but that they actually knew, through information collected by the trade association, that children were injured in accidents involving blasting caps. According to statistics submitted by the plaintiffs, the number of such accidents between 1955 and 1959 which were known to the manufacturers ranged from 86 to 137 per year. See statistical tables said to be based on I.M.E. data submitted as Exhibits 2A and 2B, Plaintiffs' Memorandum in Opposition, August 26, 1971, in *Hall v. Du Pont,* 69-C-273.

Defendants do not deny that they had knowledge of these accidents. They claim to have taken all reasonable feasible steps to reduce the risk of their occurrence.

Moreover, they argue that they did not deal with plaintiffs, never saw them, and are in court today only through a third party's carelessness, thus invoking (in part) the familiar doctrine that limits a manufacturer's liability to injuries caused by his product when put to its "intended use."

A manufacturer's liability for failure to exercise reasonable care ordinarily extends only to "those who use [the product] for a purpose for which the manufacturer should expect it to be used and . . . those whom [the manufacturer] should expect to be endangered by its probable use" when "physical harm is caused to them by [the product's] lawful use in a manner and for a purpose for which it is supplied." Rest. 2d Torts § 395 (1965). Comment j to section 395 of the Second Restatement of Torts, titled "Unforeseeable use or manner of use," explains that:

> The liability stated in this Section is limited to persons who are endangered and the risks which are created in the course of uses of the chattel which the manufacturer should reasonably anticipate. In the absence of special reason to expect otherwise, the maker is entitled to assume that his product will be put to a normal use, for which the product is intended or appropriate; and he is not subject to liability when it is safe for all such uses, and harm results only because it is mishandled in a way which he has no reason to expect, or is used in some unusual and unforeseeable manner. *See also Mazzi v. Greenlee Tool Co.,* 320 F.2d 821, 823 (2d Cir. 1963) (applying New York law and collecting cases and authorities).

This doctrine has been applied in two cases involving explosives manufacturers to insulate them from liability when their products, manufactured for specialized purposes, came into the possession of untrained third parties who were injured while using them. *See Littlehale v. E. I. Du Pont De Nemours & Co.,* 268 F.Supp. 791 (S.D.N.Y. 1966), *aff'd,* 380 F.2d 274 (2d Cir. 1967); *Harper v. Remington Arms Co.,* 156 Misc. 53, 280 N.Y.S. 862 (Sup. Ct. 1935), *aff'd mem.,* 248 App. Div. 713, 290 N.Y.S. 130 (1st Dep't. 1936), leave to appeal denied, 272 N.Y. 675 (1936). Despite the general validity of the intended use principle, it does not warrant a conclusion that the blasting cap manufacturers in this case had no duty of reasonable care to the plaintiff-children. The doctrine of intended use is an illustration of the broader doctrine of foreseeability. A manufacturer cannot ignore a probable "misuse" of his product. This interpretation is shared by many courts including the Fourth Circuit in *Spruill v. Boyle-Midway, Inc.,* 308 F.2d 79 (1962), the Eighth Circuit in *Larsen v. General Motors Corp.,* 391 F.2d 495 (1968), and the Second Circuit in *Mazzi v. Greenlee Tool Co.,* 320 F.2d 821 (1963). As the Fourth Circuit pointed out, in a case involving a child's death from eating furniture polish, "Intended use" is but a convenient adaptation of the basic test of "reasonable foreseeability" framed to more specifically fit the factual situations out of which arise questions of a manufacturer's liability for negligence. "Intended use" is not an inflexible formula to be apodictically applied to every case. Normally a seller or manufacturer is entitled to anticipate that the product he deals in will be used only for the purposes for which it is manufactured and sold; thus he is expected to reasonably foresee only injuries arising in the course of such use.

However, he must also be expected to anticipate the environment which is normal for the use of his product and where, as here, that environment is the home, he must anticipate the reasonably foreseeable risks of the use of his product in such an environment. These are risks which are inherent in the proper use for which his product is manufactured. Thus where such a product is an inherently dangerous one, and its danger is not obvious to the average housewife from the appearance of the product itself, the manufacturer has an obligation to anticipate reasonably foreseeable risks and to warn of them, though such risks may be incidental to the actual use for which the product was intended. *Spruill v. Boyle-Midway, Inc.,* 308 F.2d 79, 83-84 (1962).

Applying this analysis to the field of automobile safety, the Eighth Circuit concluded that Automobiles are made for use on the roads and highways in transporting persons and cargo to and from various points. This intended use cannot be carried out without encountering in varying degrees the statistically proved hazard of injury-producing impacts of various types. The manufacturer should not be heard to say that it does not intend its product to be involved in any accident when it can easily foresee and when it knows that the probability over the life of its product is high, that it will be involved in some type of injury-producing accident. *Larsen v. General Motors Corp.,* 391 F.2d 495, 501-502 (1968).

The Second Circuit endorsed a similar approach in *Mazzi,* when it held that the evidence in the case would support a jury verdict "that such usage was intended or that defendant should have reasonably foreseen that its [product] would be so used. *Mazzi v. Greenlee Tool Co.,* 320 F.2d 821, 825 (1963). *See also* 2 Harper & James, The Law of Torts § 28.4 at 1541, n. 2 (1956) and Supplement at 215 (1968). In the context of this approach to the problem of intended use, we find the complaint in this case easily distinguishable from the plaintiffs' position in *Littlehale v. E. I. Du Pont De Nemours & Co.,* 268 F. Supp. 791 (S.D.N.Y. 1966), *aff'd,* 380 F.2d 274 (2d Cir. 1967) and in *Harper v. Remington Arms Co.,* 156 Misc. 53, 280 N.Y.S. 862 (Sup. Ct. 1935), *aff'd mem.,* 248 App. Div. 713, 290 N.Y.S. 130 (1st Dep't. 1936). In *Littlehale* defendant Du Pont had manufactured blasting caps under government contract for use by Army Ordnance personnel. The trial court found that "the user [Army Ordnance] was as well or more fully informed of the hazards involved and the correct methods of use as was the manufacturer" (268 F. Supp. at 803), and hence the manufacturer was under no duty to warn its customer of "generally known risks." 268 F. Supp. at 798. Such a duty could not arise, the trial court concluded, "at some later date by reason of some unforeseeable disposition of the product by [the] initial purchaser." 268 F. Supp. at 803. In reaching this conclusion, the trial court stressed that [this] is not a case involving a product manufactured for sale or resale to the general public. It is not a case involving negligence in the manufacture, design or use of materials. It is not a case where the manufacturer had any freedom of choice as to manufacture, design, or use of materials. It is not a case where evidence has been submitted upon which foreseeability of the particular use involved herein could be predicated. 268 F. Supp. at 801-02 (citations omitted).

In these circumstances, the Second Circuit found the trial court justified in concluding that "as a matter of law du Pont . . . could not have foreseen that its detonators would be used by a person untrained in the handling of such explosives and in a manner that was never intended." *Littlehale v. E. I. Du Pont De Nemours & Co.,* 380 F.2d 274, 276 (2d Cir. 1967).

Plaintiffs' allegations in this case present a different picture. The complaint promises submission of evidence that the manufacturers not only could have foreseen, but actually did foresee that "[their] detonators would be used by [persons] untrained in the handling of explosives and in a manner that was never intended." *Id.* In contrast to the rigid wartime specifications involved in the production of the caps in *Littlehale,* the defendants in this case apparently had complete freedom of choice as to manufacture, design, and use of materials, and exercised that choice, in the words of a Du Pont employee, in a manner "keyed to the needs of our customers." Ramsdell affidavit, Sept. 3, 1971, p. 3. While no allegations have been made about whether the caps involved in this case were manufactured for sale to "the general public," it is clear that their use and circulation was expected to be considerably more widespread than purchase and use by a specialized government agency. *Cf.* 34 Fed.Reg. 5838 (March 28, 1969) (warning re blasting caps to "Keep out of the reach of children"). Because of these differences, we cannot conclude, as did the trial court in *Littlehale,* that (1) there is no factual dispute "as to the identity of the intended and actual purchaser [or user]" and (2) that, as a matter of law, plaintiffs are excluded from the foreseeable "orbit of danger." *Littlehale v. E. I. Du Pont De Nemours & Co.,* 268 F. Supp. 791, 801 (S.D.N.Y. 1966).

The *Harper* case is distinguishable on similar grounds. In that case the defendant manufacturer had produced shot-gun shells of special explosive force for use in arms testing and they were marked to warn the class who would use them for this purpose. A jury verdict for the plaintiff was reversed because the plaintiff "failed to show that he was a person whom the defendant might reasonably have anticipated would use these shells" and hence was not owed a duty of warning and reasonable care by the manufacturer. *Harper v. Remington Arms Co.,* 156 Misc. 53, 58, 280 N.Y.S. 862, 868 (Sup. Ct. 1935), *aff'd mem.,* 248 App. Div. 713, 290 N.Y.S. 130 (1st Dep't. 1936). The allegations in the present case preclude a decision at this stage that children were not foreseeable users of blasting caps. Even if the blasting cap manufacturers' own definition of their product's intended use were accepted as controlling, plaintiffs have alleged that the manufacturers had, in the words of comment *j* of section 395 of the Second Restatement of Torts, "special reason to expect" unusual uses of their product by children. A manufacturer's actual knowledge of unusual risks is the archetype reason for extending his duty of reasonable care beyond the scope of his product's normally intended use. *See, e.g., Simpson Timber Co. v. Parks,* 369 F.2d 324, 327-28 (9th Cir. 1966), *vacated on other grounds sub nom. Parks v. Simpson Timber Co.,* 388 U.S. 459, 87 S. Ct. 2115, 18 L. Ed.2d 1319 (1967). As the Eighth Circuit has pointed out, the *Simpson* case now stands for the broad proposition that a manufacturer has a duty of reasonable care with respect to unintended uses "where the injury resulting from that unintended use was *foreseeable or should have been anticipated.*" *Larsen v. General Motors Corp.,* 391 F.2d 495, 501 (1968) (citations omitted) (emphasis supplied).

Application of general principles of foreseeability and reasonable care to unintended uses is not peculiar to modern products liability cases. A similar approach can be found in numerous cases decided in the nineteenth and early twentieth centuries involving children playing with railroad turntables, dynamite blasting caps, and other dangerous instruments and machines. Even in an era when landowners had very limited duties of care to trespassers, many courts recognized that the likelihood of children playing with dangerous instruments was sufficiently foreseeable to impose a duty of care on the owners to provide appropriate locks, fences, notices, storage sheds, and other safety devices. *See, e.g., Sioux City and P. R. Co. v. Stout,* 84 U.S. 657, 17 Wall. 657, 21 L. Ed. 745 (1873) (affirming jury finding of owner's negligence to children in failing to provide turntable lock); *Edgington v. Burlington, C. R. & N. Ry. Co.,* 116 Iowa 410, 90 N.W. 95 (1902) (discussing numerous aspects of foreseeable danger to children from turntables); *Lone Star Gas Co. v. Parsons,* 159 Okla. 52, 14 P.2d 369 (1932) (finding liability of landowner to trespassing children for negligent storage of blasting caps); *see also Lynch v. Nurdin,* 1 Q.B. 29, 113 Eng. Rep. 1041 (1841); Prosser, Law of Torts § 59 at 364-376 (4th ed. 1971); 2 Harper & James, The Law of Torts § 18.2 at 1020 (1956).

The doctrines evolved in these cases are now embodied in section 339 of the Second Restatement of Torts. According to Dean Prosser's commentary on this section and its judicial antecedents, the foreseeability elements of landowners' liability to children are very similar to the foreseeability issues involved in manufacturers' liability for unintended uses. The possessor must know "or have reason to know that children are likely to trespass," and the condition in question "must be one which the occupiers should recognize as involving an unreasonable risk of harm to such children." Prosser, Law of Torts § 59 at 368, 369 (4th ed. 1971). Whether failing to guard against the known risk is unreasonable is in turn determined by the general negligence principles of probability (including obviousness), seriousness of harm and cost of taking appropriate precautions. *Id.* at 369-71, 375-76.

Plaintiffs' allegations provide a basis for finding that injuries to children were a foreseeable risk of the use and circulation of blasting caps, and that this risk was known to, or should have been known to, the individual manufacturers. It must be emphasized that we are not holding, at this stage, that the defendants in this case had a duty of reasonable care to each of the plaintiff-children. That decision can be made only after presentation of facts relevant to the risk and cost analysis, and determination of any conflict of laws issues.

(ii)   *Costs and Social Utility*

While foreseeability of risk is an essential element of a finding that a manufacturer is under a duty of care to persons in a particular position, it is not the only element in the decision. An important factor is the cost of taking precautions against the danger. The declaration that a duty or standard of reasonable care is applicable to an injury-causing situation involves various and sometimes delicate policy judgments. The social utility of the activity out of which the injury arises, compared with the risks involved in its conduct; the kind of person with whom the actor is dealing; the workability of a rule of care, especially in terms of the parties' relative ability to adopt practical means of preventing injury; the relative ability of the parties to bear the financial burden of injury and the availability of means by which the loss may be shifted or spread; the body of statutes and judicial precedents which color the parties' relationship; the prophylactic effect of a rule of liability; . . . and finally, the moral imperatives which judges share with their fellow citizens-such are the factors which play a role in the determination of duty. *Raymond v. Paradise Unified School Dist. of Butte County,* 218 Cal. App.2d 1, 8, 31 Cal. Rptr. 847, 851-52 (3d Dist. 1963). *See*

41

also Lone Star Gas Co. v. Parsons, 159 Okla. 52, 56-57 14 P.2d 369, 373-74 (1932); *Chicago B. & Q. R. Co. v. Krayenbuhl,* 65 Neb. 889, 902-04, 91 N.W. 880, 882-83 (1902); Prosser, Palsgraf Revisited, 52 Mich. L. Rev. 1, 15 (1953).

In many situations the "cost" or "social utility" side of the initial calculus of duty is relatively clear-cut. For example, the cost of printing and attaching labels and other warning devices is often regarded as trivial compared to the risk of any substantial harm. *See, e.g., Butler v. L. Sonneborn Sons, Inc.,* 296 F.2d 623, 625-26 (2d Cir. 1961); *Wright v. Carter Products, Inc.,* 244 F.2d 53, 59 (2d Cir. 1957); *Pease v. Sinclair Refining Co.,* 104 F.2d 183, 186 (2d Cir. 1939).

This may not be such a case. The defendants have indicated that there was doubt about the technical feasibility of labeling individual blasting caps during the 1950's, or of producing caps which could be less easily detonated by children, and that in any event the costs would have been substantial. Such facts, if proven, are clearly relevant to the question of defendants' duty of care, but they do not warrant a judgment in their favor on a motion to dismiss. Where the foreseeable risks of a product's use are sufficiently serious—particularly to large numbers of people—courts have not hesitated to require manufacturers to face substantial costs in warnings, testing, inspection, and safety design. *See, e.g., Larsen v. General Motors Corp.,* 391 F.2d 495 (8th Cir. 1968); *Manos v. Trans World Airlines,* 324 F. Supp. 470 (N.D. Ill. 1971); *Noel v. United Aircraft Corp.,* 219 F. Supp. 556 (D. Del. 1963), *aff'd in pertinent part,* 342 F.2d 232 (3d Cir. 1965); *Ambriz v. Petrolane Ltd.,* 49 Cal.2d 470, 319 P.2d 1 (1957), *reversing* 312 P.2d 11, 17 (4th Dist. Ct. App.1957). As with the issue of foreseeability, the issue of costs, social utility, and potential practical remedies can only be decided after a full factual presentation and analysis of applicable law.

(b)   Duty to Warn and Proximate Cause

In addition to showing that warnings (or other safety features) were required by the standard of reasonable care and that defendants failed to give such warnings or failed to give them in an adequate manner, plaintiffs must establish a causal connection. They must show (1) that defendants' failure to warn was a "cause in fact" of their injuries, i.e., the warnings might have averted the particular accident, and (2) that defendants' failure to warn was a "proximate cause" of their injuries, i.e., intervening events, remoteness or general policy considerations do not prevent a finding of liability. *See, e.g.,* Green, The Causal Relation Issue in Negligence Law, 60 Mich. L. Rev. 543, 548-569 (1962); 2 Harper & James, The Law of Torts §§ 20.1-.6 at 1108-1161 (1956) and Supplement at 92-104 (1968). *But cf.* Harper and James, *id.* Supplement at 93 ("the dichotomy is not a clear one").

Existence of the I.M.E. safety program and the possibility of intervening acts by others are relevant to the question of defendants' liability for failure to warn, but they do not entitle defendants at this stage to a judgment as a matter of law. The practice of the explosives industry of supplying warnings to customers and users through notices printed on and inserted in packages of blasting caps has already been the subject of litigation. In *Eck v. E. I. Du Pont De Nemours & Co.,* 393 F.2d 197 (7th Cir. 1968), the Seventh Circuit held that whether such warnings had adequately served notice on an injured workman, "either personally or vicariously, raised an issue of fact which the court should have submitted to the jury." 393 F.2d 197, 201. The adequacy of printed warnings and the I.M.E. safety program is even less clear-cut in this case, where the manufacturers cannot claim that children, in contrast to workmen using blasting caps, are aware of risks generally known in the trade. *Cf. Hopkins v. E. I. Du Pont De Nemours & Co.,* 199 F.2d 930, 933 (3d Cir. 1952), judgment reversed on basis of Pennsylvania law, 212 F.2d 623 (3d Cir. 1954); *Canifax v. Hercules Powder Co.,* 237 Cal. App.2d 44, 54-55, 46 Cal. Rptr. 552, 559 (3d Dist. 1965).

The defendants' contention that warnings on the caps might have been ineffective had they been given, refers to problems of proof which clearly cannot be resolved prior to a full factual presentation. See 2 Harper & James, The Law of Torts, § 20.2 at 1113-14 (1956) and Supplement at 94-95 (1968); Green, The Causal Relation Issue in Negligence Law, 60 Mich. L. Rev. 543, 559-60 (1962); *cf. Jacobs v. Technical Chemical Co.,* 472 S.W.2d 191, 196-200 (Tex. Ct. Civ. App. 1971); *Haft v. Lone Palm Hotel,* 3 Cal.3d 756, 768-69, 91 Cal. Rptr. 745, 752, 478 P.2d 465, 472 (1970).

The general rule on intervening acts and proximate cause includes the element of foreseeability: an intervening act by a third person (even if negligent) relieves the original negligent actor from liability only if "the subsequent wrongdoer's act could not have been anticipated by the first actor in the exercise of due care." *Boeing Airplane Co. v. Brown,* 291 F.2d 310, 317-18 (9th Cir. 1961); *see also* Rest.2d Torts § 447(a) (1965); 2 Harper & James, The Law of Torts, § 28.10 at 1555, § 20.5 at 1141-46 (1956).

In many cases the defendant's negligence rests precisely on his failure to guard against the risks of foreseeable misconduct by others, and the occurrence of such misconduct, "whether innocent, negligent, intentionally tortious, or criminal does not prevent the actor from being liable for harm caused thereby." Rest.2d Torts § 449 (1965). Alternatively stated, "[t]he happening of the very event the likelihood of which makes the actor's conduct negligent cannot relieve him from liability." Rest.2d Torts § 449, comment *b* (1965); *cf. Petition of Kinsman Transit Co.,* 338 F.2d 708, 723-24 (2d Cir. 1964), *cert. denied sub nom. Continental Grain Co. v. City of Buffalo,* 380 U.S. 944, 85 S. Ct. 1026, 13 L. Ed.2d 963 (1965).

A typical application of this principle is found in numerous cases holding that trespassing, tampering, and other misconduct by children, particularly in relation to dangerous instruments and machinery, is a foreseeable risk whose occurrence does not insulate a defendant who has failed to provide reasonable safeguards. See 2 Harper & James, The Law of Torts, § 20.5 at 1144 n. 34 (1956) and Supplement at 100 (1958); Rest.2d Torts § 449, Appendix at 245-57 (1966). Even if it were determined that such acts, or certain kinds of acts, constituted superseding causes, it would still be a question for the jury (assuming sufficiency of the plaintiffs' evidence) as to whether they actually occurred. *See McLaughlin v. Mine Safety Appliances,* 11 N.Y.2d 62, 71-72, 226 N.Y.S.2d 407, 413-14, 181 N.E.2d 430, 435 (1962).

(2)   *Strict Liability*

A duty to warn may be imposed on a manufacturer under strict liability principles if without a warning his product would be "in a defective condition unreasonably dangerous to the user or consumer." Rest.2d Torts § 402A and comment *j* (1965). Whether a product is "defective" or "unreasonably dangerous" depends on the same considerations respecting harm already discussed in the context of negligence: foreseeability, seriousness and cost of preventing. Under strict liability principles, however, they are applied in a somewhat different manner. The plaintiff does not have to identify and prove a particular failure to exercise reasonable care on the part of the manufacturer, nor can the manufacturer assert in defense that the product's design or manufacture was carried out with reasonable care. *See, e.g., O'Keefe v. Boeing Co.,* 335 F. Supp. 1104, 1118-19, 1132 (S.D.N.Y. 1971); *Cunningham v. MacNeal Memorial Hospital,* 47 Ill.2d 443, 453-54, 266 N.E.2d 897, 902 (1970); Rest.2d Torts § 402A(a) (1965).

There are two reasons for imposing strict liability on manufacturers. They may be summarized by the phrases "incentive" and "risk allocation."

A manufacturer is in the best position to discover defects or dangers in his product and to guard against them through appropriate design, manufacturing and distribution safeguards, inspection and warnings. *See, e.g., Vandermark v. Ford Motor Co.,* 61 Cal.2d 256, 260-63, 37 Cal. Rptr. 896, 898-900, 391 P.2d 168, 170-72 (1964); *Escola v. Coca-Cola Bottling Co. of Fresno,* 24 Cal.2d 453, 461, 150 P.2d 436, 440-41 (1944) (Traynor, J., concurring); James, General Products—Should Manufacturers Be Liable Without Negligence?, 24 Tenn. L. Rev. 923 (1957). A rigorous rule of liability with enhanced possibilities of large recoveries is an "incentive" to maximize safe design or a "deterrence" to dangerous design, manufacture, and distribution. *See, e.g., Vandermark v. Ford Motor Co.,* 61 Cal.2d 256, 260-63, 37 Cal. Rptr. 896, 898-900, 391 P.2d 168, 170-72 (1964); Katz, The Function of Tort Liability in Technology Assessment, 38 U. Cinn. L. Rev. 587, 607-08, 631-36 (1969).

The fact that the safety practices of entire industries have been held to be below the standard of reasonable care indicates the need for broad safety incentives. *See Marsh Wood Products Co. v. Babcock and Wilcox Co.,* 207 Wis. 209, 218-19, 240 N.W. 392, 396 (1932); *The T. J. Hooper,* 60 F.2d 737, 740 (2d Cir. 1932); cf. *Canifax v. Hercules Powder Co.,* 237 Cal. App.2d 44, 55, 46 Cal. Rptr. 552, 559 (3d Dist. 1965); Katz, The Function of Tort Liability in Technology Assessment, 38 U. Cinn. L. Rev. 587, 631-36 (1969).

A second approach has been variously expressed as "loss distribution," "risk allocation," or "enterprise liability." Regardless of safety measures taken by manufacturers and distributors, accidents and injuries will inevitably occur which can be fairly said to have been wholly or partly caused by some defective characteristic of the product involved. Accidents and injuries, in this view, are seen as an inevitable and statistically foreseeable "cost" of the product's consumption or use. *See, e.g., Greenman v. Yuba Power Products, Inc.,* 59 Cal.2d 57, 63-64, 27 Cal. Rptr. 697, 701, 377 P.2d 897, 901 (1962).

The policy question of who should bear this cost has already been resolved in the great majority of jurisdictions which have adopted the principle of strict tort liability for manufacturers and suppliers, or its equivalent, implied warranty without privity.

§ 2.17A SPECIAL TYPES OF LIABILITY

See, for compilations of jurisdictions which have adopted these doctrines, Prosser, The Fall of the Citadel (Strict Liability to the Consumer), 50 Minn. L. Rev. 791, 794-99 (1966); 2 Frumer & Friedman, Products Liability, § 16A [3] (1970 rev.). These jurisdictions include seven of the ten states in which plaintiffs' injuries occurred, three of the four states in which the manufacturers have their principal places of business, and the state of New York in which the trade association is located and in which the action has been brought.

Strict liability concepts do not require the manufacturer to produce a product incapable of doing harm; the very utility of many products, such as knives and automobiles, presupposes characteristics which can inflict harm. A "defect" must "cause" the harm. [A] plaintiff must trace his injury to a quality or condition of the product which was unreasonably dangerous either for a use to which the product would ordinarily be put, or for some special use which was brought to the attention of the defendant. These are the risks and losses which may fairly be regarded as typical of the enterprise and so fairly allocable to it. James, General Products—Should Manufacturers Be Liable Without Negligence? 24 Tenn. L. Rev. 923, 927 (1957) (citation omitted).

It is important to note that there is no sharp boundary between foreseeability, i.e., probability of harm, under negligence and under strict liability principles. On the contrary, there has been a continual interplay between the two doctrines. See, for an example of strict liability as influenced by foreseeability under negligence principles, *Davis v. Wyeth Laboratories, Inc.,* 399 F.2d 121, 129-30 (9th Cir. 1968) citing *Wright v. Carter Products, Inc.,* 244 F.2d 53, 56, 58 (2d Cir. 1957); for the converse example see the broad concept of foreseeability adopted under negligence principles in *Larsen v. General Motors Corp.,* 391 F.2d 495, 501-03 (8th Cir. 1968).

Reduction of the threshold probability required before a defendant-manufacturer can be held liable in either negligence or strict liability has resulted from the abandonment of rigid categorical judgments about what kinds of uses and users are foreseeable, and from an increased willingness to submit such issues to juries where the determination "depends on policy values underlying the 'common affairs of life.'" Passwaters v. General Motors Corp., 454 F.2d 1270, 1275 n.5 at 1276 (8th Cir. 1972). *See also* Noel, Defective Products: Abnormal Use, Contributory Negligence, and Assumption of Risk, 25 Vand. L. Rev. 93, 128 (1972).

In enterprise liability terms, what is important is "the foreseeability of the kinds of risks which the enterprise is likely to create" as distinguished from the negligence standard's focus on foreseeably unreasonable risks of specific conduct in particular circumstances. James, General Products—Should Manufacturers Be Liable Without Negligence?, 24 Tenn. L. Rev. 923, 925 (1957). Scope of possible liability is measured not by what "can and should reasonably be avoided" (though it may include such risks) but rather "the more or less inevitable toll of a lawful enterprise." 2 Harper & James, The Law of Torts § 26.7 at 1377 (1956). As in the areas of workmen's compensation and (in some jurisdictions) respondeat superior, the enterprise's liability extends to "the harm . . . typical for [the enterprise's] activities, and thus calculable and reasonably insurable." Ehrenzweig, Negligence Without Fault, 54 Calif. L. Rev. 1422, 1457 (1966).

Courts have used both "incentive" and "risk allocation" theories in applying strict liability. In a case holding a drug manufacturer liable for failure to warn users of the statistically small but qualitatively severe danger of a polio vaccine, the Ninth Circuit emphasized the fact of the manufacturer's actual knowledge of the risks involved. While the manufacturer was immune from liability during an initial period when "there was no known or foreseeable risk involved in taking [the drug]," "after further experience, the danger became apparent [and] a duty to warn attached." *Davis v. Wyeth Laboratories, Inc.,* 399 F.2d 121, 129 (9th Cir. 1968). *See also Basko v. Sterling Drug Co., Inc.,* 416 F.2d 417, 426 (2d Cir. 1969).

In cases where manufacturers have more experience, more information, and more control over the risky properties of their products than do drug manufacturers, courts have applied a broader concept of foreseeability which approaches the enterprise liability rationale. *See generally* Noel, Defective Products: Extension of Strict Liability to Bystanders, 38 Tenn. L. Rev. 1, 7-10 (1970) and cases cited therein.

A number of jurisdictions, including California, Texas, Indiana, New Jersey, Connecticut, Arizona, Michigan and New York have extended strict liability beyond its limitation in the Restatement to "users and consumers" (Rest.2d Torts § 402A and comment *o* on Caveat (1965)) to include third parties and "bystanders" injured by products such as automobiles, shotguns, and power lawnmowers. *See Elmore v. American Motors Corp.,* 70 Cal.2d 578, 75 Cal. Rptr. 652, 451 P.2d 84 (1969); *Darryl v. Ford Motor Co.,* 440 S.W.2d 630 (Tex. 1969); *Sills v. Massey-Ferguson, Inc.,* 296 F. Supp. 776 (N.D. Ind. 1969); *Lamendola v. Mizell,* 115 N.J. Super. 514, 280 A.2d 241 (1970); *Mitchell v. Miller,* 26 Conn. Super. 142, 214 A.2d 694 (1965); *Caruth v. Mariani,* 11 Ariz. App. 188, 463 P.2d 83 (1970); *Piercefield v. Remington Arms,* 375 Mich. 85, 133 N.W.2d 129 (1965); *Codling v. Paglia,* 38 A.D.2d 154, 327 N.Y.S.2d 978 (3d Dep't. 1972). These courts reason that defects in, for example, automobiles pose a thoroughly foreseeable risk to other persons on or near the road, and that the policies underlying strict liability—control of the risk and spreading of loss—are applicable regardless of the "user or consumer" limitation. *See, e.g., Elmore v. American Motors Corp.,* 70 Cal.2d 578, 586, 75 Cal. Rptr. 652, 657, 451 P.2d 84, 88-89 (1969); *cf.* for discussion of enterprise liability and products other than automobiles: *Sills v. Massey-Ferguson, Inc.,* 296 F. Supp. 776, 781 (N.D. Ind. 1969) (power lawnmower); *Klimas v. International Telephone and Telegraph Corp.,* 297 F. Supp. 937, 941- 42 (D.R.I. 1969) (electrical fuse).

As in the case of negligence, the greater the product's dangers when defects are present, the less the power of the court to preclude recovery by foreclosing a jury judgment of culpability. *Davis v. Wyeth Laboratories, Inc.,* 399 F.2d 121, 129-30 (9th Cir. 1968). Similarly, where tampering by children is involved, negligence's tenderness towards youth is reflected in a reluctance to dismiss a strict liability claim. *Thomas v. General Motors Corp.,* 13 Cal. App.3d 81, 91 Cal. Rptr. 301 (4th Dist. 1970).

If the standard of strict liability is found applicable to the absence of warnings on the caps, the range of intervening acts which will insulate the defendants from liability will be even narrower than under negligence principles. See Rest.2d Torts § 402A, comment *n* (1965); 2 Frumer & Friedman, Products Liability § 16A [5] [f]. However that range of intervening acts is defined under the laws of the various states, it will remain a jury question as to whether they occurred. See *Sills v. Massey-Ferguson, Inc.,* 296 F. Supp. 776, 782 (N.D. Ind. 1969).

D.   *Joint Liability*

The central question raised by defendants' motion is whether the defendants can be held responsible as a group under any theory of joint liability for injuries arising out of their individual manufacture of blasting caps. Joint tort liability is not limited to a narrow set of relationships and circumstances. It has been imposed in a wide range of situations, requiring varying standards of care, in which defendants cooperate in various degrees, enter into business and property relationships, and undertake to supply goods for public consumption. Developments in negligence and strict tort liability have imposed extensive duties on manufacturers to guard against a broad spectrum of risks with regard to the general population. The reasoning underlying current policy justifies the extension of established doctrines of joint tort liability to the area of industry-wide cooperation in product manufacture and design.

(1)   The *Elements of Joint Liability*

Joint liability has historically been imposed in four distinguishable kinds of situations: (1) the actors knowingly join in the performance of the tortious act or acts; (2) the actors fail to perform a common duty owed to the plaintiff; (3) there is a special relationship between the parties (e.g., master and servant or joint entrepreneurs); (4) although there is no concerted action nevertheless the independent acts of several actors concur to produce indivisible harmful consequences. 1 Harper & James, The Law of Torts § 10.1 at 697-98 (1956). *See also* Prosser, Joint Torts and Several Liability, 25 Calif. L. Rev. 413, 429 et seq. (1937).

These categories reflect three overlapping but distinguishable problems with which the law of joint liability has been concerned. The first is the problem of joint or group control of risk: the need to deter hazardous behavior by groups or multiple defendants as well as by individuals. The second is the problem of enterprise liability: the policy of assigning the foreseeable costs of an activity to those in the most strategic position to reduce them. The third is the problem of fairness with respect to burden of proof: the desire to avoid denying recovery to an innocent injured plaintiff because proof of causation may be within defendants' control or entirely unavailable. The complaint and defendants' motion to dismiss raise all three problems for consideration.

(2)   *Joint Control of Risk*

The problem of joint control of risk was early posed in a case of group assault. In imposing joint liability, the court reasoned that ". . . [with] all coming to do an unlawful act, and of one party, the act of one is the act of all (*See* Sir John Heydon's Case, 11 Co. Rep. 5, 77 Eng. Rep. 1150 (1613), and other English cases cited in Prosser, Law of Torts § 46 at 291 (4th ed. 1971)). Even in its earliest form the doctrine of joint liability for concerted action contained all the elements necessary for its future development: (1) causing harm (2) by cooperative or concerted activities (3) which violated a legal standard of care.

INITIATION OF THE SUIT

American courts have imposed joint liability for concerted action in cases involving a complex interaction of the three elements of the doctrine. "Cooperation" or "concert" has been found in various business and property relationships, group activities such as automobile racing, cooperative efforts in medical care or railroad work, and concurrent water pollution. "Express agreement is not necessary; all that is required is that there shall be a common design or understanding." Prosser, Joint Torts and Several Liability, 25 Cal. L. Rev. 413, 429-30 (1937).

The standard of care to which defendants have been jointly held has ranged from assault and reckless driving to negligence in building maintenance, brush burning, water pollution, and manufacture of explosives. *See, e. g., Simmons v. Everson,* 124 N.Y. 319, 25 N.E. 911 (1891) (collapsed wall supported by interlocking walls); *Prussak v. Hutton,* 30 App. Div. 66, 51 N.Y.S. 761 (3d Dep't. 1898) (powder house used and maintained by several defendants); *Troop v. Dew,* 150 Ark. 560, 234 S.W. 992 (1921) (defendant contractors breaking fences allowing cattle to enter); *Hanrahan v. Cochran,* 12 App. Div. 91, 42 N.Y.S. 1031 (4th Dep't. 1896) (racing horses); *Bierczynski v. Rogers, Del.,* 239 A.2d 218 (1968) (racing cars); *Sprinkle v. Lemley,* 243 Or. 521, 414 P.2d 797 (1966) (doctors treating same patient); *Michigan Millers Mut. Fire Ins. Co. v. Oregon-Washington R. & Nav. Co.,* 32 Wash.2d 256, 201 P.2d 207 (1948) (railroads burning brush); *Moses v. Town of Morgantown,* 192 N.C. 102, 133 S.E. 421 (1926) (independent discharging of refuse into stream); *Thompson v. Johnson,* 180 F.2d 431 (5th Cir. 1950) (assault by several individuals); *Dement v. Olin-Mathieson Chemical Corp.,* 282 F.2d 76 (5th Cir. 1960) (manufacturers of components).

These diverse cases impose joint liability on groups whose actions create unreasonable hazards of risks of harm, even though only one member of the group may have been the "direct" or physical cause of the injury. Where courts perceive a clear joint control of risk—typically the racing and assault cases, as well as those involving common duties or joint enterprise—the issue of who "caused" the injury is distinctly secondary to the fact that the group engaged in joint hazardous conduct.

This rationale was recognized in the nineteenth century. In a case involving a horse race in a crowded street, a New York court noted that the collision was "not willful or intentional on the part of the defendants," but it upheld a jury determination that the negligent racing of the defendants was the joint cause of injury. *Hanrahan v. Cochran,* 12 App. Div. 91, 94, 42 N.Y.S. 1031, 1032-33 (4th Dep't. 1896). Imposing liability on the defendant not involved in the actual collision, the court stated that "these defendants were acting together and in concert in this race. It was the race that created the condition that resulted in the accident." 12 App. Div. at 95, 42 N.Y.S. at 1033. By participating in a joint creation of negligent risk, both defendants were held liable for the consequences. See, for a modern application of this rule to automobile racing, *Lemons v. Kelly,* 239 Or. 354, 360-61, 397 P.2d 784, 787 (1964), and Annot., 13 A.L.R.3d 431 (1967) (collecting cases). Analogous language focusing on the joint creation of risk can be found in the "common duty" cases, as when several defendants neglect to maintain a party wall. *Simmons v. Everson,* 124 N.Y. 319, 25 N.E. 911 (1891).

Joint control of risk can also arise through business relations or joint enterprise. Thus a New York court found that the owner and lessee of a powder magazine, as

48

well as the purchaser of the powder, all "participated in the maintenance of the powder house" and hence were jointly liable for damages caused by explosion. *Prussak v. Hutton,* 30 App. Div. 66, 67, 51 N.Y.S. 761, 763 (3d Dep't. 1898). *See also Lindsay v. Acme Cement Plaster Co.,* 220 Mich. 367, 190 N.W. 275 (1922) (two defendants under a duty to keep track in repairs); *Walton, Witten & Graham Co. v. Miller's Adm'x,* 109 Va. 210, 63 S.E. 458 (1909) (employer and contractor both under duty to warn employee as to blasting); *Troop v. Dew,* 150 Ark. 560, 234 S.W. 992 (1921) (independent contractors both under duty to repair fences). The opinions frequently refer to the defendants' violations of a common duty of care not only in terms of joint control of risk, but also as concurrent causes which combine to produce injury. *See, e.g., Walton, Witten & Graham Co. v. Miller's Adm'x,* 109 Va. 210, 213-14, 63 S.E. 458, 460 (1909).

Defendants argue that their participation in the I.M.E. safety program, and their cooperative or parallel activities regarding the safety features of blasting caps do not give them joint control over the risks of injury for purposes of tort liability. Joint control of risk and consequent joint responsibility arises, in their view, only when manufacturers enter into a conspiracy to commit intentional harm, or into a partnership or joint venture. The key to a joint venture, they assert, is an agreement to share profits and to pursue a limited number of business objectives over a short period of time. Since the defendants' membership in their trade association involves neither profit-sharing nor a limited time-span, they contend that no joint responsibility arises from the association and its members' activities.

The problem with this argument is that the elements of joint control of risk do not coincide with those in the formal doctrine of joint venture. The distinction was the basis for decision in *Connor v. Great Western Savings & Loan Assn.,* 69 Cal.2d 850, 73 Cal. Rptr. 369, 447 P.2d 609 (1968). The court found that a savings bank (Great Western) and a housing developer (Conejo) had, as a matter of practical economics, combined their property, skill, and knowledge to carry out the tract development, that each shared in the control of the development, that each anticipated receiving substantial profits therefrom, and that they cooperated with each other in the development. 69 Cal.2d 850, 863, 73 Cal. Rptr. 369, 375, 447 P.2d 609, 615.

Despite this extensive cooperation and shared control of the venture the court found that there is no evidence of a community or joint interest in the undertaking. Great Western participated as a buyer and seller of land and lender of funds, and Conejo participated as a builder and seller of homes. Although the profits of each were dependent on the overall success of the development, neither was to share in the profits or the losses that the other might realize or suffer. *Id.* Applying the rule that [A] joint venture exists when there is "an agreement between the parties under which they have . . . a joint interest, in a common business undertaking, and understanding as to the sharing of profits and losses, and a right of joint control." *Id.* (citations omitted), the court declined to hold the bank vicariously liable as a joint venturer for the negligence of the developer. The court did find the bank liable for its own negligence in exercising what in practical effect was its joint control of the venture.

In undertaking these relationships [with the developer] Great Western [the bank] became much more than a lender content to lend money at interest on the security of real property. It became an active participant in a home construction enterprise. It had the right to exercise extensive control of the enterprise. Its financing, which made the enterprise possible, took on ramifications beyond the domain of the usual money lender. 69 Cal.2d 850, 864, 73 Cal. Rptr. 369, 376, 447 P.2d 608, 616. The bank, it held, should have realized that the thinly capitalized builder would be under great pressure to put up shoddy housing. The lesson is clear that joint control of risk can exist among actors who are not bound in a profit-sharing joint venture. This point is thoroughly confirmed by cases imposing joint liability on "joint enterprises," which are distinguished from "joint ventures" as being "non profit undertaking[s] for the mutual benefit or pleasure of the parties" (*Connor v. Great Western Savings & Loan Assn.,* 69 Cal.2d 850, 863-64 n. 6, 73 Cal. Rptr. 369, 376 n. 6, 447 P.2d 609, 616 n. 6 (1968)) and on which joint liability is imposed because of the parties' effective joint control of the risk. *See* Prosser, Law of Torts § 72 at 475-80 (4th ed. 1971).

Joint control may be shown in one of three ways. First, plaintiffs can prove the existence of an explicit agreement and joint action among the defendants with regard to warnings and other safety features—the classic "concert of action." Second, plaintiffs can submit evidence of defendants' parallel behavior sufficient to support an inference of tacit agreement or cooperation. Such cooperation has the same effects as overt joint action, and is subject to joint liability for the same reasons. *Cf.* Prosser, Joint Torts and Several Liability, 25 Calif. L. Rev. 413, 430 (1937); Posner, Oligopoly and the Antitrust Laws: A Suggested Approach, 21 Stan. L. Rev. 1562, 1576-78 (1969). Third, plaintiffs can submit evidence that defendants, acting independently, adhered to an industry-wide standard or custom with regard to the safety features of blasting caps. Regardless of whether such evidence is sufficient to support an inference of tacit agreement, it is still relevant to the question of joint control of risk. The dynamics of market competition frequently result in explicit or implicit safety standards, codes, and practices which are widely adhered to in an entire industry. *See, e.g.,* 1 Frumer & Friedman, Products Liability § 5.04 (1970 rev.). Where such standards or practices exist, the industry operates as a collective unit in the double sense of stabilizing the production costs of safety features and in establishing an industry-wide custom which influences, but does not conclusively determine, the applicable standard of care. *See* Prosser, Law of Torts § 33 at 166-68 (4th ed. 1971) (on relationship of industry custom to standard of care). As our decision in *Hall* below indicates, the existence of industry-wide standards or practices alone will not support, in all circumstances, the imposition of joint liability. But where, as here in *Chance,* individual defendant-manufacturers cannot be identified, the existence of industry-wide standards or practices could support a finding of joint control of risk and a shift of the burden of proving causation to the defendants. See discussion of Rest.2d Torts § 433B (1965) below. In view of the allegations of explicit cooperation among members of the industry, it is apparent that plaintiffs have chosen the first of the above three alternative theories. We have set forth the other two lines of possible proof only to suggest the *a fortiori* position presented in the instant case.

There is thus no support for defendants' argument that to establish joint control of risk, plaintiffs must demonstrate that the explosives industry was "rigidly controlled" through the trade association with regard to blasting cap design, manufacture, and labeling, and that the object of such control was some particularly reprehensible breach of duty. The variety of business and property relationships in which joint control of risk has been found demonstrates the flexibility of the doctrine. Liability is not limited to particular formal modes of cooperation, nor to illegal or grossly negligent activities. Two recent cases provide examples under both strict liability and negligence standards. In *Vandermark v. Ford Motor Co.,* 61 Cal.2d 256, 37 Cal. Rptr. 896, 391 P.2d 168 (1964), the applicable standard of care was strict liability; the duty of an automobile manufacturer was defined as having "its cars delivered to the ultimate purchaser free from dangerous defects" whether "negligently or nonnegligently caused." 61 Cal.2d 256, 261, 37 Cal. Rptr. 896, 899, 898, 391 P.2d 168, 171, 170. The court clearly perceived the manufacturer of the completed product as the strategic link in the complex chain of production and distribution and held that it could not delegate its duty backward to the manufacturers of component parts or forward to dealers and distributors.

For purposes of strict liability, the retail automobile distributor was also held to be "an integral part of the overall producing and marketing enterprise that should bear the costs of injuries resulting from defective products." 61 Cal.2d 256, 262, 37 Cal. Rptr. 896, 899, 391 P.2d 168, 171. This conclusion was based in part on the fact that the retailer himself may play a substantial part in insuring that the product is safe or may be in a position to exert pressure on the manufacturer to that end; the retailer's strict liability thus serves as an added incentive to safety. 61 Cal.2d 256, 262, 37 Cal. Rptr. 896, 899-900, 391 P.2d 168, 171-72.

Holding the retailer strictly liable was also justified on the grounds that "in some cases the retailer may be the only member of [the] enterprise reasonably available to the injured plaintiff." 61 Cal.2d 256, 262, 37 Cal. Rptr. 896, 899, 391 P.2d 148, 171. Joint liability "affords maximum protection to the injured plaintiff and works no injustice to the defendants, for they can adjust the costs of such protection between them in the course of their continuing business relationship." 61 Cal.2d 256, 262-63, 37 Cal. Rptr. 896, 900, 391 P.2d 168, 172.

In the *Vandermark* case, the factors considered relevant to the issue of joint liability were (1) the standard of care—itself a function of the foreseeability and gravity of risk and the capacity of avoiding it; (2) the participants' capabilities of promoting the requisite safety in the risk-creating process; (3) the need to protect the consumer, both in terms of ascertaining responsible parties and providing compensation; and (4) the participants' ability to adjust the costs of liability among themselves in a continuing business relationship.

The Fifth Circuit looked to similar considerations in a case involving the question of joint control of risk in the context of *res ipsa loquitur.* The plaintiff in *Dement v. Olin-Mathieson Chemical Corp.,* 282 F.2d 76 (5th Cir. 1960), had been injured while working with an explosive charge containing three component parts. Evidence indicated that two of the components—the blasting cap and the dynamite—might have caused the accident. One of the defendant-manufacturers argued that the plaintiff was not entitled to the aid of *res ipsa,* since only one of the components had been under its exclusive control.

This "musical chairs argument" was rejected on the grounds it was not necessary that in order for res ipsa to apply one particular force must be severed out, identified and held as a matter of law to be the cause of the premature explosion. The various components were manufactured to be a part of one combination. . . . Even in cases in which there is no combination as there obviously is here, the Texas courts recognize joint liability against actors completely independent and unrelated to each other in circumstances where their conduct has caused indivisible injury which cannot be accurately apportioned and identified by the plaintiff. *Dement v. Olin-Mathieson Chemical Corp.,* 282 F.2d 76, 82 (5th Cir. 1960) (citation omitted).

Like the Supreme Court of California in *Vandermark,* the Fifth Circuit emphasized the defendant-manufacturers' high duty of care to guard against defects in explosives, the defendants' control over the products at the critical stage when care was needed, the necessity of not imposing impenetrable procedural and burden of proof requirements on injured plaintiffs, and the possibility of cost-adjustment among the defendants. *See* 282 F.2d at 81, 82, 83, and 82 n. 3. *Cf. Ybarra v. Spangard,* 25 Cal.2d 486, 154 P.2d 687 (1944) (patient not required to show which doctor or nurse responsible for injury). Plaintiffs' allegations in this case raise genuine issues under these criteria. As discussed in detail above, the allegation that defendants had actual knowledge of risks to children and of feasible safety measures provides a basis for finding an applicable duty of care under negligence and strict liability principles. Plaintiffs further allege that the defendant manufacturers obtained this knowledge through a jointly-sponsored trade association; the manufacturers delegated, in effect, at least some functions of safety investigation and design (such as labeling) to an industry-wide entity. Whether defendants collected and shared this knowledge as a group, and made joint or cooperative decisions on the basis of the known risks, are critical issues which require full factual development.

Factors which must be explored to determine both the existence of joint control of risk and appropriate remedies (if any) include the size and composition of the trade association's membership, its announced and actual objectives in the field of safety, its internal procedures of decision-making on this issue, the nature of its information-gathering system with regard to accidents, the safety program and its implementation by the association and member manufacturers, and any other activities by the association and its members (such as legislative lobbying) with regard to safety during the time period in question. *See generally* Developments in the Law-Judicial Control of Private Associations, 76 Harv. L. Rev. 983, 994-998, 1037-1055, 1080-1095 (1963).

(3)   *Enterprise Liability*

Joint liability has been traditionally imposed on multiple defendants who exercise actual collective control over a particular risk-creating product or activity. In a related but distinguishable fashion, joint or vicarious liability has been imposed on the most strategically placed participants in a risk-creating process, even though injuries are caused "directly" or partially by other participants under their general supervision. *See* 2 Harper & James, The Law of Torts, ch. 26, esp. at 1361-69, 1375-78 (1956) and Supplement (1968). As Judge Cardozo noted in a workmen's compensation case involving injury to one employee by another's carelessness:

> The risks of injury incurred in the crowded contacts of the factory through
> the acts of fellow workmen are not measured by the tendency of such acts

to serve the master's business. Many things that have no such tendency are done by workmen every day. The test of liability under the statute is not the master's dereliction, whether his own or that of his representatives acting within the scope of their authority. The test of liability is the relation of the service to the injury, of the employment to the risk. *Leonbruno v. Champlain Silk Mills,* 229 N.Y. 470, 473, 128 N.E. 711, 712 (1920).

A similar principle of enterprise liability is embedded in the doctrine of respondeat superior—an employer's vicarious liability to third parties for employees' wrongs committed "in the scope of their employment." Rest. 2d Agency § 219(1) (1958). In the pure vicarious liability case, an employer is not charged himself with violating a standard of care—such as failing to properly supervise the inspection or labeling of a product. Rather, the employer is held liable because, despite reasonable precautions, his employee has violated the applicable standard of care. *See* Rest. 2d Agency §§ 219(1), 228, 229 (1958); 2 Harper & James, The Law of Torts, ch. 26 at 1361-63, 1368-69, 1372-74, 1390 (1956). The employer may be held liable even though the employee's acts (or failure to act) were forbidden or intentionally wrongful. Rest. 2d Agency § 230 (forbidden acts); § 231 (consciously criminal or tortious acts); § 232 (failure to act); *cf. Roberts v. Gagnon,* 1 A.D.2d 297, 300, 149 N.Y.S.2d 743, 747 (3d Dep't. 1956).

The rationale for an employer's vicarious liability to third parties has been analyzed as being very close to the enterprise liability basis of workmen's compensation. In both types of cases [w]e are not . . . looking for the master's fault but rather for risks that may fairly be regarded as typical of or broadly incidental to the enterprise he has undertaken. . . . [O]ne of the purposes for such a quest is to mark out in a broad way the extent of tort liability (as a cost item) that it is fair and expedient to require people to expect when they engage in such an enterprise, so there can be some reasonable basis for calculating this cost. . . . What is reasonably foreseeable in this context, however, is quite a different thing from the foreseeably unreasonable risk of harm that spells negligence. In the first place, we are no longer dealing with specific conduct but with the broad scope of a whole enterprise. Further, we are not looking for that which can and should reasonably be avoided, but with the more or less inevitable toll of a lawful enterprise. The foresight that should impel the prudent man to take precautions is not the same measure as that by which he should perceive the harm likely to flow from his long-run activity in spite of all reasonable precautions on his own part. The proper test here bears far more resemblance to that which limits liability for workmen's compensation than to the test for negligence. The employer should be held to expect risks, to the public also, which arise "out of and in the course of" his employment of labor. 2 Harper & James, The Law of Torts, § 26.7 at 1376-78 (1956) (citations omitted). *See also* Calebresi, Some Thoughts on Risk Distribution and the Law of Torts, 70 Yale L.J. 449, 543 (1961).

Enterprise liability is also apparent in the long line of cases imposing joint and vicarious liability on owners, employers and manufacturers for breach of "nondelegable duties," or for miscarriage of "inherently dangerous activities" by their contractors, employees, and distributors. *See* Prosser, Law of Torts § 71 at 470-74 (4th ed. 1971) (collecting cases).

INITIATION OF THE SUIT

A review of the cases demonstrates that the range of non-delegable duties is very broad; Dean Prosser suggests that the only unifying criterion is "the conclusion of the courts that the responsibility is so important to the community that the employer [in the broad sense of one who utilizes the services of another] should not be permitted to transfer it to another." Prosser, Law of Torts § 71 at 471 (4th ed. 1971). The list of "inherently dangerous activities" is also long, running from classic categories such as the keeping of vicious animals or blasting to any activity "in which there is a high degree of risk in relation to the particular surroundings" and which thus requires definite or special precautions. Prosser, *supra,* at 73; see Rest.2d Torts §§ 416, 427 (1965); Rest.2d Agency § 214, comment *c* (1958).

This body of precedent, whether couched in the language of non-delegable duty or inherently dangerous activity or both, is addressed essentially to the problem of when it is justifiable for an owner, employer, or manufacturer to rely on the services of another to guard against known or foreseeable risks. *See, e.g., Besner v. Central Trust Co.,* 230 N.Y. 357, 362-63, 130 N.E. 577, 578-79 (1921). The factors which must be considered in deciding whether such reliance is justifiable include the competence and reliability of the person upon whom reliance is placed, his understanding of the situation, the seriousness of the danger and the number of persons likely to be affected, the length of time elapsed, and above all the likelihood that proper care will not be used, and the ease with which the actor himself may take precautions. Prosser, Law of Torts § 33 at 177 (4th ed. 1971) (citations omitted).

In many instances the most strategic point of foresight, precaution and risk distribution may be the individual manufacturer, supplier, or employer. In other situations— typically water or air pollution by multiple emitters—the only feasible method of ascertaining risks, imposing safeguards and spreading costs is through joint liability or other methods of joint risk control. *See, e.g., Moses v. Town of Morgantown,* 192 N.C. 102, 133 S.E. 421 (1926); *Tackaberry Co. v. Sioux City Service Co.,* 154 Iowa 358, 378, 132 N.W. 945, 952-53 (1911) (Weaver, J. dissenting); *cf.* Katz, The Function of Tort Liability in Technology Assessment, 38 U. Cinn. L. Rev. 587, 616-20 (1969); Rheingold, Civil Cause of Action for Lung Damage Due to Pollution of Urban Atmosphere, 33 Brooklyn Law Rev. 17, 31-32 (1966). The point is not only that the damage is caused by multiple actors, but that the sole feasible way of anticipating costs or damages and devising practical remedies is to consider the activities of a group. We do not, of course, suggest that private actions are the best way to meet these problems but only that in the absence of preemptive legislation, tort principles will support a remedy. *Cf. Connecticut Action Now, Inc. v. Roberts Plating Company, Inc.,* 457 F.2d 81 (2d Cir. 1972); Michelman, Pollution as a Tort: A Non-Accidental Perspective on Calabresi's *Costs,* 80 Yale L.J. 647 (1971); Roberts, River Basin Authorities: A National Solution to Water Pollution, 83 Harv. L. Rev. 1527, 1540-1556 (1970); Calabresi and Melamed, Property Rules, Liability Rules, and Inalienability: One View of the Cathedral, 85 Harv. L. Rev. 1089, 1108-1110 (1972).

The allegations in this case suggest that the entire blasting cap industry and its trade association provide the logical locus at which precautions should be taken and liability imposed. It is unlikely that individual manufacturers would collect information about the nation-wide incidence and circumstances of blasting-cap accidents involving children, and it is entirely reasonable that the manufacturers should delegate this function to a jointly-sponsored and jointly-financed association.

In the event that the evidence warrants it, the imposition of joint liability on the trade association and its members should in no way be interpreted as "punishment" for the establishment of industry-wide institutions. Such liability would represent rather the law's traditional function of reviewing the risk and cost decisions inherent in industry-wide safety practices, whether organized or unorganized. *See, e.g., The T. J. Hooper,* 60 F.2d 737 (2d Cir. 1932).

To establish that the explosives industry should be held jointly liable on enterprise liability grounds, plaintiffs, pursuant to their pleading, will have to demonstrate defendants' joint awareness of the risks at issue in this case and their joint capacity to reduce or affect those risks. By noting these requirements we wish to emphasize their special applicability to industries composed of a small number of units. What would be fair and feasible with regard to an industry of five or ten producers might be manifestly unreasonable if applied to a decentralized industry composed of thousands of small producers.

(4)   *Causation and Burden of Proof*

Plaintiffs contend that they should be relieved of the usual burden of proving a causal connection between each of their injuries and a particular manufacturer. Their problem is that a blasting cap found and exploded by a child often destroys what will be the only reliable evidence of its manufacturer—markings on the casing. As a solution they invoke Section 433B of the Second Restatement of Torts, which provides in pertinent part:

> (2) Where the tortious conduct of two or more actors has combined to bring about harm to the plaintiff, and one or more of the actors seeks to limit his liability on the ground that the harm is capable of apportionment among them, the burden of proof as to the apportionment is upon each such actor. (3) Where the conduct of two or more actors is tortious, and it is proved that harm has been caused to the plaintiff by only one of them, but there is uncertainty as to which one has caused it, the burden is upon each such actor to prove that he has not caused the harm.

Subsection (2) is based primarily on cases in which water pollution has been caused by independent actors. Its applicability depends on an initial showing by the plaintiff that each defendant has done something—not necessarily simultaneously—to cause the damage although it cannot be demonstrated "that any one defendant was responsible for the entire injury or any specified part of it." 1 Harper & James, The Law of Torts § 10.1 at 708 (1956). Courts have held that where the injury "cannot be apportioned with reasonable certainty among the individual wrongdoers, all of the wrongdoers will be held jointly and severally liable for the entire damages. . . ." *Landers v. East Texas Salt Water Disposal Co.,* 151 Tex. 251, 256, 248 S.W.2d 731, 734 (1952); *see also* cases cited in 1 Harper & James, *supra,* § 10.1 at 706-09.

In the instant case plaintiffs have alleged that defendants' conduct combined to cause injury at the point of the labeling and designing of the caps. The rule embodied in section 433B(2) of the Second Restatement of Torts, shifting the burden of apportionment to the defendants, is applicable only as a corollary principle of proof to plaintiffs' main theories that defendants engaged in concerted action, or operated as a joint enterprise, with respect to the labeling and design of the caps. Subsection (3) of Section 433B shifts the burden of proving causation to independently-acting defendants. It arises not from the problem of combined causation but rather from alternative causation of injury. The best known example is *Summers v. Tice,* 33 Cal.2d 80, 199 P.2d 1 (1948), in which a hunter's injury could have been caused by only one of his two independently negligent companions. The reason for shifting the burden of proving causation, as with the burden of proving apportionment, is the injustice of permitting proved wrongdoers, who among them have inflicted an injury upon the entirely innocent plaintiff, to escape liability merely because the nature of their conduct and the resulting harm has made it difficult or impossible to prove which of them has caused the harm. Rest.2d Torts § 433B, comment *f* (1965). *See also* Wigmore, Joint Tortfeasors and Severance of Damages: Making the Innocent Party Suffer Without Redress, 17 Ill. L. Rev. 458 (1923).

Plaintiffs must first demonstrate that defendants breached a duty of care as to them. *See Summers v. Tice,* 33 Cal.2d 80, 85-86, 199 P.2d 1, 4 (1948); Rest.2d Torts § 433B, comment *g* (1965). We have already concluded that plaintiffs may be able to demonstrate such a breach.

Second, plaintiffs must establish some causal connection between the group—created risk and their injuries—"that the harm has resulted from the conduct of some one" of the tortious actors. Rest.2d Torts § 433B, comment *g* (1965). Defendants argue that the complaint fails to allege this connection between the named defendants and the injuries because it concedes that the caps may have been made by other, unnamed manufacturers. In their supporting papers defendants raise the possibility that the caps involved in the accidents may have come from Canadian or other foreign manufacturers or from domestic firms no longer in business and not named in the complaint. Defendants' Reply Memorandum, Sept. 2, 1971, at p. 4; Defendants' Reply Memorandum, Dec. 24, 1970, at p. 12.

The possibility—admitted by plaintiffs—that the caps may have come from other, unnamed sources, does not affect plaintiffs' burden of proof. Plaintiffs must show by a preponderance of the evidence—i. e., that it is more probable than not that the caps involved in the accidents were the products of the named defendant-manufacturers. Plaintiffs do not have to identify which one of the defendant-manufacturers made each injury-causing cap. To impose such a requirement would obviate the entire rule of shifting the burden of proving causation to the defendants. It must be more probable than not that an injury was caused by a cap made by some one of the named defendant manufacturers, though which one is unknown. *See, e.g.,* Ball, The Moment of Truth: Probability Theory and Standards of Proof, 14 Vand. L. Rev. 807 (1961); Tribe, Trial by Mathematics: Precision and Ritual in the Legal Process, 84 Harv. L. Rev. 1329, 1341 n. 37 (1971); J. M. Maguire et al., Cases and Materials on Evidence, 547-550 (5th ed. 1965); citations in *Rosado v. Wyman,* 322 F.Supp. 1173 (E.D.N.Y. 1970).

Defendants argue further that the requisite causal connection between the unknown member or members of the group and the injuries cannot be established because the defendants' conduct was not in "close physical and chronological connection to the injurious results." Defendants' Surrebuttal Memorandum at p. 10. While the hunting cases involve such conduct, a sufficient causal connection has been found in other circumstances involving more complex interaction between multiple defendants and injury. *See* Saint Pierre v. McCarthy [1957] Que. Rep. 421 (merchants selling cartridges to boys). The key requirement thus far imposed in the cases has been that the risk-creating conduct be "simultaneous in time, or substantially so, and [be] . . . of substantially the same character, creating substantially the same risk of harm, on the part of each actor." Rest.2d Torts § 433B, comment *h* (1965). The required chronological nexus, in other words, is not between defendants' conduct and injury, but among the conduct of the several defendants. Plaintiffs' allegations satisfy these criteria.

If plaintiffs can establish by a preponderance of the evidence that the injury-causing caps were the product of some unknown one of the named defendants, that each named defendant breached a duty of care owed to plaintiffs and that these breaches were substantially concurrent in time and of a similar nature, they will be entitled to a shift of the burden of proof on the issue of causation.

E.   *Joinder, Transfer and Conflict of Laws*

To justify permissive joinder of parties plaintiffs must show both a "common question of law or fact" and a right to relief "arising out of the same transaction or occurrence or series of transactions or occurrences." Fed. R. Civ. P. 20(a). Defendants move for severance of plaintiffs on the ground that the complaint fails to satisfy either requirement, and for dismissal or transfer of the claims thus severed. 28 U.S.C. § 1404(a). They assert that the substantive law of the ten states will govern liability, and hence the claims present no common question of law.

The question of which state's law will govern which aspects of this case cannot be settled by assertion. In diversity cases, a federal court is bound to apply the choice-of-law principles of the state in which it sits. *Klaxon v. Stentor Electric Mfg. Co.,* 313 U.S. 487, 61 S. Ct. 1020, 85 L. Ed. 1477 (1941). Under New York law, the choice of applicable law in personal injury cases is not determined by the traditional "place of injury" test, but by "the flexible principle that the law to be applied to resolve a particular issue is 'the law of the jurisdiction which, because of its relationship or contact with the occurrence or the parties, has the greatest concern' with the matter in issue and 'the strongest interest' in its resolution." *Long v. Pan American World Airways,* 16 N.Y.2d 337, 341, 266 N.Y.S.2d 513, 515, 213 N.E.2d 796, 798 (1965), quoting *Babcock v. Jackson,* 12 N.Y.2d 473, 481, 484, 240 N.Y.S.2d 743, 749, 751, 191 N.E.2d 279, 282, 285 (1963) (Fuld, J.). *Cf.* Reese, Products Liability and Choice of Law: The United States Proposals to the Hague Conference, 25 Vand. L. Rev. 29, 31-32, 37-38 (1972); Leflar, The Torts Provisions of the Restatement (Second) of Conflict of Laws, 72 Colum. L. Rev. 267, 270-71, 276-77 (1972).

The locus of defendants' joint activity was allegedly at least in part in New York, the location of the I.M.E. Whether proof of this connection would be sufficient to support the application of New York law to some or all of the claims is a complex question involving consideration of New York choice-of-law principles and federal constitutional law. The parties are directed to supply briefs on this issue and on the general question of the law applicable to the different aspects of this case. Prior to a full consideration of the choice-of-law question, this court cannot rule on whether the plaintiffs' claims contain a common question of law. It should be noted, however, that Rule 20(a) requires only *"any* common question of law or fact." Thus the presence of questions of law not common to all the plaintiffs will not, in itself, defeat joinder. *See Music Merchants v. Capitol Records,* 20 F.R.D. 462 (E.D.N.Y. 1957); 7 Wright & Miller, Federal Practice and Procedure § 1653 at 274 (1972).

Plaintiffs' claims do contain, moreover, common questions of fact-for example, whether the defendants exercised joint control over the labeling of blasting caps and operated, for purposes of tort liability, as a joint enterprise with respect to such labeling. The presence of these questions satisfies the requirement of Rule 20(a) that "any question of law or fact common to all these persons" arise in the action. Defendants also contend that because the accidents occurred at different times and places, plaintiffs' rights to relief do not arise out of the same transaction or occurrence, or series of transactions or occurrences. There is no rigid rule as to what constitutes "the same transaction or occurrence" for purposes of joinder under Rule 20(a). "[T]he approach must be the general one of whether there are enough ultimate factual concurrences that it would be fair to the parties to require them to defend jointly" against the several claims. *Eastern Fireproofing Co., Inc. v. United States Gypsum Co.,* 160 F. Supp. 580, 581 (D. Mass. 1958). Application of this flexible standard presents a certain challenge in this case. It would be neither fair nor convenient to any of the parties nor to the court to determine in this court all the relevant issues of fact involved in each accident. At the same time it would be unfair and burdensome to require each plaintiff to prove the alleged joint activities in ten separate and (to that extent) repetitive actions.

The solution does not lie in wholesale severance, and the cases cited by defendants do not support that result. *See, e.g., Kenvin v. Newburger, Loeb & Co.,* 37 F.R.D. 473 (S.D.N.Y. 1965), distinguishable from this case on the grounds that here, plaintiffs' right to relief arises to a significant (but not complete) extent on alleged joint activity which constitutes a single "transaction or occurrence." Rather, fairness to the parties may be maximized by permitting plaintiffs to litigate the issues of joint activity in this court, and then transferring the questions which turn on the particular facts of each accident to the federal districts in which the accidents occurred. *See* 28 U.S.C. § 1404(a), Rules 20(b) and 42(a) and (b), Federal Rules of Civil Procedure. Whether this procedure would entail full separate trials of different issues, or special findings of fact in this court, or other possible procedures, will be decided after consideration of the choice-of-law problem and in consultation with the parties.

II.   THE HALL CASE
A.   *Facts and Proceedings*

In *Hall v. Du Pont,* plaintiffs' first complaint was filed in 1969. In its original form, the complaint presented 230 claims on behalf of forty-three plaintiffs against fifteen defendants, comprising almost all American manufacturers of blasting caps and their trade association, the I.M.E.

The original *Hall* complaint, like the present complaint in *Chance,* did not link the plaintiffs' injuries to the products of particular manufacturers. Rather, the complaint alleged that virtually the entire blasting cap industry had cooperated with regard to certain safety features of its product, particularly with regard to warning labels. The results of this cooperation, according to the complaint, were inadequate safety provisions which in turn caused plaintiffs' injuries.

Two sets of legal theories were relied upon to support joint liability and federal jurisdiction. The first was grounded in federal anti-trust law: the defendants were said to have conspired to eliminate competition in the field of safety, in violation of the Sherman Anti-Trust Act, 15 U.S.C. § 1 *et seq.* A second set of claims was based on state law—including negligence, common law conspiracy, assault, and strict liability in tort—and was brought within federal jurisdiction by pendant jurisdiction and diversity of citizenship, 28 U.S.C. § 1332. The Sherman Act claims were dismissed because of the expiration of the applicable statute of limitations and plaintiffs were granted leave to amend. *Hall v. Du Pont,* 312 F. Supp. 358 (E.D.N.Y. 1970).

An amended complaint was filed. The plaintiffs in the *Hall* case now comprise the children of three families and their parents: the Halls, citizens of New York; the Balls, citizens of Ohio; and the Brieses, citizens of North Dakota. Each of the plaintiff-children claims damages against two manufacturers of blasting caps, Du Pont and Hercules, both citizens of Delaware, on grounds of negligence, common law conspiracy, assault, and strict liability in tort. Claims are also made by the parents of these children for loss of services and medical expenses. The sole basis of federal jurisdiction is diversity of citizenship.

I.M.E., an unincorporated New York association, was also named as a defendant. On plaintiffs' motion I.M.E. was dropped as a defendant to retain diversity jurisdiction. Fed. R. Civ. P. 21.

The new pleading resembles the original in most of its factual allegations. Each of three groups of children is said to have "come into possession" of a dynamite blasting cap which was not labeled or marked with a warning of danger, and which could be easily detonated by a child. In each instance an injurious explosion occurred.

One significant detail with regard to each injury is added in the amended complaint: the name of a particular manufacturer. In the case of the Hall children, the accident which occurred on April 17, 1956, in Suffolk County, New York, involved a cap "manufactured, labeled, and designed," according to the complaint, by Hercules. A cap similarly alleged to have been produced by Hercules is said to have been responsible for the injuries sustained by the Briese children in Bismarck, North Dakota, on July 31, 1956. The Ball child was allegedly injured in Caton, Ohio, on April 23, 1961, by a cap produced by Du Pont.

While the amended complaint links each injury to the product of a particular manufacturer, it also seeks to preserve the joint liability approach of the earlier pleading. The plaintiffs press their claims against "all defendants"; the Halls, for example, seek relief not only against Hercules, which allegedly produced the cap involved in the New York accident, but against Du Pont as well. Defendants responded to the amended complaint with several motions attacking the legal sufficiency of certain claims, the timeliness of the parents' claims, the joinder of the parties, and the appropriateness of the forum. While this court recognized that defendants' motions might have merit, they were denied pending discovery. *See* Memorandum and Order, Hall v. Du Pont, 69-C-273, February 16, 1971. After an extensive discovery period defendants' motions have been renewed.

B.   Joint Liability

The central question raised by defendants' motions is whether the amended complaint presents a claim of joint liability against the manufacturers. We hold that the amended complaint in *Hall* does not preserve the joint liability aspects of the case. After dismissal of the I.M.E. as a defendant on plaintiffs' motion, the defendants numbered only two manufacturers—Du Pont and Hercules—out of a larger group of active producers. The basis of selection of these two defendants is clear. Du Pont and Hercules happen to be the only two manufacturers whom three groups of plaintiffs can identify as the producers of injury-causing caps. Plaintiffs' assertion that Du Pont and Hercules "will fairly and adequately protect the interests of the unincorporated association and its members" is not sufficient to overcome the arbitrary method by which these two firms were selected by plaintiffs to defend against a claim of industry-wide responsibility.

A plaintiff is not required to implead all joint tort-feasors as indispensible parties. *See Lawlor v. National Screen Service Corp.,* 349 U.S. 322, 330, 75 S. Ct. 865, 869, 99 L. Ed. 1122 (1955); *Bigelow v. Old Dominion Copper Mining & Smelting Co.,* 225 U.S. 111, 132, 32 S. Ct. 641, 644, 56 L. Ed. 1009 (1912). Moreover, the courts will normally honor the plaintiff's choice of theory and the Federal Rules of Civil Procedure recognize his right to plead more than one claim or the same claim supported by different theories alternatively, hypothetically and even inconsistently. Fed. R. Civ. P. 8(a), (e) (2). Yet, there are limits on the plaintiff's choice. One consideration is that some remedies and theories pose substantially more difficult problems of administration than others. Another is the degree of avoidable cost and expense placed on the defendant.

The problem is most clearly posed in class actions where foreseeable burdens are so great that the court can exercise discretion to compel plaintiffs to use a less onerous alternative. *See* Fed. R. Civ. P. 23(b) (3); *Green v. Wolf Corp.,* 406 F.2d 291, 301 (2d Cir. 1968), *cert. denied,* 395 U.S. 977, 89 S. Ct. 2131, 23 L. Ed.2d 766 (1969). Thus, for example, in explaining Rule 23(b) (3) requiring a finding that "a class action is superior to other available methods for the fair and efficient adjudication of the controversy" the draftsmen of the Rule noted, "another method of handling the litigious situation may be available which has greater practical advantages . . . the court with the aid of the parties ought to assess the relative advantages of alternative procedures for handling the total controversy." 3B Moore's Federal Practice, ¶ 23.01 [10.3].

A "novel or boundary line" principle (Patterson, The Scope of Restitution and Unjust Enrichment, 1 Mo.L.Rev. 223, 231 (1936)), particularly where it requires courts and litigants to assume heavy burdens, need not be extended to situations where traditional remedies are perfectly satisfactory. In this respect the *Hall* case—where the manufacturer of the cap in question is known—is quite different from *Chance*— where it is not. It is true that the doctrine of adequacy and the exercise of judicial discretion denying alternative remedies is most often associated with specific performance. 2 Restatement of the Law of Contracts § 358 (1932). But we hardly need remind ourselves that equity and law have been merged in the federal courts; the principles of one need not be ignored in administering the other. *Cf.* Fed. R. Civ. P. 2 (one form of action); *Ross v. Bernhard,* 396 U.S. 531, 539-542, 90 S. Ct. 733, 738-740, 24 L. Ed.2d 729 (1970).

Plaintiffs, by joining defendants, rely upon equitable antecedents. *See, e.g.,* references to Equity Rules and Practice in the Committee Notes to Rules 19, 20 and 21 of the Federal Rules of Civil Procedure in 3A Moore's Federal Practice ¶¶ 19.01[3], 19.01[5-2], 20.01[2], 21.01[2]; 1 Harper & James, The Law of Torts, § 10.1 at 695-697 (1956). The hoary principle that he who seeks equity must do equity applies. McClintock, Handbook of Principles of Equity, 22 (2d ed.1948). Plaintiff will not be permitted to burden the court and defendants by an unnecessary and inappropriate joinder of a party having no real interest in the suit. McClintock, Handbook of Principles of Equity, 22 (2d ed.1948); 3A Moore's Federal Practice ¶ 20.08. *Cf. Dorsey v. Community Stores Corporation,* 52 F.R.D. 13 (E.D. Wis. 1971).

We do not justify this position on the ground that we "feel free to fashion an independent law of remedies in equitable actions." Wright, Handbook of the Law of Federal Courts, 242 (2d ed. 1970). *See also Zunamon v. Brown,* 418 F.2d 883, 888-889 (8th Cir.1969). Rather, it is an exercise of our procedural power to "secure the just, speedy, and inexpensive determination" of this action. Fed. R. Civ. P. 1.

No appropriate benefit to plaintiff is suggested by joining with the defendant who manufactured the damaging blasting cap another manufacturer of similar caps. Neither law nor equity encourages people to be "churlish about their rights." Lord Bowen quoted in Behrens v. Richards, [1905] 2 Ch. 614, Chaffee & Re, Equity, 893 (5th ed. 1967). In fact, as we have already noted, the redundant naming of an additional manufacturer results from the happenstance of joinder of claims by unrelated plaintiffs; a manufacturer whose cap was known to have caused the damage to any one plaintiff named in the complaint was carried over into the claims of another plaintiff for typographical rather than legal reasons.

The claims by the Halls and the Brieses against Du Pont and the claims by the Balls against Hercules must be dismissed.

INITIATION OF THE SUIT

C. *Appropriate Forum*

With each plaintiff now having claims only against the manufacturer of the injury-causing cap, defendants' motion for severance under Rule 20(a) of the Federal Rules of Civil Procedure must be granted. While evidence of joint action or responsibility may well be relevant in the claims against each manufacturer, proof of such responsibility will not be necessary for recovery on each plaintiff's claims. Recovery in each case will turn on the legal-factual questions of negligence and strict liability, and on evidence about the circumstances of the separate accidents. The claims by the three groups of plaintiffs present sufficiently diverse questions of law and fact to require severance.

This brings us to defendants' final contention, that the claims arising in North Dakota against Hercules and in Ohio against Du Pont should be dismissed as inappropriate to a New York forum, or alternatively, transferred to federal courts in North Dakota and Ohio. Section 1404(a) of title 28 of the United States Code provides that "for the convenience of parties and witnesses, in the interest of justice, a district court may transfer any civil action to any other district or division where it might have been brought."

Arguing for dismissal rather than transfer, defendants contend that the doctrine of *forum non conveniens* is "substantive" law and binding on a federal court in a diversity case under *Erie R. Co. v. Tompkins,* 304 U.S. 64, 58 S. Ct. 817, 82 L. Ed. 1188 (1938). Faced with a tort suit between nonresidents based on a tortious act outside New York, a New York state court would have only the remedy of dismissal. *See, e.g., Jones v. United States Lines, Inc.,* 36 A.D.2d 601, 318 N.Y.S.2d 557 (1st Dep't. 1971). Defendants' contention is that where a New York state court would dismiss on the grounds of inappropriate forum, a federal court sitting in New York must do likewise. Defendants' position has no support in prior cases or in the policy objectives of federal practice. Putting aside the question of whether New York practice would apply to the North Dakota and Ohio actions and whether New York courts would condition a dismissal on a defendant's agreement to submit to another jurisdiction, state law and remedies are not controlling. Federal courts, unlike state courts, have both the power and responsibility to coordinate and switch cases on a national scale in aid of the more efficient administration of justice. *See* 28 U.S.C. § 1404(a); *Thompson v. Palmieri,* 355 F.2d 64, 66 (2d. Cir. 1966). *Cf. Parsons v. Chesapeake & Ohio R. Co.,* 375 U.S. 71, 84 S. Ct. 185, 11 L. Ed.2d 137 (1963) (holding that prior dismissal of complaint by state court on basis of state doctrine of *forum non conveniens* does not divest federal court of discretionary power to rule on motion for transfer under 28 U.S.C. § 1404(a)). In any event, there is no inconsistency between the transfer policy of section 1404(a) and New York's *forum non conveniens* doctrine.

The relevant factors are well known. In terms of the private interests of the litigants, they include relative ease of access to proof, availability of witnesses (including compulsory process) and "all other practical problems which make trial of a case easy, expeditious, and inexpensive." *Gulf Oil Corp. v. Gilbert,* 330 U.S. 501, 508, 67 S. Ct. 839, 843, 91 L. Ed. 1055, 1062 (1947). The public interest in fairness and judicial administration is of at least equal importance and involves such considerations as familiarity with applicable local law, and avoidance of having litigation "piled up in congested centers instead of being handled at its origin." *Gulf Oil Corp. v. Gilbert, supra,* 330 U.S. at 508-509, 67 S. Ct. at 843. *See also Parsons v. Chesapeake & Ohio R. Co.,* 375 U.S. 71, 73-74, 84 S. Ct. 185, 197, 1 L. Ed.2d 137 (1963).

In the North Dakota and Ohio cases, local questions of fact and law will predominate. Transfer under 28 U.S.C. § 1404(a) is particularly appropriate because it secures the advantages of forums in which the accidents occurred while preserving the discovery already obtained in this court.

The claims of Dennis and Daryl Briese and their father, George Briese, against Hercules must be transferred to the United States District Court, District of North Dakota. The claims of Christopher Ball and his father, Harley Ball, against Du Pont must be transferred to the United States District Court, Northern District of Ohio. The claims of Philip and Douglas Hall and their father, Lloyd Hall, against Hercules, based on an accident which occurred in this district, remain in this court.

D.   *Parents' Claims for Loss of Services and Medical Expenses*

Defendants have moved to dismiss the claims by the parent-plaintiffs for loss of services and medical expenses on the grounds that they are barred by the applicable statutes of limitations. Since the claims arising in North Dakota and Ohio will be transferred to their respective federal districts, the statute of limitations question should be decided in those forums. The motions in this court to dismiss the parents' claims in the Briese and Ball cases are accordingly denied without prejudice.

The claim by Lloyd Hall, father of Philip and Douglas Hall, against Hercules, arises out of an accident which occurred in Suffolk County, New York, on April 17, 1956. In diversity cases, this court is bound to apply the New York statute of limitations. *See Guaranty Trust Co. v. York,* 326 U.S. 99, 65 S. Ct. 1464, 89 L. Ed. 2079 (1945). Under New York law, actions to recover damages for personal injury must be commenced within three years of the occurrence of the injury. CPLR 214; *Golia v. Health Ins. Plan of Greater New York,* 6 A.D.2d 884, 177 N.Y.S.2d 550 (2d Dep't. 1958), *aff'd,* 7 N.Y.2d 931, 197 N.Y.S.2d 735, 165 N.E.2d 578 (1960). For purposes of determining the applicable statute of limitations, a parent's action for a child's medical expenses is considered an action for "personal injury." *Bailey v. Boat,* 178 Misc. 870, 36 N.Y.S.2d 465 (Sup. Ct. Tioga Co. 1942); *Ballantine v. Ahearn,* 170 Misc. 651, 10 N.Y.S.2d 937 (Sup. Ct. Kings Co. 1939). While CPLR 208 provides for tolling of the statute of limitations during infancy, neither this section nor its predecessor, section 60 of the Civil Practice Act, tolls the statute for the parent's claims. *Kratz v. Dussault,* 33 A.D.2d 826, 305 N.Y.S.2d 734 (3d Dep't. 1969); *Francies v. County of Westchester,* 3 A.D.2d 850, 161 N.Y.S.2d 501 (2d Dep't. 1958).

No circumstances of a special nature militate against the application of the New York statute in this case. *Moviecolor Ltd. v. Eastman Kodak Co.,* 288 F.2d 80 (2d Cir.), *cert. denied,* 368 U.S. 821, 82 S. Ct. 39, 7 L. Ed. 26 (1961). Defendant Hercules' motion to dismiss Lloyd Hall's claim for medical expenses is accordingly granted.

III. CONCLUSION AS TO CHANCE AND HALL CASES
A. *Chance v. Du Pont*

In Chance v. Du Pont, 70-C-1107, plaintiffs cannot identify the particular manufacturers of the injury-causing caps. They have joined substantially the entire blasting cap industry and its trade association as defendants, and their recovery turns on theories of joint liability.

Plaintiffs' allegations of joint knowledge and action raise issues of fact and law sufficient to defeat dismissal, and to require full consideration of the choice-of-law issues in the case. Defendants' motion to dismiss the plaintiff-children's claims is denied, and the parties are directed to submit briefs on the law applicable to the issues in the case. Decision on defendants' motion to dismiss the parents' claims for medical expenses on statute of limitations grounds is reserved pending decision on the law applicable to that issue.

Defendants' motions for severance and transfer are denied. They may be renewed after consideration of the choice-of-law issues and appropriate procedures for trying the issues in the case.

The complaint sounds in assault (counts 3, 7, 11, 15, 19, 23, 28, 32, 36, 40, 44, 48 and 52) as well as in strict liability and negligence but no allegations to show intent are incorporated. On the basis of the argument to date, it seems unlikely that this theory is seriously urged. The assault claims are dismissed.

Separate claims are also made for conspiracy (counts 2, 6, 10, 14, 18, 22, 27, 31, 35, 39, 43, 47 and 51). But, as already pointed out, the conspiracy allegations merely support the negligence and strict liability theories as evidence of joint activity. They supply no separate basis for recovery and are dismissed.

An amended complaint need not be filed.

B. *Hall v. Du Pont*

In Hall v. Du Pont, 69-C-273, three groups of plaintiffs brought claims against two manufacturers of blasting caps. In each instance one of the two manufacturers was identified as the producer of the injury-causing cap; the other was joined on a theory of industry-wide responsibility for certain features of the cap's design.

The arbitrary basis of plaintiffs' selection of the non-producer defendants, and the absence of any demonstrable need for joint liability in administrative or remedial terms, requires dismissal of each plaintiff's claims against the non-producer defendants. The remaining claims against the individual manufacturers present sufficiently diverse questions of law and fact to defeat joinder under Rule 20(a) of the Federal Rules of Civil Procedure. The severed claims arising in Ohio and North Dakota are transferred to their respective federal districts.

The children's claims arising in this district remain in this court. The parent's claim for loss of services and medical expenses is dismissed under the applicable statute of limitations.

So ordered.

D.C.N.Y., 1972.

C. Joint and Several Liability

Under normal liability doctrines, a tortfeasor is responsible, or liable, only for his portion of the tort or incident. When there are two or more tortfeasors, the plaintiff may, in some states, sue each defendant for the entire amount of the damages, under the concept of indivisible or non-apportionable fault. This is a highly controversial doctrine, and some states, such as California, have even legislated to outlaw it. The plaintiff may not recover more than once for the original amount of damages, but often, the defendant with the "deep pockets" ends up paying more than his proportionate degree of liability. Many defendants settle out of cases early where they have been sued jointly and severally liable, leaving the remaining defendant or defendants to shoulder the rest of the damages, regardless of fault.

There is a chance that defendants may be able to recover damages from each other under the doctrine of contribution and indemnification. Many business contracts, however, contain hold harmless clauses, making this impossible. The case below is evidence of joint and several liability.

Phelan v. Lopez
701 S.W.2d 327 (Tex. App. 9 Dist.,1985)

James Clyde Lopez brought suit as a result of injuries he suffered in two separate accidents. The cause of both accidents and the resulting injuries were hotly contested. The first accident occurred on October 12, 1978. Mr. Lopez was working at a construction site in Beaumont, Texas, where a grocery store was being built. The property and the building being built were owned by Michael and Pat Phelan. Mr. Lopez alleged that while working on a raised mobile platform, a Mite-E-Lift, a wheel of the Mite-E-Lift fell into a utility hole in the building foundation. The Mite-E-Lift toppled, throwing Mr. Lopez to the ground. He claimed he suffered a knee injury and a back injury. He brought suit against the Phelans and their architect, Thomas C. McKnight, alleging various acts of negligence as to each.

The second accident occurred in Port Arthur, Texas on February 26, 1980. Mr. Lopez was working at the Port Arthur Civic Center which was under construction. Once again Mr. Lopez was on top of a Mite-E-Lift when a pen sheared and the platform suddenly fell. He claimed he suffered neck and back injuries as a result of this accident. He brought suit against the owner, distributor and manufacturer of the Mite-E-Lift alleging negligence and product liability.

INITIATION OF THE SUIT

Trial began and during the trial, Mr. Lopez settled with all the defendants sued as a result of the second accident. The jury found Mr. Lopez, the Phelans and Mr. McKnight negligent regarding the first accident. They failed to find that McKnight's negligence was a proximate cause of the injuries. Based upon the jury's answers the trial court entered judgment in favor of Mr. Lopez against the Phelans. The Phelans bring forth eleven points of error.

The Phelans' first point of error states: "The trial court erred in overruling Phelans' objections to the court's charge because there was no evidence that on the occasion in question, the Phelans were under a duty to supervise the work of an employee of a subcontractor."

The special issue in question was:

SPECIAL ISSUE NO. 1

Find from a preponderance of the evidence which of the defendants, if any, was negligent with respect to the accident of October 12, 1978. Answer "yes" or "no" on each line in Column 1. If any of your answers are "yes" in Column 1, was any such negligence a proximate cause of the occurrence in question? Answer "yes" or "no" on the corresponding line of Column 2.

In answering this Issue you shall consider only the following acts or omissions, if any, which plaintiff alleges were negligence on the part of defendant McKnight and defendants, Mike Phelan and Pat Phelan:

(1) Failure to provide covers and/or barricades for the holes which were left in the floor of the building;
(2) Failure to properly supervise and coordinate construction activities on the premises;
(3) Failure to provide a reasonably safe place to work.

	Column 1 Negligence	Column 2 Proximate Cause
Thomas McKnight		
(1) Covers and/or barricades	Yes	No
(2) Supervise and coordinate	No	
(3) Safe place to work	No	
Mike Phelan and Pat Phelan		
(1) Covers and/or barricades	Yes	No
(2) Supervise and coordinate	Yes	Yes
(3) Safe place to work	Yes	No

The Phelans' objections to the issue, which are relevant to this point of error, were:

> Defendants further object to special issue no. 1 because the evidence as a matter of law establishes that the responsibility to cover the holes and to supervise and coordinate the construction activities on the premises rested with Thomas McKnight who was an independent contractor.
>
> Defendant further objects to the submission of special issue no. 1 as the evidence is undisputed that the defendants Phelan were the owners of the piece of property in question and under no duty to cover or barricade the holes in question, supervise or coordinate the construction activities or to supply a reasonably safe place to work. Further, there is no evidence that the failure to cover or barricade the holes in question was negligence nor is there any evidence that it was a proximate cause of the accident in question. There is also no evidence that the failure to supervise and coordinate the construction activities on the premises was negligence nor is there any evidence that the negligence, if there were negligence, it was a proximate cause of the accident in question.

Both the objections to the charge and this point of error urge no evidence points. It was undisputed that the Phelans were the owners of the property and the building being constructed. It was hotly disputed as to what part the Phelans played in the construction process or whether the Phelans exercised any control over the premises while under construction.

An owner of land has a duty to use reasonable care to keep the premises under his control in a safe condition. *Smith v. Henger,* 148 Tex. 456, 226 S.W.2d 425 (1950). In *Redinger v. Living, Inc.,* 689 S.W.2d 415 (Tex. 1985), our state adopted the Restatement (Second) of Torts sec. 414 (1977) which provides: "One who entrusts work to an independent contractor, but who retains the control of any part of the work, is subject to liability for physical harm to others for whose safety the employer owes a duty to exercise reasonable care, which is caused by his failure to exercise his control with reasonable care." *See also, Tovar v. Amarillo Oil Co.,* 692 S.W.2d 469 (Tex. 1985).

There was no issue given the jury as to the extent of the Phelans' control, if any, over the work place. There was no specific objection to the lack of such an issue. When some, but not all, of a cluster of issues are necessary to sustain a ground of recovery are given and answered by the jury without objection or request, the trial court may make written findings on omitted issues raised by the evidence. If no written findings are made, the omitted issues are deemed to have been found by the court in such a manner to support the judgment. *Harmes v. Arklatex Corp.,* 615 S.W.2d 177 (Tex. 1981). Thus, the trial court is deemed to have found that the Phelans exercised some control over the property during the construction period. There is sufficient evidence to support this deemed finding. Point of error number one is overruled.

Points of error numbers two and three question the legal and factual sufficiency of the evidence of the jury's finding of proximate cause. In this regard, the Phelans argue that "conceptually the jury's answers to the liability issue do not make sense. . . .

if the Phelans' negligence in failing to provide covers and barricades for the holes and negligence in failing to provide a safe place to work were not proximate causes of the occurrence, then their failure to supervise and coordinate could not have been either." This court may not look to the answers of other issues for the purpose of determining whether an answer to a particular issue has support in the evidence. *C & R Transport, Inc. v. Campbell,* 406 S.W.2d 191 (Tex. 1966). There was extensive testimony about the types of supervisors on a construction site and their respective duties and responsibilities. There was testimony that proper coordination and supervision could have avoided the "open hole" problem. It is reasonable to infer from all of this testimony that the Phelans' failure to supervise and coordinate the construction work was a proximate cause of the accident. Proximate cause, as any other ultimate fact, may be established and inferred from the circumstances surrounding the event. *Whitman v. Campbell,* 618 S.W.2d 935 (Tex. App. Beaumont 1981, *no writ*). Points of error numbers two and three are overruled.

The next point of error states: "The trial court erred in overruling Phelans' objections to the charge and denying their requested instruction regarding proximate cause because its submission of the definition of proximate cause contained language which was confusing to the jury." The crux of this argument is that it was reversible error for the trial court to use the term "new and independent cause" in its definition of proximate cause without defining it. The Phelans properly objected to the failure of the trial court to include a definition of "new and independent cause" and tendered a definition which was refused by the court. They allege the error was harmful in that it was a source of confusion and the jury was confused as to the definition of proximate cause.

It has been held several times that when the term "new and independent cause" is used, it must be defined. *Texas & N.O.R. Co. v. Warden,* 107 S.W.2d 451 (Tex. Civ. App.—El Paso 1937, *writ dism'd*); *Railway Express Inc. v. Gaston,* 91 S.W.2d 883 (Tex. Civ. App.—El Paso 1936, *writ dism'd*); *Texas & P. Ry. Co. v. Mercer,* 127 Tex. 220, 90 S.W.2d 557 (1936). However, in none of these cases, was the failure to define the phase held to be reversible error. In *Young v. Massey,* 128 Tex. 638, 101 S.W.2d 809 (1937) we find the following language:

> It is the settled law of this state that if the evidence in a negligence case raises the issue of new and independent cause, it is reversible error not to include the term in the definition of proximate cause. Also, if such term is necessary to be used in the definition of proximate cause, it is reversible error not to define it.

This was a case where the term was not included in the definition of "proximate cause." We find no cases such as the instant one, i.e., where the term is included in "proximate cause," but then not defined. We believe the most prudent rule to adopt in this situation is the one enunciated in *Dennis v. Hulse,* 362 S.W.2d 308 (Tex. 1962). In order to obtain a reversal of the trial court, the complaining party must show the error complained of amounted to such a denial of the rights of appellant as was reasonably calculated to cause and probably did cause the rendition of an improper judgment. Further, this is to be determined from an evaluation of the whole case. *First*

Employees Ins. Co. v. Skinner, 646 S.W.2d 170 (Tex. 1983). The jury did not request the trial court to define "new and independent cause." They did not request the trial court to explain the relationship between proximate cause and new and independent cause. The jury only requested the judge to give them a clearer definition of proximate cause. Their request has been echoed by numerous juries and judges. While it was error not to define the term, in this instance, it was not reversible error. Point of error number four is overruled.

Point of error number five alleges the trial court erred in failing to sever the two different accidents. The Phelans recognize that severance is a matter within the sound discretion of the trial court. They say the trial court abused its discretion in that the controversy involved more than one cause of action, the severed cause would be the proper subject of an independently asserted lawsuit and the severed causes were not so intertwined as to involve the same identical factors and issues. In contesting the motions to sever, Mr. Lopez, relying on the common questions of fact respecting the cause of his low back injury, stated:

> The defendants involved in each accident are going to maintain that the other incident was the immediate, or producing cause, of the injury to plaintiff's low back. There is some evidence in the record to support either view, and in fact it is plaintiff's contention that the first accident did cause a low back injury, as diagnosed by Dr. Siff, and that the second accident aggravated this injury, both instances constituted sufficient trauma to be a producing cause of some portion of the disability which plaintiff is now experiencing as a result of the back injury.
> The only practical, fair, economical and just manner to adjudicate the issue of responsibility for the disability arising out of the back injury is to join these defendants in one suit where a jury can pass upon the preponderance of the evidence preceived by the jury. Any other approach would run the serious risk of either denying plaintiff recovery for the back injury (if each separate jury were to conclude the other accident caused the disability) or would lay a predicate for defendants to contend on appeal from separate judgments that plaintiff was recovering twice from the same loss. . . .

The Phelans have not demonstrated where they were prejudiced in trying the two accidents together. In fact, the trial court instructed the jury not to include any amount for any injuries sustained resulting from the February 26, 1980, accident. The trial court did not abuse its discretion. Point of error number five is overruled. Point of error number six alleges the trial court erred in not allowing a credit for the settlement reached with the defendants involved in the February 26, 1980, accident. This argument is based upon the premise that Mr. Lopez sued all the defendants as co-tortfeasors and when no issues were presented to the jury as to the fault of the second accident defendants, the Phelans' became entitled to a credit under Tex. Rev. Civ. Stat. Ann. art. 2212a, sec. 2(d) (Vernon Supp. 1985). The Phelans' analysis would be correct if the first accident defendants and the second accident defendants were joint tortfeasors. Defendants become joint tortfeasors when their negligence concur in producing a single, indivisible injury. *Austin Road Co. v. Pope,* 147 Tex. 430, 216

INITIATION OF THE SUIT

S.W.2d 563 (1949). Here, Mr. Lopez suffered some separate and distinct injuries from the second accident. Moreover, as previously noted, the trial court expressly instructed the jury not to include any award based upon the injuries sustained in the second accident. Point of error number six is overruled. Points of error numbers seven and eight state:

> The trial court erred in failing to have the jury deliberate further as to the apportionment of negligence between Lopez and the Phelans after McKnight was absolved from liability.
>
> The trial court erred in entering judgment against Phelans for seventy (70%) percent of the amount of damages awarded rather than disregarding the percentage assessed against McKnight.

These points are based upon special issue number 3, and the jury's answers as follows:

SPECIAL ISSUE NO. 3

What percentage of the negligence that caused the occurrence do you find from a preponderance of the evidence to be attributable to each of the parties found by you to have been negligent?

The percentage of negligence attributable to a party is not necessarily measured by the number of acts or omissions found.

Answer by stating the percentage opposite each name.

Phelan Defendants	50%
Thomas C. McKnight, Jr	20%
James Clyde Lopez	30%
Total	100%

Point of error number seven focuses on the failure of the trial court to have the jury deliberate further. Here, there was no apparent conflict in the jury's answers, thus there was no duty on the trial court to have them deliberate further. See Tex. R. Civ. P. 295, *Harris County v. Patrick,* 636 S.W.2d 211 (Tex. App.—Texarkana 1982, *no writ*).

The real thrust of the Phelans' argument is contained in point of error eight. Tex. Rev. Civ. Stat. Ann. art. 2212a, secs. 1, 2(b) (Vernon Supp. 1985) is the controlling statute. *Section 1* states:

> Contributory negligence shall not bar recovery in an action by any person or party or the legal representative of any person or party to recover damages for negligence resulting in death or injury to persons or property if such negligence is not greater than the negligence of the person or party or persons or parties against whom recovery is sought, but any damages

allowed shall be diminished in proportion to the amount of negligence attributed to the person or party recovering.

Section 2(b) states:

> In a case in which there is more than one defendant, and the claimant's negligence does not exceed the total negligence of all defendants, contribution to the damages awarded to the claimant shall be in proportion to the percentage of negligence attributable to each defendant.

Section 1 is quite specific when it states that "damages allowed shall be diminished in proportion to the amount of negligence attributed to the party recovering." Here, the jury attributed 30 percent of the negligence to Mr. Lopez and the trial court diminished the jury's award by 30 percent. The Phelans rely on *section 2(b)* and the case of *Haney Electric Co. v. Hurst,* 624 S.W.2d 602 (Tex. Civ. App.—Dallas 1981, *writ dism'd*). Their reliance, however, is misplaced. *Section 2(b)* deals with contribution among defendants. Here, there was no other defendant with which to compare a percentage of negligence. *Haney, supra,* is distinguishable in that it involved multiple claimants and a single defendant. Thus, the trial court was correct in following *section 1*. Points of error numbers seven and eight are overruled.

The next two points of error challenge the legal and factual sufficiency of the evidence in the jury's award of $30,000.00 in past medical expenses. Keeping in mind that the trial court had instructed the jury not to include any amount for injuries sustained resulting from the accident of February 26, 1980, the trial court's charge asked the jury to find "(g) Medical expenses in the past which were necessary for treatment of injuries resulting from the occurrence of October 12, 1978."

The medical expenses in question were incurred as a result of surgery to the lower back. A first surgery was performed in Beaumont, Texas in October, 1980, and a second surgery in Houston, Texas in February, 1982. The question of the cause of Mr. Lopez's lower back problem was highly contested. There was testimony from Mr. Lopez and his wife that he first began to have lower back problems after the first accident. There was expert testimony that Mr. Lopez was experiencing lower back problems two months prior to the second accident. There is conflicting expert testimony whether the second accident was the type that could have caused a lower back disc injury. The jury was confronted with days of testimony, much of it conflicting, and much of it based upon hypothetical questions. After reviewing the voluminous medical testimony and records, we are unable to say the jury's award is erroneous either legally or factually. Points of error numbers nine and ten are overruled.

The Phelans' final point of error contends the trial court erred in not allowing the jury to receive a compromise settlement agreement wherein Mr. Lopez settled one of his workers compensation claims. The Phelans offered the compromise settlement agreement for the purpose of showing Mr. Lopez has made a prior inconsistent statement. The offer was made by the Phelans, not to show any collateral source, but to show that Mr. Lopez had, in the workers compensation claim, alleged only a knee injury and had not mentioned a back injury. Mr. Lopez claimed the evidence was cumulative and its prejudicial force outweighed its probative value. In the manner offered by the Phelans, neither argument has merit. The evidence, in the manner proposed, should have been admitted. In light of the entire record, we are unable to say the error was reasonably calculated to cause and probably did cause the rendition of an improper judgment. This point of error is overruled.

Mr. Lopez brings forth two points of error which seek a remand on the issues regarding McKnight's negligence. Lopez seeks only to urge these points in the event of a remand as to the Phelans. We, therefore, overrule these two points of error.

The judgment of trial court is affirmed.

Page 123, add new § 2.28A:

§ 2.28A   Complaint for Declaratory Judgment (New)

IN THE UNITED STATES DISTRICT COURT
FOR THE [judicial district] DISTRICT OF [state]
[judicial division] DIVISION

[name]	)	
	)	
Plaintiff	)	Civil Action No. [case number]
	)	
v.	)	
	)	
[name]	)	
	)	
Defendant	)	

COMPLAINT FOR DECLARATORY JUDGMENT AND
SPEEDY HEARING PURSUANT TO FED. R. CIV. P. 57

Plaintiffs [name] by their attorneys [firm name] for their complaint filed pursuant to Federal Rules of Civil Procedure Rule [___] against Defendant [name], allege as follows:

NATURE OF ACTION, SUMMARY OF CLAIMS AND NEED
FOR SPEEDY HEARING

1. This is a declaratory judgment action under federal as well as state statutory and common law in which Plaintiffs [name] and [name] seek a declaration of non-infringement and non-dilution of Defendant [name] trademarks with respect to the [plaintiff name] use of several composite trademarks, each of which consists of the [trademark] design (in use since [19__]) in conjunction with other indicia of the Club, on footwear. These composite trademarks include, without limitation, the [plaintiff

name] football helmet logo bearing the [trademark] design (the _____), the mark _____, and the mark _____ (all of the [trademark] design marks are referred to collectively as the _____).

2.   As set forth in greater detail below, officially licensed footwear products bearing [trademark design] and other source identifying indicia of the [plaintiffs name] will be introduced into the marketplace nationally, and in particular in substantial quantities in this District, during the next sixty (60) days.

3.   The demand for officially licensed _____ products will increase dramatically in the next several weeks, as the start of the new _____ season is anticipated with enormous interest and enthusiasm by the fans of the _____, including [plaintiff name] fans. The [plaintiff name] open training camp for the upcoming [date] _____ season on [date]. The Club's first pre-season game is [date] against the _____ and its opening regular season game is on [date] against the _____.

4.   Based upon the actions of [defendant name] as described more fully below, the [plaintiffs name] have a real and reasonable apprehension that [defendant name] will commence legal action to prevent the distribution and sale of said officially licensed footwear products which bear the [trademark design].

5.   Any effort by [defendant name] to interfere with sales of licensed footwear products bearing [trademark design] at the start of the [date] _____ season and the start of the back-to-school sales season would severely damage the [plaintiffs name] by impeding their licensee's introduction of licensed merchandise at a time of peak marketplace demand. Such interference would also materially damage the relationship between [plaintiff name] and said licensee, which relies on [plaintiff name] to ensure that licensed products can be marketed without interference from third parties.

6.   Therefore, advancement of this action on the Court's calendar and a speedy hearing pursuant to Rule [___] of the Federal Rules of Civil Procedure is required prior to the commencement of the [date] _____ season in order to prevent injury to the [plaintiffs name] and to their business relationships with their footwear licensee and retailers.

PARTIES, JURISDICTION AND VENUE

7.   Plaintiff [name] is one of the thirty (30) active _____ member clubs (the "Member Clubs") whose teams play professional football games. The Club is a [state] limited partnership with its principal place of business in this District in [city, state].

8.   Plaintiff [name] is a [state] corporation with its principal place of business in [city, state]. _____, which is owned by the _____, was created in [date] to exploit commercially the various trademark rights of the _____ for the collective benefit of all of the Member Clubs.

9.   Upon information and belief, Defendant [name] is a [state] corporation with its principal place of business at [location]. Upon information and belief, [defendant

name] is doing business in this District through, inter alia, the advertisement and sale of its products.

10.   This case presents and actual controversy within the jurisdiction of this Court pursuant to 28 U.S.C. para 2201, *et seq*. The subject matter of this action involves the provisions of the Trademark Act, 15 U.S.C. para. 1114(1), 1125(a) and 1125(c), which gives rise to jurisdiction in this Court pursuant to 28 U.S.C. para 1331 and 1338. Venue is proper pursuant to 28 U.S.C. para 1391.

THE _____ AND THE HISTORY AND FAME OF THE [PLAINTIFF NAME]

11.   Each of the Member Clubs of the _____, including the [plaintiff name], owns and operates a professional football team engaged in providing entertainment services by playing competitive professional football games in various locations primarily in the United States.

12.   The business objective of each _____ Member Club, including the [plaintiff name], is to create and sustain fan interest in the _____ in general and in its professional football team in particular. _____ football is the most popular professional team sport in the United States. Millions of persons attend the games each year and millions more follow the respective teams and games in the electronic and print media, and access and download information and images related to the game via the Internet. Fan interest and support is further created and sustained by the sale of officially licensed products, including footwear, bearing the names, logos and other trademarks of the _____ and Member Clubs.

13.   The [plaintiff name] began operating a professional football team in [date], when the _____ awarded an expansion franchise to the original owners. Over their thirty-eight (38) year history, the [plaintiff name] have become one of the most legendary and storied professional sports franchises in the world. The [plaintiff name] success on the field is unmatched in the annals of the _____. The Club holds the _____ record for the number of Super Bowl appearances with [number] and shares the _____ record for Super Bowl championships with [number], having won the Super Bowl [game numbers] games.

14.   From the Club's inception in [date] through the [date] season, over forty-four (44) million fans have attended [plaintiff name] football games. The level of fan interest in the [plaintiff name], both in this District and nationally is such that as of the end of the [date] _____ season, the Club had played its games before one hundred and thirteen (113) consecutive sold out stadiums (both home and away games.)

15.   The [plaintiff name] football games are consistently telecast regionally and have also been telecast nationally during prime time approximately [number] times. Nationally televised [plaintiff name] games have been a Thanksgiving Day tradition for over [number] years. In addition, the [plaintiff name] three (3) most recent Super Bowl appearances (Super Bowls [game numbers]) rank among the top ten (10) most watched television programs in history, with the Super Bowl [number] game ranking as the second most watched program of all time with approximately ninety four (94)

million viewers. As a result of this pervasive media exposure, the nationwide fame and public recognition of the Club's trademarks, in particular the [trademark], is among the greatest of all professional sports team trademarks.

THE [PLAINTIFF NAME] TRADEMARKS

16. To identify and distinguish their respective professional football teams, the entertainment services which they provide, and the officially licensed merchandise related thereto, the _____ Member Clubs, including the [plaintiff name], adopt and use in interstate commerce various names, terms, symbols, emblems, slogans, designs, colors and other identifying ("_____ Trademarks"). Among the _____ Trademarks are full team names and nicknames, game uniform designs, helmet logos and other names, symbols and slogans which identify the _____ and the Member Clubs.

17.   For many years, the [plaintiff name] have adopted and used several trademarks in connection with the business of organizing, conducting and promoting the [plaintiff name] professional football franchise in the _____, including, inter alia, the famous [trademark design] (collectively the "[trademark name]"). The [plaintiff name] own several federal and state trademark registrations for the [trademark] for use in connection with entertainment services in the form of football games and exhibitions and for use on and in connection with articles of apparel. The [trademark], including the [trademark design], are famous to the public because of the widespread use of said marks, the great popularity of _____ football and the [plaintiff name], and the extensive media coverage of the _____ and, in particular, the [plaintiff name].

18.   A [trademark design] used in a professional football context is a trademark of the [plaintiff name] and embodies and symbolizes the history, fame and enormous goodwill associated with the Club and its legendary football team.

THE BUSINESS OF _____ AND THE SALE OFFICIALLY LICENSED [PLAINTIFF NAME] MERCHANDISE

19.   _____ is authorized to license the _____ Trademarks on behalf of the [plaintiff name] and the other _____ Member Clubs to third parties for commercial exploitation. To fulfill its obligations as the exclusive trademark licensing agent of the Member Clubs, [plaintiff name] has entered into license agreements for use of the _____ Trademarks on a wide variety of products. There are currently approximately [number] [plaintiff name] licensees that manufacture and sell approximately one thousand (1,000) products which bear the _____ Trademarks. Examples of officially licensed products bearing the [trademark] include shirts, caps, socks, slippers, other articles of apparel, footwear, sports equipment, games and novelties. The [trademark], including the [trademark design], can be found on virtually all types of apparel products—from headgear to footwear.

20.   The [trademark] embody substantial goodwill and have achieved fame and secondary meaning as identifiers of the [plaintiff name] and the _____ as the source or sponsor of merchandise upon which the [trademark] appear. The [plaintiff name] have ranked among the top ten Member Clubs in terms of merchandise sales in

twelve (12) of the past fourteen (14) years. In six (6) of those years, including each year from [date] through [date], the [plaintiff name] were the top selling _____ Member Club in merchandise sales and in [date] they were ranked second. From [date] through [date], sales of merchandise bearing the [trademark] accounted for over [____%] of all [plaintiff name] retail sales. As a result, said marks are extremely valuable commercial assets and embody goodwill of incalculable value.

21.   [Plaintiff name] licensees have invested significant amounts of capital and have devoted substantial amounts of time and effort to the production, marketing and promotion of merchandise bearing the [trademark], including the [trademark], and have established on behalf of the [plaintiff name] a significant consumer demand for these items through such efforts. Consumers readily identify merchandise bearing the [trademark] as being sponsored and approved by the [plaintiff name] and the _____.

22.   Over the years, [plaintiff name], on behalf of the [plaintiff name] and other _____ Member Clubs, has granted a number of licenses for use of the _____ Trademarks, including the [trademark design], on footwear. Licensed footwear products bearing the _____ Trademarks, including the [trademark], have included, inter alia, team-identified children's and adults' sneakers, boots, slippers, turf shoes and cleats. Photographs of licensed footwear products bearing the [trademark design] contained in various [plaintiff name] Merchandise Catalogs are attached hereto as Exhibit I. [Exhibit omitted.]

23.   Upon information and belief, [defendant name] has been aware for several years that [plaintiff name] has licensed the _____ Trademarks, including the [trademark], for use on footwear products.

THE BUSINESS OF [DEFENDANT NAME]

24.   Upon information and belief, [defendant name] is one of the established manufacturers, marketers and sellers of certain types of athletic footwear and related products in the United States. Upon information and belief, [defendant name] manufactures markets and sells its athletic footwear and related products under the [name] brand name and trademark. Upon information and belief, [defendant name] best selling and most well known products are [name] brand basketball shoes.

25.   [Defendant name] owns United States Trademark Registration No. [number] for a five-pointed star design alone (the "[trademark]"), which is limited to use on "canvas-topped rubber soled athletic shoes." Upon information and belief, all use by [defendant name] of the [trademark] on footwear products is made in conjunction with other source-identifying indicia of [defendant name] on said products. Upon information and belief, all footwear products marketed and sold by [defendant name] are marketed and sold under or in conjunction with use of the brand name [name].

26.   Upon information and belief, in connection with its business of manufacturing, marketing and selling athletic footwear in the [name] brand name context, [defendant name] uses, and owns several United States Trademark Registrations for,

a number of composite trademarks which consist of the [trademark design] in conjunction with other source-identifying indicia of [defendant name]. These composite marks include a design mark consisting of a five pointed star together with a distinctive arrow shape, a design mark consisting of a five pointed star inside a shaded square box, as well as the marks [name].

27.   The [trademark], which are used to indicate Club sponsorship, and the [trademark], which are used to indicate an athletic footwear brand and manufacturer, have coexisted and continue to coexist in the marketplace without confusion.

28.   Upon information and belief, in 1995, [defendant name] acquired all of the stock of [company name], which was at that time a _____ licensee for footwear. In [date], [plaintiff name] terminated all license agreements with [company name] and entered into a license agreement with [defendant name] for the right to use, inter alia, the [trademark], including the [trademark] consisting of the [trademark design], on footwear.

THREATS BY [DEFENDANT NAME] WITH RESPECT TO USE OF THE [PLAINTIFF NAME] [TRADEMARK] ON FOOTWEAR: THE PARTIES' PRIOR DEALINGS

a.   The Prior Opposition Proceedings

29.   On [date], the [plaintiff name] filed United States Trademark Application Serial No. [number] for the [trademark] consisting of the [trademark design], for use on men's, women's, and children's clothing and footwear, including sneakers (the "Application"). A United States Patent and Trademark Office ("PTO") Examining Attorney determined that there was no similar registered or pending trademark which would bar registration of this mark and the mark was published for opposition on [date].

30.   On [date], [defendant name] filed a Notice of Opposition in the PTO against registration of the Application. The PTO proceeding is [proceeding name] (hereinafter, the "Opposition Proceeding"). In its Notice of Opposition, [defendant name] alleged that a likelihood of confusion exists between the [trademark design] and the [trademark] as used on the goods listed in the Application, in particular, in connection with use on footwear.

b.   [Defendant name] Settlement Demands

31.   In [date], the parties agreed to suspension of the Opposition Proceeding so that settlement discussions could be pursued. The Opposition Proceeding remained suspended for over two years, during which time periodic settlement negotiations were conducted.

32.   In [date], solely as an effort to amicably resolve the parties' dispute with respect to the registrability of the [trademark design], the [plaintiff name] made a settlement proposal to [defendant name] which included, inter alia, an offer always to use said mark on footwear in a professional football context indicative of sponsorship by the [plaintiff name].

33. On [date], [defendant name], through outside counsel [firm name], counsel of record in the Opposition Proceeding, rejected the [plaintiff name] proposal and declared that "[defendant name] cannot permit the use of a prominent star (such as the subject logo) on footwear regardless of the limitations" on such use offered in the [plaintiff name] settlement proposal. A copy of the [date] letter is attached hereto as Exhibit 2. [Exhibit omitted.]

34. Additional settlement negotiations took place in late [19___] and early [19___]. On [date], the [plaintiff name] made a second settlement proposal to [defendant name]. This proposal, while differing from the [plaintiff name] first proposal in several material respects, likewise contained an offer always to use the [trademark design] on footwear in a professional football context indicative of sponsorship by the [plaintiff name].

35. On [date], [defendant name], through its counsel, rejected this settlement proposal and counter proposed that, as a condition for settlement of the pending Opposition Proceeding, the [plaintiff name] agree "never to use the [trademark design] on any type of footwear." A copy of the [date] letter is attached hereto as Exhibit 3. [Exhibit omitted.]

c. Threat to [plaintiff name] Right to License the [trademark] for Footwear

36. On [date] and [date], [plaintiff name], on behalf of the _____ Member Clubs, including the [plaintiff name], entered into two license agreements with [company name], located in [location], for use of the _____ Trademarks, including the [trademark], on adult and youth casual comfort footwear, winter boots and shower footwear. Pursuant to these licenses, [company name] will produce footwear products bearing the trademarks of several of the _____ Member Clubs, including the [trademark].

37. [Company name]-identified styles have been finalized and it will produce and offer for sale two (2) [plaintiff name]-identified styles, Nos. [number] and [number] (color photographs of which are attached hereto as Exhibit 4), [Exhibit omitted] bearing several of the [trademark], in particular, the composite marks [trademark], [trademark], and [trademark].

d. Need for Declaratory Relief

38. The distribution and sale of [company name] licensed footwear bearing the [trademark] is imminent. [Company name] will begin shipping footwear products bearing the [trademark] to retailers by mid-August, [19___], in an effort to capitalize on the strong demand for _____ merchandise at that time.

39. Based on (1) [defendant name] institution of the Opposition Proceeding, in which it asserted a likelihood of confusion with respect to use of the [trademark design] on footwear, (2) the declaration in the [date] letter that [defendant name] could not permit the [plaintiff name] use of a prominent star on footwear, even in a composite mark, despite the [plaintiff name] offer to couple its use of the [trademark design] with other indicia of sponsorship by the [plaintiff name] and the _____, and

(3) the requirement set forth in the [date] letter that any settlement of the Opposition Proceeding include an agreement by the [plaintiff name] never to use their famous [trademark design] on any type of footwear, the [plaintiff name] have a real and reasonable apprehension that: (a) [defendant name], upon notice of the imminent introduction into the marketplace of footwear bearing the [trademark], will sue for trademark infringement, dilution and/or for other violations of its perceived rights in the [trademark]; (b) [defendant name] will interfere with the [plaintiffs name] efforts to license the [trademark] for use on footwear and related products in a professional football context indicative of Club sponsorship; (c) the [plaintiffs name] relationships with their footwear licensee, [company name], will be damaged and interfered with by [defendant name]; and (d) said footwear licensee's relationships with its retailers will be damaged and interfered with by [defendant name].

FIRST COUNT

(Declaration of Non-Infringement)

40.   The [plaintiff name] use of the [trademark], including, without limitation, the composite marks [trademark designs], on footwear (as set forth in Exhibit 4 [Exhibit omitted] and otherwise) in a professional football context indicative of sponsorship by the [plaintiff name] does not, and will not, (a) cause confusion or mistake or deceive the public in violation of Section 32(1) of the Lanham Act, 15 U.S.C. sec. 1114(1); (b) constitute unfair competition or a false designation of origin in violation of Section 43(a) of the Lanham Act, 15 U.S.C. sec. 1125(a); and (c) constitute unfair competition or trademark infringement under state statutory or common law.

SECOND COUNT

(Declaration of Non-Dilution)

41.   The [plaintiffs name] repeat and reallege the allegations of paragraphs 1 through 39 of the Complaint as if fully set forth herein.

42.   The [plaintiffs name] use of the [trademark], including, without limitation, the composite marks [trademark designs], on footwear (as set forth in Exhibit 4 [Exhibit omitted] and otherwise) in a professional football context indicative of sponsorship by the [plaintiff name] does not, and will not (a) diminish and blur the meaning of the [trademark], [trademark design], in the athletic footwear brand and manufacturer context; (b) constitute dilution of the [trademark], including the [trademark design], in the athletic footwear brand and manufacturer context in violation of Section 43(c) of the Lanham Act, 15 U.S.C. sec. 1125(c); (c) constitute dilution of the [trademark], including the [trademark], in the athletic footwear brand and manufacturer context in violation of state statutory or common law, and (d) otherwise violate state or federal statutory or common law.

FOR BOTH COUNTS

43.   Unless this Court immediately declares the rights of the parties to this action, the [plaintiffs name] will be irreparably harmed because their investment in the

goodwill embodied in the [trademark] will be harmed in a manner beyond monetary calculation.

44. The [plaintiffs name] have no adequate remedy at law.

WHEREFORE, The [plaintiffs name] request this Court to enter judgment:

(a) declaring that the [plaintiffs name] use of the [trademark], including, without limitation, the composite marks [trademark designs], on footwear (as set forth in Exhibit 4 [Exhibit omitted] and otherwise) in a professional football context indicative of sponsorship by the [plaintiff name] does not, and will not:

> (i) cause confusion or mistake or deceive the public in violation of Section 32(I) of the Lanham Act, 15 U.S.C. para. 1114(I); (ii) constitute unfair competition or a false designation of origin in violation of Section 43(a) of the Lanham Act, 15 I/S/C/ 1125(a), (iii) constitute unfair competition or trademark infringement under state statutory or common law; (iv) constitute dilution of the [trademark] in the athletic footwear brand and manufacture context in violation of Section 43(c) of the Lanham Act, 15 U.S.C. para 1125 (c), state statutory or common law; and (v) otherwise infringe upon or violate any rights of [defendant name] in the use of its [trademark] on footwear on related goods;

(b) declaring that the [plaintiffs name] and [defendant name] have and can continue to co-exist with respect to use of their respective five-pointed star composite marks on footwear, with the [plaintiff name] using the [trademark], including, without limitation, the composite marks [trademark designs], and [defendant name] using the [trademark];

(c) declaring that the [plaintiffs name] use and enforcement of the [trademark design] in connection with the items of footwear listed in Application Serial No. [number] will not interfere with any rights of [defendant name] in the [trademark];

(d) entering judgment in favor of the [plaintiffs name] and against [defendant name] as to each of the foregoing declarations;

(e) granting the [plaintiffs name] their costs and expenses of this action; and

(f) awarding the [plaintiffs name] such other and further relief as this Court may deem proper.

Dated: [location]
[date]

Respectfully submitted,

_____ [Attorneys for Plaintiffs]

CHAPTER 4

DISCOVERY

§ 4.1 Introduction

Page 209, add at end of section:

DISCOVERABILITY
1. RELEVANT 2. MATERIALITY
A. PROBATIVE VALUE (TIME AND SCOPE)
2. CALCULATED TO LEAD TO THE DISCOVERY OF ADMISSIBLE EVIDENCE 3. NOT PROTECTED BY PRIVILEGE OR PROHIBITED BY OTHER RULES OF CIVIL PROCEDURE

FORM 4–01
SAMPLE DISCOVERY CONTROL PLAN AND
SCHEDULING ORDER

NO. [case number]

IN THE DISTRICT

[name]   COURT OF [county]

Plaintiff   COUNTY, TEXAS

vs.   [judicial district] JUDICIAL DISTRICT

[name(s)]

Defendant(s)

DISCOVERY

DISCOVERY CONTROL PLAN AND SCHEDULING ORDER

BE IT REMEMBERED that a pretrial conference was held in the above cause pursuant to a request by the Court previously notifying the parties that an informal conference would be held prior to a trial setting in this matter. The following parties and/or attorneys were present or agreed to this Order:

_____

The following was signed and stipulated by the parties AND/OR Ordered by the Court.

a. This is a Discovery Control Plan for Level   1   2   3   (Circle One) (If this case is a Level 1 or 2 case, nothing herein shall be construed as altering the limitations set forth in the Texas Rules of Civil Procedure; for Level 1 and 2 cases this order shall be construed only as a Pretrial Scheduling Order unless otherwise expressly stated.) Parts a.1 through a.8 to be completed for Level 3 cases only.

    1. Amended Pleadings. The deadline for filing amended pleadings is

    _____

    2. Special Exceptions: The deadline for filing exceptions to pleadings is

    _____

    3. Discovery. All discovery shall be completed by

    _____

    Discovery requests shall be served or filed, as appropriate, in sufficient time to allow for a timely response to such discovery requests to be served or filed by the discovery deadline.
    4. Time Limits for Depositions: _____
    5. Limitations on Interrogatories: _____
    6. Limitations on Requests for Production: _____
    7. Other Limitations: _____
    8. Deadline for Designations of Experts. Plaintiff shall file a designation of the testifying experts by _____
    Any expert not designated shall not be permitted to testify. A designation shall include the subject matter and opinions to be offered by the expert.

b. Dispositive Motions (Summary Judgments, Plea to Jurisdiction, Plea in Abatement, etc.) All dispositive motions shall be filed and heard by

_____

c. Mediation. Mediation IS ____ IS NOT____ required.
d. Formal Pre-Trial Conference. This case is set for formal pre-trial on

_____

e. Each party shall be prepared to consider such other matters as may aid in the disposition of the case, including any matter raised pursuant to Rule 166a. All

Pre-Trial motions (Motions *in Limine,* etc.) shall be filed 10 days before the formal pretrial conference and will be heard at the formal pretrial conference.

f.   Jury Trial: This matter is set for jury trial on _____.

Signed and approved this [date] day of [month], 20 [year].

_____
                                                                      Judge Presiding

_____Plaintiff/Petitioner

_____Defendant/Respondent

_____Other

§ 4.37   Witness/Client Deposition Preparation Checklist

Page 293, add at end of section:

___   24.   Do not use language such as "to tell the truth . . . ," or "honestly speaking." It implies that you did not tell the truth before.

___   25.   Pause before answering all questions to give your lawyer an opportunity to object if he wants to.

§ 4.64   Checklist for Responding to Request for Production of Documents

Page 333, add at end of section:

> SMOKING GUN: A document or piece of evidence so important to the case that it is called the smoking gun. It is also referred to sometimes as a "hot document."

CHAPTER 5

INVESTIGATION

Page 376, add new § 5.24A:

§ 5.24A   Where to Locate Public Records (New)

A.   County Clerk/Recorder's Office

The County Recorder or Clerk's office is created by each state's constitution in each of the state's counties. The county clerk or recorder is an elected position. The various job descriptions of this position vary from jurisdiction to jurisdiction. In some areas, the clerk or recorder also acts as the tax assessor and property appraiser. In others, that is a totally separate position. Generally, the clerk handles all the recorded documents in that jurisdiction, such as deeds and liens. In small, rural areas, the county recorder or clerk's office is generally found in the county courthouse. In large cities, the office is generally separate.

In Harris County, Texas, the County Clerk serves three main purposes. She maintains the records of Commissioners' Court (the equivalent of the county government), Probate Courts (because the sheer size of Harris County necessitates that that function be separated from District courts and given to County Courts, for which the county clerk is responsible) and County Civil Courts at Law (more legislatively created courts to help take a load off the District Courts by separating out lesser offenses and civil actions). As the county recorder, she is also responsible for real property records including state and federal tax liens; vital statistics records including marriage licenses; assumed names and uniform commercial code records, and various other records including military discharge records, hospital liens and livestock brands. As chief election official for the third largest county in the country, she administers county and state elections and also contracts for election services for political parties and smaller jurisdictions.

The County Clerk's Office maintains all Real Property Records . . . Deeds, Mortgages, Contracts, Leases, Tax Liens, Abstracts of Judgment, Lis Pendens, Mechanics and Materialmans Liens, Powers of Attorney, and various other instruments. The titles to, and the ownership of, all real estate in Harris County are determined from the records in the County Clerk's Office.

The County Clerk's office maintains Uniform Commercial Code Records, Powers of Attorney, and various other instruments. The County Clerk's office maintains Birth and Death Certificates for Harris County that are not filed with the City of Houston, Vital Statistics. The clerk's office issues Marriage Licenses and is the only official authorized in Harris County to issue Marriage Licenses. The County Clerk's office is also the place to file assumed names and acquire fishing and hunting licenses and to file liquor applications and permits. The office also records and keeps for public record Subdivision Map Records, Partnership Agreements, School Budgets, Embalmers Registry, Optometry Licenses, Cattle Animal Tattoos, Tax Receipts, State Tax Liens, and Federal Tax Liens. Additionally there are Landlords Liens, Serviceman's Discharges, Beer License Certificates, Hospital Liens, Bills of Sale, Utility Reports, Polygraph Examiners License, and Lay Midwife Identifications. The County Clerk's office serves four County Civil Courts-at-Law of Harris County. The County Clerk's office is the custodian and keeper of the records, documents, papers, and judgments in all County Civil Courts-at-Law cases.

The clerk's office also has the custody of all funds placed in Registry of the Courts pending the outcome of litigation. The County Clerk's office serves four Probate Courts of Harris County The department handles all records of the Estates of Deceased, Incapacitated Persons (including Minors), Cases of the Mentally Ill, Trust Funds, and Wills for Safekeeping. The County Clerk's office serves as the Clerk of the Commissioners' Court. The County Clerk's office serves as the Chief Election Official for Harris County. . . .

B. District Court Clerk's Office

The District Court Clerk handles all the filings of the pleadings, motions and other papers which are a part of district court lawsuits. If you were looking for the custody agreement which is a part of a divorce proceeding, or a copy of the divorce decree, you would look in the lawsuit file at the District Court Clerk's office. If, however, you wanted a copy of the marriage license, you would look at the County Clerk or Recorder's office.

Page 379, add new section § 5.30A:

§ 5.30A Uniform Commercial Code (UCC) and Secured Transactions (New)

The Uniform Commercial Code is an aggregate of laws which define and regulate interstate commerce. The major purpose of the Code is to protect both debtor and creditor, and an adaptation version of the uniform code exists in every state except Louisiana. Every time a debtor purchases something on the installment plan, or obtains a bank loan, a UCC-1 financing statement is used to publicly record the fact that the creditor has a security interest (a lien) in the property now owned by the debtor, or purchaser. When the creditor files the UCC-1 financing form with either the county or the Secretary of State, he is said to have perfected his interest in the collateral. This means that the debtor's security interest in the collateral supersedes the claims of most other creditors and the creditor is henceforth referred to as a secured creditor. The UCC-1 form varies slightly from state to state. You can generally find a copy of your state's UCC-1 financing form from an office supply store, the Office of the Secretary of State for your state, in your firm's form files, or on the Internet. Although an elaborate official form and instructions follow, a simple example of the UCC-1 form for the State of Texas is shown here:

TO BE FILED IN THE OFFICE OF THE SECRETARY OF STATE
FINANCING STATEMENT

This instrument is intended to be a Financing Statement complying with the requisites therefor as set forth in the Texas Business and Commerce Code.

1.   The name and address of the debtor ("Debtor") is:

2.   The name and address of the secured party ("Secured Party") is:

3.   This Financing Statement covers the following types of property (the "Collateral"): All fixtures, equipment, furniture, furnishings and other personal property now or hereafter located upon any part of the property (the "Land") described in Exhibit "A" which is attached hereto and incorporated herein by reference [Exhibit omitted], in which Debtor (or Debtor's heirs, representatives, successors or assigns) now has, or at any time hereafter acquires, an interest, and which are now, or at any time hereafter, either a part of the Land or situated in, on or about the Land and utilized in connection with the operation of the Land, or acquired or delivered to the Land for use or incorporation in construction of any improvements on the Land, including, but not limited to:

(a)   building and construction materials and equipment; all plans, specifications and drawings for any improvements to be placed on the Land; all contracts and subcontracts relating to the Land; all deposits (including tenant's security deposits), fund, accounts, contract rights, instruments, documents, general intangibles (including trademarks, trade names and symbols used in connection with the Land or the improvements thereon), and notes or chattel paper arising from or by virtue of any transactions related to the Land; all permits, licenses, franchises, certificates and other rights and privileges obtained in connection with the Land; all proceeds arising from or by virtue of the sale, lease or other disposition of any of the real or personal property described herein; all heating, lighting, refrigeration, plumbing, ventilating, incinerating, water-heating, transportation, communications, electrical and air-conditioning systems and equipment, sprinkler and fire-extinguishing systems, computers and computer systems, maintenance equipment;

(b)   rentals, deposits and other sums as may become due Debtor as landlord under any leases, written or verbal, with respect to the Land or any improvements now or hereafter thereon;

(c)   deposits for taxes, insurance or otherwise made under any Deed of Trust or other instrument securing payment of the indebtedness of Debtor to Secured Party;

(d)   all replacements, betterments, substitutions and renewals of, and additions to, any of the Collateral;

(e)   all proceeds, including without limitation all condemnation or insurance proceeds arising out of or with respect to the Collateral or the Land;

(f)   all products of Collateral;

(g)   any and all proceeds arising from or by virtue of the sale, lease or other disposition of any of the foregoing property items set forth above;

(h)   any and all proceeds rising from the taking of all or a part of the Land for any public or quasi-public use under any law, or by right of eminent domain, or by private or other purchase in lieu thereof;

(i)   all gross proceeds due to Debtor under and pursuant to that certain Assignment by and between Debtor and Secured Party, dated of even date herewith (the "Assignment"), including without limitation, all cash, notes, drafts, acceptances and chattel paper arising therefrom, together with all additions and accessions thereto, substitutions and replacements therefor.

Dated:

DEBTOR:

BY: _____

SECURED PARTY:

BY: _____

FORM 5–10A
FINANCING STATEMENT

THIS SPACE FOR USE OF FILING OFFICER

FINANCING STATEMENT — FOLLOW INSTRUCTIONS CAREFULLY
This Financing Statement is presented for filing pursuant to the Uniform Commercial Code
and will remain effective, with certain exceptions, for 5 years from date of filing.

A. NAME & TEL. # OF CONTACT AT FILER (optional)	B. FILING OFFICE ACCT. # (optional)

C. RETURN COPY TO: (Name and Mailing Address)

D. OPTIONAL DESIGNATION [if applicable]	LESSOR/LESSEE	CONSIGNOR/CONSIGNEE	NON-UCC FILING

1. DEBTOR'S EXACT FULL LEGAL NAME - insert only one debtor name (1a or 1b)

1a. ENTITY'S NAME

OR

1b. INDIVIDUAL'S LAST NAME	FIRST NAME	MIDDLE NAME	SUFFIX

1c. MAILING ADDRESS	CITY	STATE	COUNTRY	POSTAL CODE

1d. S.S. OR TAX I.D.#	OPTIONAL ADD'NL INFO RE ENTITY DEBTOR	1e. TYPE OF ENTITY	1f. ENTITY'S STATE OR COUNTRY OF ORGANIZATION	1g. ENTITY'S ORGANIZATIONAL I.D.#, if any	NONE

2. ADDITIONAL DEBTOR'S EXACT FULL LEGAL NAME - insert only one debtor name (2a or 2b)

2a. ENTITY'S NAME

OR

2b. INDIVIDUAL'S LAST NAME	FIRST NAME	MIDDLE NAME	SUFFIX

2c. MAILING ADDRESS	CITY	STATE	COUNTRY	POSTAL CODE

2d. S.S. OR TAX I.D.#	OPTIONAL ADD'NL INFO RE ENTITY DEBTOR	2e. TYPE OF ENTITY	2f. ENTITY'S STATE OR COUNTRY OF ORGANIZATION	2g. ENTITY'S ORGANIZATIONAL I.D.#, if any	NONE

3. SECURED PARTY'S (ORIGINAL S/P or ITS TOTAL ASSIGNEE) EXACT FULL LEGAL NAME - insert only one secured party name (3a or 3b)

3a. ENTITY'S NAME

OR

3b. INDIVIDUAL'S LAST NAME	FIRST NAME	MIDDLE NAME	SUFFIX

3c. MAILING ADDRESS	CITY	STATE	COUNTRY	POSTAL CODE

4. This FINANCING STATEMENT covers the following types or items of property:

5. CHECK BOX — This FINANCING STATEMENT is signed by the Secured Party instead of the Debtor to perfect a security interest [if applicable] (a) in collateral already subject to a security interest in another jurisdiction when it was brought into this state, or when the debtor's location was changed to this state, or (b) in accordance with other statutory provisions [additional data may be required]	7. If filed in Florida (check one) Documentary □ Documentary stamp □ stamp tax paid □ tax not applicable □
6. REQUIRED SIGNATURE(S)	8. □ This FINANCING STATEMENT is to be filed [for record] (or recorded) in the REAL ESTATE RECORDS Attach Addendum [if applicable]
	9. Check to REQUEST SEARCH CERTIFICATE(S) on Debtor(s) [ADDITIONAL FEE] (optional) All Debtors □ Debtor 1 □ Debtor 2 □

Office of the Secretary of State of Texas Web Form

(1) FILING OFFICER COPY — NATIONAL FINANCING STATEMENT (FORM UCC1) (TRANS) (REV. 12/18/95)

INVESTIGATION

General Instructions for National Financing Statement (Form UCC1) (Trans)

Please type or laser-print this form. Be sure it is completely legible. Read all Instructions.

Fill in form very carefully; mistakes may have important legal consequences. Follow Instructions completely. If you have questions, consult your attorney. Filing officer cannot give legal advice.

Do not insert anything in the open space in the upper portion of this form; it is reserved for filing officer use.

When properly completed, send Filing Officer Copy, with required fee, to filing officer. If you want an acknowledgment, also send Acknowledgment Copy, otherwise detach. If you want to make a search request, complete item 9 and send Search Request Copy, otherwise detach. Always detach Debtor and Secured Party Copies.

If you need to use attachments, use 8-1/2 X 11 inch sheets and put at the top of each additional sheet the name of the first Debtor, formatted exactly as it appears in item 1 of this form; you are encouraged to use Addendum (Form UCC1Ad).

Item Instructions

1. **Debtor name:** Enter only one Debtor name in item 1, an entity's name (1a) or an individual's name (1b). Enter Debtor's exact full legal name. Don't abbreviate.

1a. Entity Debtor. "Entity" means an organization having a legal identity separate from its owner. A partnership is an entity; a sole proprietorship is not an entity, even if it does business under a trade name. If Debtor is a partnership, enter exact full legal name of partnership; you need not enter names of partners as additional Debtors. If Debtor is a registered entity (e.g., corporation, limited partnership, limited liability company), it is advisable to examine Debtor's current filed charter documents to determine correct name, entity type, and state of organization.

1b. Individual Debtor. "Individual" means a natural person and a sole proprietorship, whether or not operating under a trade name. Don't use prefixes (Mr., Mrs., Ms.). Use suffix box only for titles of lineage (Jr., Sr., III) and not for other suffixes or titles (e.g., M.D.). Use married woman's personal name (Mary Smith, not Mrs. John Smith). Enter individual Debtor's family name (surname) in Last Name box, first given name in First Name box, and all additional given names in Middle Name box.

   For both entity and individual Debtors: Don't use Debtor's trade name, D/B/A, A/K/A, F/K/A, etc. in place of Debtor's legal name; you may add such other names as additional Debtors if you wish.

1c. An address is always required for the Debtor named in 1a or 1b.

1d. Debtor's social security or tax identification number is required in some states. Enter social security number of a sole proprietor, not tax identification number of the sole proprietorship.

1e,f,g "Additional information re entity Debtor" is optional. It helps searchers to distinguish this Debtor from others with the same or a similar name. Type of entity and state of organization can be determined from Debtor's current filed charter documents. Organizational I.D. number, if any, is assigned by the agency where the charter document was filed; this is different from taxpayer I.D. number; this should be entered preceded by the 2-character U.S. Postal identification of state of organization (e.g., CA12345, for a California corporation whose organizational I.D. number is 12345).

Note: If Debtor is a transmitting utility as defined in applicable Commercial Code, attach Addendum (Form UCC1Ad) and check box Ad8.

2. If an additional Debtor is included, complete item 2, determined and formatted per Instruction 1. To include further additional Debtors, or one or more additional Secured Parties, attach either Addendum (Form UCC1Ad) or other additional page(s), using correct name format. Follow Instruction 1 for determining and formatting additional names.

3. Enter information, determined and formatted per Instruction 1. If there is more than one Secured Party, see Instruction 2. If there has been a total assignment of the Secured Party's interest prior to filing this form, you may provide either assignor Secured Party's or assignee's name and address in item 3.

4. Use item 4 to indicate the types or describe the items of collateral. If space in item 4 is insufficient, put the entire collateral description or continuation of the collateral description on either Addendum (Form UCC1Ad) or other attached additional page(s).

5, 6. All Debtors must sign. Under certain circumstances, Secured Party may sign instead of Debtor; if applicable, check box in item 5 and provide Secured Party's signature in item 6, and under certain circumstances, in some states, you must also provide additional data; use Addendum (Form UCC1Ad) or attachment to provide such additional data.

7. If filing in the state of Florida you must check one of the two boxes in item 7 to comply with documentary stamp tax requirements.

8. If the collateral consists of or includes fixtures, timber, minerals, and/or mineral-related accounts, check the box in item 8 and complete the required information on Addendum (Form UCC1Ad). If the collateral consists of or includes crops, consult applicable law of state where this Financing Statement is to be filed and complete Ad3b, and Ad4 if required, on Addendum (Form UCC1Ad) and, if required, check box in item 8.

9. Check box 9 to request Search Certificate(s) on all or some of the Debtors named in this Financing Statement. The Certificate will list all Financing Statements on file against the designated Debtor currently effective on the date of the Certificate, including this Financing Statement. There is an additional fee for each Certificate. This item is optional. If you have checked box 9, file copy 3 (Search Request Copy) of this form together with copies 1 and 2. Not all states will honor a search request made via this form; some states require a separate request form.

Instructions re Optional Items A-D

A. To assist filing officers who might wish to communicate with filer, filer may provide information in item A. This item is optional.

B. If filer has an account with filing officer or is authorized to pay fees by means of a card (credit or debit) and wishes to use such means of payment, check the appropriate box and enter filer's account number in item B, or, in the alternative, filer may present this information by a cover letter.

C. Complete item C if you want acknowledgment copy returned and you have presented simultaneously a carbon or other copy of this form for use as an acknowledgment copy.

D. If filer desires to use titles of lessee and lessor, or consignee and consignor, instead of Debtor and Secured Party, check the appropriate box in item D. This item is optional. If this is not a UCC security interest filing (e.g., a tax lien, judgment lien, etc.), check the appropriate box in item D, complete items 1-9 as applicable and attach any other items required under other law.

FORM 5–10B
FINANCING STATEMENT ADDENDUM

FINANCING STATEMENT ADDENDUM — FOLLOW INSTRUCTIONS

THIS SPACE FOR USE OF FILING OFFICER

AdA. NAME OF FIRST DEBTOR ON RELATED FINANCING STATEMENT

ENTITY'S NAME

INDIVIDUAL'S LAST NAME	FIRST NAME	MIDDLE NAME, SUFFIX

AdB. MISCELLANEOUS:

Ad1. ADDITIONAL DEBTOR'S EXACT FULL LEGAL NAME - insert only one name (Ad1a or Ad1b)

Ad1a. ENTITY'S NAME

OR

Ad1b. INDIVIDUAL'S LAST NAME	FIRST NAME	MIDDLE NAME	SUFFIX

Ad1c. MAILING ADDRESS	CITY	STATE	COUNTRY	POSTAL CODE

Ad1d. S.S. OR TAX I.D.#	OPTIONAL ADD'NL INFO RE ENTITY DEBTOR	Ad1e. TYPE OF ENTITY	Ad1f. ENTITY'S STATE OR COUNTRY OF ORGANIZATION	Ad1g. ENTITY'S ORGANIZATIONAL I.D.#, if any ☐ NONE

Ad2. ADDITIONAL SECURED PARTY'S EXACT FULL LEGAL NAME - insert only one name (Ad2a or Ad2b)

Ad2a. ENTITY'S NAME

OR

Ad2b. INDIVIDUAL'S LAST NAME	FIRST NAME	MIDDLE NAME	SUFFIX

Ad2c. MAILING ADDRESS	CITY	STATE	COUNTRY	POSTAL CODE

Ad3a. ☐ This FINANCING STATEMENT covers timber to be cut, minerals, or mineral-related accounts, or is filed as a fixture filing

Ad3b. ☐ This FINANCING STATEMENT covers crops growing or to be grown on the real estate described below

Ad4. Description of real estate:

Ad7. Additional collateral description:

Ad5. Name and address of a RECORD OWNER of above-described real estate (if Debtor does not have a record interest):

Ad6. REQUIRED SIGNATURE

Ad8. ☐ Debtor is a TRANSMITTING UTILITY (if applicable)

Office of the Secretary of State of Texas Web Form

(1) FILING OFFICER COPY — NATIONAL ADDENDUM (FORM UCC1Ad) (TRANS) (REV. 12/18/95)

INVESTIGATION

Instructions for National Addendum (Form UCC1Ad) (Trans)

AdA.   Insert name of first Debtor shown on Financing Statement to which this Addendum is related, exactly as shown in item 1 of Financing Statement.

AdB.   Miscellaneous: Under certain circumstances, additional information not provided on Financing Statement (Form UCC1) is required; also, some states have non-uniform requirements. Use this space to provide such additional information or to comply with such requirements; otherwise, leave blank.

Ad1.   If this Addendum adds an additional Debtor, complete Ad1 in accordance with Instruction 1 on Financing Statement.

Ad2.   If this Addendum adds an additional Secured Party, complete Ad2 in accordance with Instruction 3 on Financing Statement.

Ad3-Ad5. If collateral is realty-related (crops, fixtures, timber, minerals or mineral-related accounts), check box Ad3a and/or Ad3b, as appropriate; provide description of real estate in item Ad4, if required; and, if Debtor is not a record owner of the described real estate, provide, in item Ad5, the name and address of a record owner. Also, provide collateral description on Financing Statement or in item Ad7.

Ad6.   If this Addendum adds an additional Debtor, additional Debtor must sign. Under certain circumstances, Secured Party may sign instead of additional Debtor; if applicable, see Instruction 5, 6 on Financing Statement.

Ad7.   You may use this space to provide continued description of collateral, if you cannot complete description on Financing Statement.

Ad8.   If Debtor is a transmitting utility as defined in the applicable Commercial Code, check box Ad8.

92

Because each state adopts the Uniform Commercial Code in whole or in part, making changes to fit the customs and traditions of that state, the rules regarding the use of the UCC-1 financing statement will vary from state to state as well. If you cannot find the words "Commercial Code" in your state statutes, try looking for terms such as "Business and Commerce Code." There is also considerable confusion on the place to file the completed UCC-1 forms. Whether the form is filed with the County Recorder or Clerk or the Secretary of State (or both) will depend on the type of property involved. In some instances (such as stock certificates), the property will actually have to be in the possession of the creditor, but in most cases, as long as the form evidences that the property has been "attached" under UCC rules, possession by the creditor is not necessary. The components of "attachment" are:

1. The debtor retains possession of the collateral but has signed a security agreement with the creditor
2. The secured creditor has given something of value to the debtor in exchange for the collateral
3. the debtor has retained some rights in the collateral

Below is an example of a security agreement. This document usually accompanies a loan agreement in a package for a bank loan.

FORM 10–C
SECURITY AGREEMENT

This SECURITY AGREEMENT is made on this _____ day of _____, 20 ___ between _____, _____, _____ ("Debtor"), and _____, _____, _____,_____ ("Secured Party").

1. **SECURITY INTEREST.** Debtor grants to Secured Party a security interest in all inventory, equipment, appliances, furnishings, and fixtures now or hereafter placed upon the premises known as _____, located at _____, _____ (the "Premises") or used in connection therewith and in which Debtor now has or hereafter acquires any right and the proceeds therefrom. As additional collateral, Debtor assigns to Secured Party, a security interest in all of its right, title, and interest to any trademarks, trade names, contract rights, and leasehold interests in which Debtor now has or hereafter acquires. The Security Interest shall secure the payment and performance of Debtor's promissory note of even date herewith in the principal amount of _____ ($_____) Dollars and the payment and performance of all other liabilities and obligations of Debtor to Secured Party of every kind and description, direct or indirect, absolute or contingent, due or to become due now existing or hereafter arising.

2. **COVENANTS.** Debtor hereby warrants and covenants: (a) The collateral will be kept at _____, _____, _____; and that the collateral will not be removed from the Premises other than in the ordinary course of

INVESTIGATION

business. (b) The Debtor's place of business is _____, _____.
_____, and Debtor will immediately notify Secured Party in writing of any change in or discontinuance of Debtor's place of business. (c) The parties intend that the collateral is and will at all times remain personal property despite the fact and irrespective of the manner in which it is attached to realty. (d) The Debtor will not sell, dispose, or otherwise transfer the collateral or any interest therein without the prior written consent of Secured Party, and the Debtor shall keep the collateral free from unpaid charges (including rent), taxes, and liens. (e) The Debtor shall execute alone or with Secured Party any Financing Statement or other document or procure any document, and pay the cost of filing the same in all public offices wherever filing is deemed by Secured Party to be necessary. (f) Debtor shall maintain insurance at all times with respect to all collateral against risks of fire, theft, and other such risks and in such amounts as Secured Party may require. The policies shall be payable to both the Secured Party and the Debtor as their interests appear and shall provide for ten (10) days written notice of cancellation to Secured Party. (g) The Debtor shall make all repairs, replacements, additions, and improvements necessary to maintain any equipment in good working order and condition. At its option, Secured Party may discharge taxes, liens, or other encumbrances at any time levied or placed on the collateral, may pay rent or insurance due on the collateral and may pay for the maintenance and preservation of the collateral. Debtor agrees to reimburse Secured Party on demand for any payment made, or any expense incurred by Secured Party pursuant to the foregoing authorization.

3. **DEFAULT.** The Debtor shall be in default under this Agreement upon the happening of any of the following: (a) any misrepresentation in connection with this Agreement on the part of the Debtor. (b) any noncompliance with or nonperformance of the Debtor's obligations under the Note or this Agreement. (c) if Debtor is involved in any financial difficulty as evidenced by (i) an assignment for the benefit of creditors, or (ii) an attachment or receivership of assets not dissolved within thirty (30) days, or (iii) the institution of Bankruptcy proceedings, whether voluntary or involuntary, which is not dismissed within thirty (30) days from the date on which it is filed. Upon default and at any time thereafter, Secured Party may declare all obligations secured hereby immediately due and payable and shall have the remedies of a Secured Party under the Uniform Commercial Code. Secured Party may require the Debtor to make it available to Secured Party at a place which is mutually convenient. No waiver by Secured Party of any default shall operate as a waiver of any other default or of the same default on a future occasion. This Agreement shall inure to the benefit up and bind the heirs, executors, administrators, successors, and assigns of the parties. This Agreement shall have the effect of an instrument under seal.

By:

_____

Date: _____

NOTE: FILE FINANCING STATEMENTS IN OR WITHIN FIVE (5) DAYS FROM DATE.

Actually, the security agreement is the document which CREATES the security interest, and the UCC-1 form is the form which PERFECTS the security interest. It is usually necessary to have the security agreement to create the initial interest before it can be perfected.

SEARCHING THE UCC-1 FINANCE FORMS

You will probably not be involved in the creation and preparation of these forms unless you are working in a banking specialty, but these UCC-1 forms are a wonderful source of information for the litigation paralegal. We use these forms to find missing witnesses, deadbeat parents, defendant assets, and on and on. The first step is WHERE to search. Because the laws vary so greatly for filing these forms, we recommend searching in any county where you think the person is living or doing business, as well as with the Secretary of State in any state where you think the person is living or doing business. Think creatively. The paralegals filing these documents live by the adage, "When in doubt, file everywhere." Let that drive your searches. This information is public information, and anyone can access it. Here is a checklist of things to remember to aid your search:

CHECKLIST FOR UCC-1 SEARCHES

1.   Check for all variations and misspellings of the name that you can think of.
2.   If you know it, check the person's county of birth and surrounding counties. If you have a social security number, use the chart in [the third edition of] this book at § **566** to determine the state of issuance of the number. Most people return to familiar areas when they are at loose ends.
3.   Watch out for metropolitan areas where several counties converge, such as Los Angeles and Houston. Search all surrounding counties. Also search the counties of popular resort areas within commuting distance of that area.
4.   Look for "dba's" (doing business as, or assumed name or fictitious name certificates) and search on those as well.
5.   A UCC-1 search will enhance your findings if you have already completed a bankruptcy search, real property search, motor vehicle search and any other public record searches available.
6.   UCC-1 searches are an excellent addition to a standard asset check or search at the beginning of a litigation case.

There are also a myriad of search agencies available ready to complete your searches for a fee. Check with your attorney and see if he or she wants you to use a search company (find them anywhere legal services are advertised) or if you are to complete the search yourself.

§ 5.39 Witness Location

Page 386, add at end of section:

20. UCC records

21. Alumni associations

22. The realtor who listed or sold his house

23. Ask the information experts in the neighborhood . . . the CHILDREN!

§ 5.41 Driver's License Records

Page 389, add at end of § 5.41:

FORM 5–12A
SAMPLE REQUEST FOR DRIVER LICENSE INFORMATION (TEXAS)

REQUEST FOR INFORMATION FROM TEXAS DRIVER LICENSE RECORDS (Mail to: Records Bureau, Texas Department of Public Safety, Box 15999, Austin, Texas 78761-5999). Make check payable to: TEXAS DEPARTMENT OF PUBLIC SAFETY. The following is to be completed by the person requesting information.

Circle the number of the type of service desired: (For Driving Safety Course, circle 3A).

1.	Date of birth—License status—Latest address	Fee $4.00
2.	Date of birth—License status—List of accidents and Violations in record within immediate past 3-year period.	Fee $6.00
2A.	Same as #2 (above) Certified. THIS RECORD IS NOT ACCEPTABLE FOR DRIVING SAFETY COURSE.	Fee $10.00
3.	Date of Birth—License status—List of all accidents and violations in record. This record is furnished to licensee only.	Fee $7.00
3A.	Same as #3 (above) Certified. THIS RECORD FURNISHED TO LICENSEE ONLY. ACCEPTABLE FOR DSC COURSE.	Fee $10.00

Information Requested on:

Date of Birth _____ Texas Driver's License No. _____

Social Security Number:_____

§ 5.65   SKIP TRACING CHECKLIST

Mail Driving Record To:

Last Name: _____First Name: _____Middle: _____

*Mailing Address: _____

City/State _____Zip _____

*Have Driving Records mailed to your home address, not to the Court.

§ 5.65   Skip Tracing Checklist

Page 418, add at end of section:

   _____   **14.**   UCC search

CHAPTER 7

INSURANCE DEFENSE

Page 476, and new § 7.7A:

§ 7.7A   Bad Faith (New)

Neither insurance defense firms nor their carrier clients enjoy hearing the words "bad faith." Insureds sometimes file such claims against their insurance companies for breach of contract, failure to pay a covered claim, or failing to investigate the insured's claim with reasonableness. Case law is very straightforward regarding the insurance companies obligations and responsibilities. See the case below.

Sawyer v. Farm Bureau Mut. Ins. Co.
619 N.W.2d 644 (S.D. 2000)

GILBERTSON, Justice.

Defendant Farm Bureau Mutual Insurance Company (Farm Bureau) appeals from a jury verdict in favor of Plaintiff, Shon Sawyer (Sawyer). The jury awarded damages for breach of contract, bad faith, and punitive damages to Sawyer arising out of a dispute as to insurance coverage relating to the death of livestock. Farm Bureau also appeals an award of Sawyer's attorney's fees. We affirm in part and reverse and remand in part.

FACTS AND PROCEDURE

Sawyer operates a cattle-feeding operation near Hurley, South Dakota. In June of 1995, Sawyer procured insurance from Farm Bureau through its agent, Kurtis Berndt, of Sioux Falls. This initial policy covered all his property except his livestock. In January of 1996, the policy was expanded to include livestock. The trial court found that Sawyer's livestock coverage was designated as "Special Form" as indicated on the Declarations page of the policy. Special Form is also referred to as "all-risks" in the industry, and applies to all loss except as otherwise excluded. Under Sawyer's original policy, Farm Bureau would not cover "loss to livestock or poultry caused in whole or in part: . . . by smothering; [or] by freezing in blizzards or snowstorms." However, for an additional premium, Sawyer obtained an endorsement to his policy. This endorsement provided that Farm Bureau would cover "Freezing and Smothering in Blizzards or Snowstorms."

INSURANCE DEFENSE

In November of 1996, 109 head of cattle died during a winter storm, defined by the parties as an "ice storm." Another 188 head died during a December blizzard. When Sawyer submitted a claim for the loss of the cattle, Farm Bureau required all the cattle to be necropsied, which is a procedure similar to an autopsy. This procedure required Sawyer to stockpile the 297 frozen carcasses in his yard, and then individually move each carcass into a building heated to 100 degrees. The carcass was left in the building to thaw, a process that took several days. Once the carcass was thawed, it was inspected to determine whether death resulted from disease rather than freezing. After inspection, the carcass was restacked outside. Farm Bureau demanded that each animal be necropsied to determine that the death was covered by the policy. It took the position that Sawyer must prove that the animals' death resulted from "freezing or smothering in snowstorms or blizzards," as defined in the policy's endorsement before coverage would apply. Sawyer argued that because his livestock coverage was "Special Form," all losses were covered unless otherwise excluded.

Farm Bureau also refused payment on the grounds that Sawyer had not told it that he was feeding other people's cattle. It based this position on a clause in the policy that stated as follows: "We cover: Direct loss to unscheduled farm personal property owned by you, being purchased by you or rented or leased to you which is used in the operation of your farm as a farm." Farm Bureau interpreted this clause as requiring 100% ownership of the livestock by Sawyer. Sawyer did not own 100% of the livestock he was feeding. During the course of his operation, he had needed to secure additional financing. Unable to secure the necessary financing through a financial institution, he instead solicited and obtained several investors in his operation. These investments were in a variety of forms, but usually involved a partial ownership in certain livestock. At all times, Sawyer continued to provide feed, medicine and other supplies for the livestock. Sawyer was responsible for insuring the livestock. All livestock was purchased and sold in Sawyer's name. However, because Sawyer did not own 100% of the livestock, Farm Bureau denied coverage under Sawyer's policy. As a result, the parties were unable to reach a settlement and the dispute went to a jury trial on July 21, 1999.

After the close of evidence at trial, both parties moved for a directed verdict. In ruling on those motions, the trial court made several findings. It found as a matter of law that Sawyer had an ownership interest in the cattle sufficient to satisfy the requirements of the policy. In addition, it found that the coverage was "Special Form" and hence, the loss during the ice storm was covered under the policy because it was not specifically excluded. It also found that the endorsement purchased by Sawyer eliminated the exclusion contained in the policy for death from freezing or smothering in a blizzard or snowstorm. As a result, the trial court granted Sawyer's motion for directed verdict as to the loss from the November ice storm. It also granted Sawyer's motion as to coverage for the loss resulting from the December blizzard. The question as to whether Sawyer was required to prove the cattle died during the blizzard rather than some time afterward, was reserved for the jury. As to Sawyer's bad faith claim, the trial court ruled there was clear and convincing evidence of a reasonable basis to believe there had been willful, wanton, and malicious behavior by Farm Bureau, sufficient to submit the claim to the jury.

§ 7.7A BAD FAITH

The jury returned a verdict in favor of Sawyer awarding $500 per head for all cattle lost in the November storm and $500 per head for 175 of the 188 cattle killed in the December blizzard, for a total of $142,000. In addition, the jury awarded bad faith damages of $34,155 and punitive damages of $125,000, as well as pre-judgment interest on the breach of contract and bad faith damages.

On appeal, Farm Bureau raises five issues for our consideration. Sawyer raises two issues by notice of review.

ANALYSIS AND DECISION

1. Whether Farm Bureau's notice of appeal was timely so as to give this Court jurisdiction to hear the appeal.

Initially we address Sawyer's contention that the appeal of Farm Bureau is not timely and the case should be dismissed for want of jurisdiction. Under SDCL 15-26A-6, an appeal must be taken within 60 days after the judgment is signed, attested, filed and notice given to the adverse party. The initial or preliminary judgment, filed on August 13, 1999, was entered with this condition, "[t]his Judgment is expressly subject to amendment, if necessary to conform to the Court's ruling on Plaintiff's Motion for Substitution of Party Defendant dated August 10, 1999." This motion to amend was previously filed by Sawyer on August 10, 1999, requesting the court to substitute Farm Bureau Mut. Ins. Co. for the originally named defendant, South Dakota Farm Bureau Mut. Ins. Co. The trial court orally granted this motion on September 16, 1999 and the order finalizing the judgment pursuant to this motion was filed on September 22, 1999.

Sawyer was the moving party on this motion. The order was significant in that it properly identified the party against whom his judgment would be enforced. As such, Sawyer will not now be heard to complain when his own motion prevented the entry of a final judgment prior to September 22, 1999 and notice of entry thereon on September 24, 1999. Therefore, the 60 day appeal period began to run from September 25, 1999 and Farm Bureau's notice of appeal on November 17 was timely.

2. Whether the trial court erred in failing to instruct the jury that Sawyer had to prove he owned the cattle for which he claimed money damages.

At the close of evidence, the trial court determined that Sawyer did have "an ownership interest in [the] cattle." As such, the jury was instructed that "[r]egardless of whether [Sawyer] was the sole owner of [the] cattle, a part-owner of [the] cattle or was custom feeding the cattle for others, [Sawyer] had an insurable interest in the cattle sufficient to obligate [Farm Bureau] to provide coverage on the cattle for their full value." Farm Bureau requested an instruction requiring Sawyer to prove "that he owned each of the animals for which he claims money damages." The request was refused. Based upon this proposed instruction, it appears Farm Bureau interprets the term "owned" in the policy to mean "100% owned by the insured." We do not agree.

We review the interpretation of an insurance contract de novo. *National Sun Indus., Inc. v. S.D. Farm Bureau Ins. Co.,* 1999 S.D. 63, 596 N.W.2d 45, 46. Whether the contract is ambiguous is also reviewed de novo. *Id.,* 596 N.W.2d at 46-7. We have previously stated that "[a]n insurance policy is ambiguous when it 'is fairly susceptible to two constructions.'" *Id.* When ambiguity is found, "the interpretation most favorable to the insured should be adopted." *Id.* Farm Bureau relies heavily on its interpretation of the term "owned." Yet, the term is not defined anywhere in the policy. While it is reasonable to conclude that ownership implies complete ownership to the exclusion of others, it is equally as reasonable to conclude that the term encompasses an infinite number and combinations of ownership interests so long as some ownership interest exists. As such, the policy is ambiguous, and the term will be construed in favor of the insured. Sawyer had at least a 25% ownership interest in the livestock that died during the storms. He is deemed to have "owned" that livestock for purposes of the Farm Bureau policy.

This decision is in line with those from other jurisdictions that have interpreted similar terms. In *Dolan v. Welch,* the Appellate Court of Illinois found the term "ownership" in an automobile insurance policy to be ambiguous. 123 Ill. App.3d 277, 78 Ill. Dec. 675, 462 N.E.2d 794, 796-97 (1984). The Minnesota Supreme Court determined that the terms "ownership" and "owned by named insured" include any insurable interest in the described property covered by the policy. *Quaderer v. Integrity Mut. Ins. Co.,* 263 Minn. 383, 116 N.W.2d 605, 608-09 (1962). Finally, in *American Indem. Co. v. Davis,* the Fifth Circuit Court of Appeals found that the term "ownership" includes joint as well as sole ownership interests in an automobile. 260 F.2d 440, 442 (5th Cir. 1958) (applying Georgia law).

In addition, there is ample evidence in the record that Farm Bureau was well aware of the fact that Sawyer would be custom feeding at his feedlot, and that as a result, he would not own 100% of all the livestock on his feedlot. At the time of application, Sawyer insured 4,000 head for $500 per head, and was charged a full premium for all 4,000 head. Three weeks after the policy went into effect, Berndt informed a Farm Bureau underwriter that Sawyer "may custom feed and plans on it." A Farm Bureau inspector reported to the underwriting division that Sawyer "d[id] some custom feeding" and he had "the impression it [was for] more than one [customer]." Additional documents produced by Farm Bureau show that the claims division was also aware that Sawyer was custom feeding. At no time after the policy went into effect, did Berndt or any other Farm Bureau personnel inform Sawyer that because of an undisclosed, internal Farm Bureau policy, he should have been insured under a different policy. Nor did any Farm Bureau personnel inform Sawyer that if he had only a partial interest in the livestock that any claims would be pro rated accordingly. Instead, Farm Bureau continued to collect the full premium on 4,000 head of cattle, insured for $500 per head. The trial court's instruction as to ownership is affirmed.

3. Whether the trial court erred in not granting a directed verdict for Farm Bureau on the issue of bad faith.

The trial court's decision not to grant a directed verdict is reviewed under the abuse of discretion standard. "The trial court's decisions and rulings on such motions are presumed correct and this Court will not seek reasons to reverse." *Martinmaas v. Engelmann,* 2000 S.D. 85, 612 N.W.2d 600, 606. Stated another way, failure to grant a directed verdict will not be overturned unless reasonable minds could not differ as to the absence of bad faith.

The test for a bad faith cause of action against an insurer was recently reiterated in *Stene v. State Farm Mut. Auto. Ins. Co.,* 1998 S.D. 95, 583 N.W.2d 399, 403. There, this Court stated:

> [F]or proof of bad faith, there must be an absence of a reasonable basis for denial of policy benefits [or failure to comply with a duty under the insurance contract] and the knowledge or reckless disregard [of the lack] of a reasonable basis for denial, implicit in that test is our conclusion that the knowledge of the lack of a reasonable basis may be inferred and imputed to an insurance company where there is a reckless disregard of a lack of a reasonable basis for denial or a reckless indifference to facts or to proofs submitted by the insured.

Id. (quoting *Walz v. Fireman's Fund Ins. Co.,* 1996 S.D. 135, 556 N.W.2d 68, 70) (alterations in original).

> An insurance company may, however, challenge claims which are fairly debatable and will be found liable only where it has intentionally denied (or failed to process or pay) a claim without a reasonable basis.

Id.

Our function here is not to determine whether we believe bad faith existed, rather whether evidence exists from which reasonable minds could find bad faith. We hold that reasonable minds could find that Farm Bureau acted in bad faith and that the trial court did not abuse its discretion in denying Farm Bureau's motion for directed verdict. Evidence of Farm Bureau's bad faith includes a tape-recorded conversation between the insurance adjuster for Farm Bureau, Wayne Nielsen, and Farm Bureau's Senior Property Supervisor, Michael McMahon. During this conversation, Nielsen and McMahon discussed strategies to make Sawyer appear fraudulent, false accusations that Sawyer had committed arson, false accusations of extra-marital affairs involving Sawyer's wife, as well as Farm Bureau's exposure under the policy and strategies to avoid paying the full loss incurred. In addition, Nielsen expressed reservations about: "having too much on paper if we go to discovery. . . . I just wonder how much at risk or how much do we get our own tit in a wringer by having too much on paper. You know. You know we don't want to create a bad faith thing. . . ."

There would have been no need to worry about creating a "bad faith thing" if Farm Bureau actually believed that they could deny coverage because Sawyer did not own 100% of the insured animals.

Further evidence of Farm Bureau's bad faith includes the fact that Farm Bureau never attempted to count or weigh the dead livestock, despite the fact that it disputed both the number and weight of the dead livestock. Finally, Sawyer was left with a mound of 297 dead cattle in his yard for several months, incurred costs associated with the necropsy of each animal, and over four and a half years later has not been paid a dime on his claims. From this evidence reasonable minds could differ whether Farm Bureau acted with a reasonable basis for denial of policy benefits and with reckless indifference to facts. The trial court's denial of Farm Bureau's motion for directed verdict on the issue of bad faith was within its discretion.

4.   Whether the trial court erred in finding clear and convincing evidence of a reasonable basis to believe there had been willful, wanton, or malicious conduct by Farm Bureau so as to submit the issue of punitive damages to the jury.

"The determination by the trial court that there was a reasonable basis to submit the punitive damages issue to the jury will not be disturbed absent a clearly erroneous interpretation of the evidence." *Kjerstad v. Ravellette Publications, Inc.,* 517 N.W.2d 419, 425 (S.D. 1994). Farm Bureau relies upon its argument that it had valid, good faith disputes as to the ownership of the dead cattle, the number of dead cattle, and the value of each, and therefore its conduct was not willful, wanton or malicious. As to the number and value of the cattle, Farm Bureau never attempted to count or weigh the dead cattle. In addition, it relied upon a strict reading of an undefined and ambiguous term in a policy written by its own employees, with the knowledge that ambiguous policy terms are construed against the insurer.

In *Isaac v. State Farm Mut. Auto. Ins. Co.,* 522 N.W.2d 752, 761 (S.D. 1994), this Court found that punitive damages were warranted when State Farm refused to settle a claim under Isaac's uninsured motorist coverage without a release of Isaac's bad faith claim against it. Punitive damages were also awarded in *Harter v. Plains Ins. Co., Inc.,* 1998 S.D. 59, 579 N.W.2d 625, 634. In that case, Plains (as Harter's insurer) intervened in a separate lawsuit between Harter and the defendant in an auto accident. As intervenors, Plains requested that Harter's claim be dismissed even though the defendant had admitted liability. The purpose behind such a request was to protect Plains from underinsured motorist liability as it was aware that the defendant was judgment proof.

When the evidence, including that discussed regarding the bad faith claim, is viewed in light of the precedent discussed, Farm Bureau has not shown that the trial court was clearly erroneous in submitting punitive damages to the jury.

5.   Whether the trial court abused its discretion in admitting Sawyer's exhibits in mass.

Evidentiary rulings made by a trial court are presumed to be correct, and are only reversed if there is an abuse of discretion. *State v. Fowler,* 1996 S.D. 78, 552 N.W.2d 92, 94 (citations omitted). At the beginning of trial, the court received Sawyer's exhibits # 1-41 to facilitate efficiency and shorten the trial. The exhibits were all produced by Farm Bureau during discovery and were admitted under the business records exception found in SDCL 19-16-10. That statute provides:

> A memorandum, report, record, or data compilation, in any form, of acts, events, conditions, opinions, or diagnoses, made at or near the time by, or from information transmitted by, a person with knowledge, if kept in the course of a regularly conducted business activity, and if it was the reg-

ular practice of that business activity to make the memorandum, report, record, or data compilation, *all as shown by the testimony of the custodian or other qualified witness,* is not excluded by § 19-16-4, even though the declarant is available as a witness, unless the source of information or the method or circumstances of preparation indicate lack of trustworthiness.

Id. (emphasis added).

Despite the emphasized language above, Sawyer's exhibits were admitted under this exception without any foundation testimony from their custodian or any other qualified witness. This is clearly a violation of the requirements specified in SDCL 19-16-10. *State v. Brown,* 480 N.W.2d 761, 764 (S.D. 1992). Therefore, the trial court abused its discretion in admitting the exhibits into evidence. "However, 'the admission of documentary exhibits does not warrant reversal absent a showing that substantial rights of the party were affected. The burden of demonstrating that such rights were affected rests with the party asserting error.'" *Brown,* 480 N.W.2d at 764 (citations omitted). Farm Bureau has not specified any substantial rights that were affected by the admission of these documents, beyond its bare assertion that the admission "affected a substantial right of the defendant to mount a defense." While we share Farm Bureau's concern regarding the apparent lack of compliance with the rules of evidence by the trial court in this instance, Farm Bureau's aforementioned assertion does not overcome the burden that it bears.

6. Whether the trial court abused its discretion when it awarded attorney's fees to Sawyer.

SDCL 58-12-3 provides in relevant part that:

> In all actions or proceedings hereafter commenced against any insurance . . . company . . . on any policy of insurance, if it appears from the evidence that such company . . . *has refused to pay the full amount of such loss, and that such refusal is vexatious or without reasonable cause,* . . . the trial court and the appellate court, shall, if judgment or an award is rendered for plaintiff, allow the plaintiff a reasonable sum as an attorney's fee to be recovered and collected as a part of the costs. . . .

Id.

Before attorney's fees may be awarded under this section, the trial court must find "that the insurance company refused to pay the full amount of the insured's loss and that said refusal was either vexatious or without reasonable cause." *Brooks v. Milbank Ins. Co.,* 2000 S.D. 16, 605 N.W.2d 173, 178 (citations omitted). The jury's "finding of bad faith on the part of an insurance company does not mean 'ipso facto' that its conduct was vexatious or without reasonable cause." *Isaac,* 522 N.W.2d at 763. These findings involve findings of fact and as such will not be reversed unless clearly erroneous. *Brooks,* 2000 S.D. 16, 605 N.W.2d at 178.

In ruling upon Sawyer's motion for attorney's fees, the trial court made the following written findings of fact as to Farm Bureau's behavior on October 26, 1999. It is clear from the evidence in this case that the conduct of Farm Bureau was "vexatious and without reasonable cause." . . . The evidence clearly shows that Farm Bureau and/or its agents repeatedly denied, minimized and attempted to discourage the claims submitted by the Plaintiff in this case. [The phone] conversation [between Nielsen and McMahon] includes attempts to undervalue Plaintiff's losses, discussions of how to make Plaintiff appear fraudulent, concerns about the need to "minimiz[e] paper" in case of discovery and the contemplated use of an allegation that Plaintiff's wife was committing adultery. The taped conversation shows specifically how far Farm Bureau and its agents were willing to go to prevent paying the entire amount of the Plaintiff's losses.

The evidence also shows that Farm Bureau failed to conduct a good faith investigation and evaluation of the Plaintiff's claims. Farm Bureau failed to count and weigh the dead animals . . . and to provide an appropriate or acceptable means of valuing the losses incurred by Plaintiff.

In *Eldridge v. Northwest G.F. Mut. Ins. Co.,* 88 S.D. 426, 221 N.W.2d 16, 21 (S.D. 1974) the trial court found that "the investigation and adjustment of plaintiff's claim by defendant's agent was incomplete and insufficient" when the agent did not even visit the site of the loss after a second storm to assess damage to the plaintiff's roof. Based on those findings, this Court affirmed the trial court's grant of attorney's fees. *Id.* An award of attorney's fees was affirmed in *Isaac* when the trial court found that State Farm had delayed its investigation, settlement and evaluation for years, finally refusing to pay any amounts due without a release of any bad faith action against it. 522 N.W.2d at 763. More recently, this Court affirmed an award of attorney's fees in *Brooks,* 2000 S.D. 16, 605 N.W.2d at 179. In that case, the insurance company refused to pay the claim because of a confession that it coerced from the insured's tenant under threat of criminal prosecution, attempting to implicate the insured in a conspiracy to defraud the insurer. *Id.* The trial court found that the insurer's refusal to pay was vexatious and without reasonable cause. Those findings were affirmed by this Court. *Id.* In light of this case law and the record before us, we cannot say that the trial court's findings that the actions of Farm Bureau were "vexatious and without reasonable cause" were clearly erroneous.

Pursuant to SDCL 58-12-3, attorney's fees are allowed only in an action against an insurer based upon the policy. Sawyer's bad faith claim against Farm Bureau is "not an action against an insurance company on a policy of insurance within the contemplation of SDCL 58-12-3." *Isaac,* 522 N.W.2d at 763 (citations omitted). Therefore, those attorney's fees relating to the bad faith claim against Farm Bureau, as opposed to the contractual claim should have been excluded. It is not clear from the record whether the trial court included attorney's fees for the bad faith claim in its award to Sawyer. Therefore, we reverse and remand for a determination of attorney's fees in accordance with this decision.

7. Whether the trial court erred in denying Sawyer's motion for judgment notwithstanding the verdict.

The trial court's decision to grant or deny a motion for judgment notwithstanding the verdict will only be overturned for an abuse of discretion. *Martinmaas,* 2000 S.D.

106

85, 612 N.W.2d at 600, 606. Sawyer argues that its motion should have been granted, directing coverage for all loss resulting from the December storm. The trial court found that the endorsement purchased by Sawyer eliminated the exclusion against death from freezing or smothering in a blizzard or snowstorm found in the policy. Therefore, Sawyer argues, all livestock deaths were covered under the Special Form ("all-risks") coverage. The basis of Sawyer's argument is that the jury award does not provide coverage for thirteen of the cattle that died as a result of the December storm. This is determined by dividing the jury verdict of $87,500 by the value of the cattle used by the jury ($500). That would equate to 175 cattle that the jury determined were covered by the policy, leaving 13 dead cattle not covered.

Despite the fact that the endorsement eliminated any exclusion for death by freezing or smothering, only those animals owned by Sawyer are covered by the policy. Even given the ambiguity of the term as discussed above, Sawyer must have *some* ownership in the cattle. Sawyer admitted in his testimony that he did not have any ownership interest in at least two of the cattle. The jury was also allowed to determine which cattle deaths were attributable to the December blizzard. The jury found that Sawyer had an ownership interest in only 175 of the cattle or that only 175 died in the storm or a combination thereof. After reviewing the testimony and evidence in the light most favorable to the verdict, we find that there is sufficient evidence to support the jury's verdict. Affirmed in part, reversed and remanded in part.

SABERS and KONENKAMP, JJ., concur.

MILLER, C.J., and AMUNDSON, J., dissent.

MILLER, Chief Justice (dissenting).

For reasons set forth below I would dismiss the appeal as untimely. I disagree with the majority's holding on that issue.

The majority holds that Farm Bureau timely filed its notice of appeal because the judgment was not final until September 25, 1999. In so holding, it incorrectly applies SDCL 15-26A-6.

The record clearly establishes that the trial court entered the judgment on August 13, 1999. Farm Bureau timely renewed its JNOV motion on August 20, 1999. The trial court's failure to rule on the parties' JNOV motions within twenty days (or enter an order extending such time for ruling) resulted in the denial of the motions on September 9, 1999 under the clear language of SDCL 15-6-50(b). Although the majority opinion inexplicably and incorrectly dismisses this point in footnote 3 as not dispositive, SDCL 15-26A-6 dictates otherwise. Accordingly, the sixty-day period began to run on September 10, 1999 not September 25, 1999 as erroneously asserted by the majority. SDCL 15-26A-6

The majority states that "an appeal must be taken within 60 days after the judgment is signed, attested, filed and notice given to the adverse party," under SDCL 15-26A-6. This is true, however that only applies when the trial court acts within the twenty-day period prescribed in the statute or the extension it has granted to itself. That is not the case here. Farm Bureau tendered the trial court an order extending the time for its determination of the motions, but it did not enter the order. Thus, the trial court's order entered on September 22, 1999 is untimely and a nullity because it was not entered within the parameters of the statute. *Bedney v. Heidt,* 1998 SD 50, 578 N.W.2d 570, 572. SDCL 15-26A-6 specifically speaks to the circumstance before this Court. It states in pertinent part:

> The running of the time for filing a notice of appeal is terminated as to all parties by a timely motion filed in the circuit court by any party pursuant to § 15-6-59 or § 15-6-50(b), or both, and the full time for appeal fixed by this section commences to run and is to be computed from the attestation and filing of an order made pursuant to such motion *or if the circuit court fails to take action on such motion or fails to enter an order extending the time for taking action on such motion within the time prescribed, then the date shall be computed from the date on which the time for action by the circuit court expires.* SDCL 15-26A-6 (emphasis added).

The statute clearly applies to this case and mandates that the sixty days began to run on the day the trial court's time for action expired, specifically September 9, 1999. Thus, Farm Bureau's notice of appeal filed on November 17, 1999 is untimely because the sixty-day period expired on November 8, 1999. The majority simply ignores the portion of SDCL 15-26A-6 quoted above, which clearly dictates the outcome in this case, choosing instead to rely on the inapplicable portion of the statute.

Furthermore, although Farm Bureau claims to have been misled by Sawyer's cooperation in scheduling the motion hearing outside the twenty-day period for trial court action, a letter from Farm Bureau's counsel belies its claim. The August 24, 1999 letter written to the trial court shows that Farm Bureau understood the statutory timeframes. The letter states in pertinent part:

> 2. *Defendant's Motion for Judgment n.o.v., or in the alternative, Motion for New Trial.*
>
> This motion has been scheduled for a hearing before you on September 8, 1999, at 3:30 P.M. I advised the court in my original cover letter that Defendant did not feel oral argument on this Motion was necessary. In cooperation with Steve Sanford and Clyde, and in your absence, we set the Motion for hearing should *the court* believe further argument on the issues would be helpful.
>
> Based upon the date of filing of the Motion the court must file its Order not later than September 9, 1999. If no order is filed the Motions are deemed to be denied. The court may extend the date for filing of its order by twenty (20) days should the court find there is good cause to extend the deadline. For your convenience I am enclosing an order extending the deadline should the court want more time to consider the motions. . . .
>
> 3. *Plaintiff's Motion for Judgment n.o.v.:*
>
> Plaintiff's Motion for Judgment n.o.v. is set for hearing on September 8, 1999 at 3:30 P.M. Defendant intends to oppose this motion, therefore,

absent the court extending the deadline for ruling on Judgment n.o.v. it will be necessary to have the hearing on September 8th unless the court advises counsel that she intends to rule based upon written submissions. Defendant will serve and file a written response. Defendant is not requesting oral argument, however, we will appear and argue should the court believe it will be helpful. **If the court extends the deadlines we could argue all Judgment n.o.v. motion's** [*sic*] **on the 16th.**

This letter clearly shows that Farm Bureau fully understood the statutory time-frames affecting any appeal it may have wished to take. Farm Bureau should not now be allowed to complain when it is clear that it was not misled by any action of Sawyer and fully understood the statutes governing its right to appeal.

Therefore, under clear and settled law, Farm Bureau's appeal should be dismissed as untimely.

AMUNDSON, J., joins this dissent.

CHAPTER 8

TRIAL READINESS AND SETTLEMENT

§ 8.18 Sample Pretrial Order

Page 511, Correct Form 8–12 to read as follows:

FORM 8–12
JOINT PRETRIAL ORDER

No. _____
: IN THE DISTRICT COURT OF
: ——————— COUNTY, _____
: _____ JUDICIAL DISTRICT _____

JOINT PRETRIAL ORDER APPEARANCE OF COUNSEL

APPEARANCE OF COUNSEL

(List the parties, their respective counsel and the address and telephone numbers of counsel in separate paragraphs.)

STATEMENT OF THE CASE

(Give a brief statement of the case for the information of the Court.)

MOTIONS

(State if there are any pending motions.)

CONTENTIONS OF THE PARTIES

(State concisely in separate paragraphs what each party claims.)

ADMISSIONS OF FACT

(List all facts which have been stipulated and admitted and require no proof.)

CONTESTED ISSUES OF FACT

(List all factual issues in controversy necessary to the final disposition of this case.)

111

TRIAL READINESS

AGREED APPLICABLE PROPOSITIONS OF LAW

(Delineate those legal propositions not in dispute.)

CONTESTED ISSUES OF LAW

(State briefly the issue of law in dispute, with a memorandum of authorities supporting each issue.)

EXHIBITS

1. Each counsel will attach to the JOINT pretrial order a copy of the list of all exhibits to be offered and will make all such exhibits available for examination by opposing counsel. This rule does not apply to rebuttal exhibits, which cannot be anticipated.

2. Any counsel requiring authentication of an exhibit must so notify in writing the offering counsel within (5) days after the exhibit is made available to opposing counsel for examination. FAILURE TO DO SO is an ADMISSION of authenticity.

3. Any other objections to admissibility of exhibits must, where possible, be made at least three (3) business days before trial, and the Court notified in writing with copies to all counsel accompanied by supporting legal authorities and copies of the exhibits *in* dispute.

4. The offering party will MARK HIS OWN EXHIBITS.

5. All exhibits will be OFFERED and RECEIVED in evidence as the FIRST ITEM OF BUSINESS at the trial.

WITNESSES

1. List the names and addresses of witnesses who will or may be used with a brief statement of the subject matter and substance of their testimony.

2. Include in this section the following:

   "In the event there are any other witnesses to be called at the trial, their names, addresses and the subject matter of their testimony shall be reported to opposing counsel as soon as they are known. This restriction shall not apply to rebuttal or impeaching witnessess, the necessity of whose testimony cannot reasonable be anticipated before the time of trial."

SETTLEMENT

(Include a statement that all settlement efforts have been exhausted, that the case cannot be settled, and will have to be tried.)

§ 8.22 TRIAL BOOK

<u>TRIAL</u>

(Include in this-paragraph the following:
a. Probable length of trial: AND
b. Availability of witnessess, including out-of-state witnessess.)

<u>ATTACHMENTS</u>

(Include the following REQUIRED attachments:

I   For a jury trial: Proposed Special Issues, including instructions or definitions.

II   For a non-jury trial: Proposed findings of fact and conclusions of law, with supporting authorities in a memorandum of law.)

_____
Judge Presiding

_____   _____
Attorney for Plaintiff   Attorney for Defendant

§ 8.22   Trial Book

Page 518, add at the end of § 8.22:

One of the best little tricks I have learned over the years is to prepare the trial book early in the case and make it work for you. Most paralegals will wait until just before trial and start to prepare the book. This is such a busy time, that the trial book becomes a real chore. Why not put the book together from the very beginning of the case, keeping it current, and taking it with you to all client meetings on the case or into your lawyer's office for in-house meetings on the case? This will provide you with ready answers to all the attorney's questions on the case without necessitating your excusal from the room to go check the file. It also takes the responsibility of putting the book together at the very busy end of the case and places it more leisurely into the ongoing day-to-day work. Keep this trial notebook on your credenza behind your desk for easy reference. Alternatively, you can keep your trial notebook on a laptop computer and have it ready for reference. You will always know the exact status of the case!

§ 8.22A — Trial Notebook Checklist (New)

TABLE OF CONTENTS

PRETRIAL ORDER

CAST OF CHARACTERS

_____ Plaintiff's name, address, home & cell phone numbers with e-mail address.

_____ Plaintiff's work address, work number and work e-mail address.

_____ Defendant's name, address and home phone number.

_____ Witnesses' name, address, home & cell phone number with e-mail address.

_____ Witnesses work address, work number and work e-mail address.

_____ Plaintiff's attorney—name, work address, work number and work e-mail address.

_____ Defendant's attorney—name, work address, work number and work e-mail address.

_____ Expert Witnesses' name, address, home & cell phone number with e-mail address.

_____ Expert Witnesses work address, work number and work e-mail address.

PLEADINGS

_____ Pleadings Index

_____ Plaintiff's Original Petition

_____ Defendant's Original Answer

_____ Plaintiff's First Amended Petition

_____ Defendant's First Amended Answer

_____ Plaintiff's First Set of Interrogatories to Defendant

_____ Defendant's Answers to Plaintiff's First Set of Interrogatories

_____ Defendant's First Set of Interrogatories to Plaintiff

_____ Plaintiff's Answers to Defendant's First Set of Interrogatories

_____ Plaintiff's First Request for Production of Documents and Inspection to Defendant

_____ Defendant's Responses to Plaintiff's First Request for Production of Documents and Inspection

_____ Defendant's First Request for Production of Documents and Inspection to Plaintiff

_____ Plaintiff's Responses to Defendant's First Request for Production of Documents and Inspection

§ 8.22A   TRIAL NOTEBOOK CHECKLIST

_____ Plaintiff's First Request for Admissions to Defendant

_____ Defendant's Response to Plaintiff's First Request for Admissions

_____ Defendant's First Request for Admissions to Plaintiff

_____ Plaintiff's Response to Defendant's First Request for Admissions

_____ Plaintiff's Motion in Limine

_____ Defendant's Response to Plaintiff's Motion in Limine

_____ Defendant's Motion in Limine

_____ Plaintiff's Response to Defendant's Motion in Limine

_____ Order Granting Plaintiff's Motion in Limine

_____ Order Granting Defendant's Motion in Limine

_____ Plaintiff's Motion for Partial Summary Judgment

_____ Defendant's Response to Plaintiff's Motion for Summary Judgment

_____ Order Granting Plaintiff's Motion for Partial Summary Judgment

DEPOSITIONS

_____ Deposition Index

_____ Deposition of Plaintiff

_____ Deposition summary of Plaintiff

_____ Deposition of Defendant

_____ Deposition summary of Defendant

_____ Deposition of Witness

_____ Deposition summary of Witness

_____ Deposition of Expert Witness

_____ Deposition summary of Expert Witness

MOTIONS IN LIMINE

EVIDENCE AND LIST OF EXHIBITS

_____ Evidence Index

_____ Medical Bills

_____ Photos of Accident Scene

_____ Enlargement of Accident Scene

_____ Photos of Plaintiff's Vehicle

_____ Time Line

_____ Diagram

TRIAL READINESS

_____ Exhibit Stickers

_____ Police reports

VOIR DIRE

_____ List of Jury Panel

_____ Information on Jury Panel

_____ Questions for Jury Panel

_____ Jury Chart

LEGAL RESEARCH AND MEMORANDAS

_____ Index

_____ Case Law

_____ Memorandums of Law

JURY INSTRUCTIONS

_____ Index

_____ Jury Instructions

WITNESS FILE

_____ Witness Index

_____ Witness Statements

_____ Summary of Witness Statement

EXPERT WITNESS FILE

_____ Expert Witness Index

_____ Expert Witness for Plaintiff (name, address home & work), phone numbers (home, work, cell), and e-mail address (home & work)

_____ Scope of Expert's Testimony

_____ Curriculum Vitae of Expert

_____ Articles Written by Expert

_____ Previous History of Expert

LATEST SETTLEMENT FIGURES OR DETERMINATION OF CASE WORTH

NOTES FOR OPENING STATEMENT

NOTES FOR CLOSING ARGUMENT

§ 8.63   DISMISSAL FOR WANT OF PROSECUTION

Page 576, add at the end of § 8.63:

FORM 8-33A
SAMPLE ORDER OF DISMISSAL (ALTERNATIVE)

Cause No. _____

_____	IN THE DISTRICT COURT OF
Plaintiff	HARRIS COUNTY, TEXAS
vs	
_____	_____ JUDICIAL DISTRICT
Defendant	

ORDER OF DISMISSAL

For failure to comply with (the notice dated _____ / TRCP _____), this cause is
ordered DISMISSED FOR WANT OF PROSECUTION. Costs of court are assessed against the plaintiff(s).

Signed_____, 20_____.

_____

JUDGE

_____ District Court

FORM 8-33B
SAMPLE DOCKET CONTROL ORDER

Cause No. _____

_____	IN THE DISTRICT COURT OF
Plaintiff	HARRIS COUNTY, TEXAS
vs	
_____	_____ JUDICIAL DISTRICT
Defendant	

DOCKET CONTROL ORDER

The following docket control order shall apply to this case unless modified by the court. If no date is given below, the item is governed by the Texas Rules of Civil Procedure.

1._____   **JOINDER.** All parties must be added and served, whether by amendment or third party practice, by this date. THE PARTY CAUSING THE JOINDER SHALL PROVIDE A COPY OF THIS SCHEDULING ORDER AT THE TIME OF SERVICE.

TRIAL READINESS

2. _____ **EXPERT WITNESS DESIGNATION.** Expert witness designations are required and must be served by the following dates. The designation must include the information listed in Rule 194.2(f). Failure to timely respond will be governed by Rule 193.6.

(a) _____ Experts for all parties seeking affirmative relief.

(b) _____ All other experts.

3. _____ **STATUS CONFERENCE.** Parties shall be prepared to discuss all aspects of the case including ADR, with the court on this date. TIME:___ .m. Failure to appear will be grounds for dismissal for want of prosecution.

4. _____ **DISCOVERY LIMITATIONS.** The discovery limitations of Rule 190.2, if applicable, or otherwise of Rule 190.3 apply unless changed below.

(a) _____ Total hours per side for oral depositions

(b) _____ Number of interrogatories that may be served by each party on any other party.

5. _____ **ALTERNATIVE DISPUTE RESOLUTION.**

(a) _____ By this date the parties must either (1) file an agreement for ADR stating the form of ADR requested and the name of an agreed mediator, if applicable; or (2) set an objection to ADR. If no agreement or objection is filed, the court may sign an ADR order.

(b) _____ ADR conducted pursuant to the agreement of the parties must be completed by this date.

6. _____ **DISCOVERY PERIOD ENDS.** All discovery must be conducted before the end of the discovery period. Parties seeking discovery must serve requests sufficiently far in advance of the end of the discovery period that the deadline for responding will be within the discovery period. Counsel may conduct discovery beyond this deadline by agreement. Incomplete discovery will not delay the trial.

7. _____ **DISPOSITIVE MOTIONS AND PLEAS.** Must be set for hearing or submission as follows:

(a) _____ Dispositive motions or pleas subject to an interlocutory appeal must be set by this date.

(b) _____ Summary judgment motions not subject to an interlocutory appeal must be set by this date.

(c) _____ Rule 166a(i) motions may not be set before this date.

8. _____ **CHALLENGES TO EXPERT TESTIMONY.** All motions to exclude expert testimony and evidence challenges to expert testimony must be filed by this date, unless extended by leave of court.

9. _____ **PLEADINGS.** All amendments and supplements must be filed by this date. This order does not preclude prompt filing of pleadings directly responsive to any timely filed pleadings.

10._____   **PRETRIAL CONFERENCE or DOCKET CALL** Parties shall be prepared to discuss all aspects of trial with the court on this date. TIME: _____ .m.

Failure to appear will be grounds for dismissal for want of prosecution.

11. _____   **TRIAL.** If not assigned by the second Friday following this date, the case will be reset.

Signed_____, 20_____.

_____

JUDGE

_____ District Court

§ 8.65   Motion for Summary Judgment

Page 584, add after **Form 8–39**:

FORM 8–39A
EXAMPLE: ACTUAL MOTION FOR SUMMARY JUDGMENT

IN THE UNITED STATES DISTRICT COURT
FOR THE [judicial district] DISTRICT OF [state]

[name]	)	
	)	
Plaintiff	)	Civil Action No. [case number]
	)	
v.	)	
	)	
[name]	)	
	)	
Defendant	)	

PLAINTIFF'S MEMORANDUM OF LAW IN SUPPORT OF MOTION FOR PARTIAL SUMMARY JUDGMENT ON LIABILITY

TABLE OF CONTENTS

STATEMENT OF THE ISSUES PRESENTED
PRINCIPAL CONTROLLING AUTHORITIES
INDEX OF EXHIBITS
INTRODUCTION
UNDISPUTED MATERIAL FACTS
  I.   The Plaintiff

STATEMENT OF THE ISSUES PRESENTED

1. Whether the record shows that there is no genuine issue of any material fact and that plaintiff and the class are entitled as a matter of law to partial summary judgment on liability because defendants' race-conscious admissions policies and practices for the [defendant name] ("Law School") violate the Equal Protection Clause of the Fourteenth Amendment and 42 U.S.C. § 2000d under the rationale articulated by Justice Powell in *Regents of University of California v. Bakke,* 438 U.S. 265 (1978).

2. Whether the record shows that there is no genuine issue of any material fact and that plaintiff and the class are entitled as a matter of law to partial summary judgment on liability under 42 U.S.C. § 2000d because defendants' race-conscious admissions policies and practices for the Law School are motivated by an interest in "diversity," which is not a "compelling governmental interest" for strict scrutiny analysis under the Equal Protection Clause of the Fourteenth Amendment.

3.   Whether the record shows that there is no genuine issue of any material fact and that plaintiff and the class are entitled as a matter of law to partial summary judgment on liability against defendants [name] and [name], acting in their official capacities, for violating 42 U.S.C. §§ 1981 and 1983.

PRINCIPAL CONTROLLING AUTHORITIES

Cases

Adarand Constructors v. Pena, 515 U.S. 200 (1995)

City of Richmond v. J.A. Croson Co., 488 U.S. 469 (1989)

Regents of University of California v. Bakke, 438 U.S. 265 (1978)

Runyon v. McCrary, 427 U.S. 160 (1976)

Shaw v. Hunt, 517 U.S. 899 (1996)

Statutes

42 U.S.C. § 1981

42 U.S.C. § 1983

42 U.S.C. § 2000d

42 U.S.C. § 2000d-7(a)(1)

INDEX OF EXHIBITS [Exhibits omitted]

INTRODUCTION

In *Regents of University of California v. Bakke,* 438 U.S. 265 (1978), the United States Supreme Court struck down as illegal a "special admissions program" that systematically employed racial classifications to grant preferences in admission to certain favored racial minorities at the expense of members from other racial groups. *Id.* at 314-24 (1978) (Powell, J., concurring in the judgment); *id.* at 414-21 (Stevens, Stewart, Rehnquist, J.J., Burger, C.J., concurring in part in the judgment and dissenting in part). Today, in open defiance of *Bakke* and subsequent Supreme Court decisions on racial classifications, the [defendant name] ("Law School") illegally employs racial classifications in order to ensure that it enrolls a "critical mass" or "meaningful numbers" of racial and ethnic minorities. Plaintiff [name] commenced this action and now brings this motion to obtain a declaration of rights that defendants' admissions policies and practices violate federal civil rights laws and the Equal Protection Clause of the Fourteenth Amendment. Plaintiff also moves for an order of this Court permanently enjoining defendants from engaging in their illegal race discrimination practices in the future.

Plaintiff [name] is a white resident of the State of [state] who applied for admission into the [19__] first-year class of the Law School. [Plaintiff name] was originally placed on a "wait list," and she was subsequently denied admission. As plaintiff's Complaint alleges, and as the deposition testimony and documents produced by defendants abundantly confirm, [plaintiff name] had her application considered and rejected under an admissions system that violated her legally protected right to equal protection of the law.

Plaintiff brings this motion, pursuant to Rule 56 of the Federal Rules of Civil Procedure, for partial summary judgment on the issue of whether the Board of Regents of the [defendant name] ("the University") violated the Equal Protection Clause of the Fourteenth Amendment and Title VI of the Civil Rights Act of 1964, 42 U.S.C. § 2000d *et seq.*, and whether defendants [name] and [name], in their official capacities, respectively, as president of the University of [name] and dean of the Law School, violated the Equal Protection Clause and 42 U.S.C. §§ 1981 and 1983. Plaintiff also brings this motion on behalf of the class she represents, as certified by this Court by order dated January 7, 1999. Specifically, the motion is brought as to the admissions policies and practices of the Law School for the academic years from [19__] forward.

UNDISPUTED MATERIAL FACTS

I. The Plaintiff

[Plaintiff name] is a white resident of the State of [state] who applied in [date] for admission into the fall [19__] first-year class of the Law School. *See* Exhibit A [Exhibit omitted] to the accompanying affidavit of [name] (Deposition testimony of [plaintiff name], pp. 42-43 [date]). Unlike most law school applicants, who apply immediately or shortly after completion of an undergraduate education, [plaintiff name] applied 18 years after graduating from college, at a time when she was married with two children and in the midst of a professional career. *See* Exhibit B [Exhibit omitted] (Law School Application File of [plaintiff name]). Among other things, her Law School Application disclosed that [plaintiff name] was applying with a cumulative 3.8 undergraduate grade point average and an LSAT score of 161, representing a score in the 86th percentile nationally. *See* Exhibit B. [Exhibit omitted]

[Plaintiff name] was notified by letter dated [date] from [name], Assistant Dean and Director of Admissions, that the Law School had placed her file on a "waiting list for further consideration should space become available." *See* Exhibit B; Exhibit A ([name] depo. pp. 94-96) [Exhibits omitted]. By letter dated [date] [19__], the Law School informed [plaintiff name] that "it is now clear that we will be unable to offer you a place in our [19__] first year class." *See* Exhibit C; Exhibit A ([name] depo. pp. 100-101) [Exhibits omitted].

[Plaintiff name] had also applied to law school at [name] Law School, where she was accepted for admission into the fall [19__] first-year class. *See* Exhibit A ([name] depo. pp. 59-60) [Exhibit omitted]. She declined the offer of admission for several reasons, including that she believed the [name] Law School offered her the better curriculum in her chosen interest: health care law. *See* Exhibit A ([name] depo. pp. 65-72) [Exhibit omitted]. As a result, [plaintiff name] is not now enrolled in any law school. She still desires, however, to attend defendants' Law School. *See* Exhibit A ([name] depo. pp. 118-19) [Exhibit omitted].

II. The Law School's Admissions Policies and Practices

A. Overview

A reading of defendants' answer is alone sufficient to establish as undisputed that defendants consider race and ethnicity in the admissions process, and that plaintiff, as a white applicant, did not have consideration of her application "enhanced" on the basis of her race. *See* Answer at Pgs 9, 19, 20, 23, 28 (Law School "uses race as a factor in admissions . . . "); *id.* at Pg 21 ("Defendants admit that plaintiff is not a member of an underrepresented minority group and that her race was not a factor that enhanced the [defendant name] consideration of her application."). Defendants justify the use of race as a factor in the admissions process on grounds that it serves a "compelling interest in achieving diversity among its student body." *See* Exhibit D (Defendants' "Objections and Responses to Interrogatory Numbers 1, 2, and 8 of Plaintiffs' Interrogatories to Defendants (Set 1)," at response to interrogatory number 9, pp. 10-11) [Exhibit omitted]. It is also undisputed that the University is a recipient of federal financial support. *See* Answer at § 16 ("Defendants admit that the [defendant name], which includes the [name] Law School, receives federal funds.").

The enormous extent to which defendants consider race and ethnicity in making admissions decisions is conclusively established by their answers to interrogatories, documents produced in the course of discovery, and the deposition testimony of the Law Schools' employees. Defendants' own documents and words make for a compelling record that is more than sufficient to support summary judgment of liability against defendants for their unlawful race discrimination.

The formal admission policy at issue in this case was adopted by the Law School faculty in the spring of [19__]. *See* Exhibit E ([date] Admissions Policy) (hereinafter the "[19__] Policy" or the "Policy") [Exhibit omitted]. The [19__] Policy explicitly states, however, that its object was "as much to ratify what had been done and to reaffirm our goals as it is to announce new policies." See Exhibit E (Policy at p. 13) [Exhibit omitted]. Consequently, there is reason to examine the Law School's policies with respect to admission of racial and ethnic minorities prior to [date].

Mr. [name] was Assistant Dean and Director of Admissions from [19__] to approximately [date]. *See* Exhibit F (Deposition of [name], p. 10 ([date])) [Exhibit omitted]. [name] made all or substantially all of the decisions on admission of students during his tenure. See *id.* ([name] depo. pp. 16-17). He testified that there was an explicit "special admissions program" for certain underrepresented racial and ethnic minorities: African Americans, Hispanics, Native Americans, and Puerto Ricans born on the U.S. mainland. *See id.* ([name] depo. pp. 23-24). Under the "special admissions program," the Law School sought to implement a policy of enrolling a class that consisted of a minimum of 10-12 percent underrepresented minorities. *See id.*

Defendants' Law School bulletins confirm the existence of a "special admissions program" for certain preferred minorities. For example, the "Law School Announcement [date]" stated as follows:

> In administering its admissions policy, the Law School recognizes the racial imbalance now existing in the legal profession and the public interest in increasing the number of lawyers from the ethnic and cultural minorities significantly underrepresented in the profession. . . . Black, Chicano, Native American, and many Puerto Rican applicants are automatically considered for a special admissions program designed to encourage and increase the enrollment of minorities.

See Exhibit G (Law School Announcement 1991-92, at pp. 89-90); *see also* Exhibit H (Law School Announcement 1988-89, at pp. 85-86). [Exhibits omitted].

In a document submitted to the American Bar Association (ABA) in 1991 or 1992, as part of an accreditation review discussed in more detail below, the Law School explained to the ABA that because "four specific ethnic groups have been particularly victimized by discrimination (African Americans, Native Americans, Mexican Americans, and Puerto Rican Americans raised on the U.S. mainland)," the Law School had "adopted a special admissions program wherein qualifications predicting success beyond the LSAT and GPA may be somewhat more emphasized in the selection process." *See* Exhibit I (Law School's submission in 1991-1992 to the ABA on compliance with ABA Standard 212) [Exhibit omitted].

B.   The Current Law School Admissions Policies

During the [date] term, then-Dean [name] appointed a committee to examine the Law School's admissions policies generally and to make recommendations on any changes. The Faculty Admissions Committee appointed for that purpose was chaired by [name] and composed of several other faculty members, including [name], [name], [name], [name] and Assistant Dean and Director of Admissions, [name]. *See* Exhibit J (Deposition of [name], pp. 38-39, 42-44 ([date])); Exhibit K (Deposition of [name], pp. 21-22 ([date]); Exhibit L (Deposition of [name], pp. 18-19 ([date])); Exhibit M (Deposition of [name], pp. 44-49 ([date])); Exhibit N (Deposition of [name], pp. 52-53 ([date])) [Exhibits omitted].

The Faculty Admissions Committee reported to the Faculty with a recommended admissions policy dated [date]. It was adopted by the faculty on [date]. *See* Exhibit E [Exhibit omitted]. The [19__] Policy remains the stated policy of the Law School on admissions, according to the current Assistant Dean and Director of Admissions, [name], *see* Exhibit O (Deposition of [name], p. 92 (June 1, 1998)) [Exhibit omitted].

The Law School admissions Policy that became effective in the spring of 1992 acknowledges that the Law School's "most general measure predicting graded law school performance is a composite of an applicants' LSAT score and undergraduate grade point average (UGPA) (. . . the 'index')." *See* Exhibit E (Policy at p. 3) [Exhibit omitted]. The Policy acknowledges that "the index does not do all the predictive work that an admissions committee might wish," but that it "should not be ignored" and that "[i]n particular, as the size of the differences in applicant index scores increases, the value of the index as a predictor of graded law school performance increases as well." *See id.* (Policy at pp. 3-4). From these premises, the Policy reaches the following conclusion:

> Bluntly, the higher one's index score, the greater should be one's chances of being admitted. The lower the score, the greater the risk the candidate poses. And when scores are extremely low, it is extremely difficult for us reliably to pick out those who would be successful at [name] and in the practice of law. So we expect the vast majority of those students we admit to have high index scores.

See id. (Policy at p. 4). Undisputably, the LSAT scores and undergraduate grade point averages of applicants are important factors in the Law School Admissions process. *See* Exhibit L ([name] depo. pp. 20-21, 61-62, 180-81, 116-18); Exhibit P (Memorandum authored by [name], dated [date], entitled, "The Gospel According to [name]," at pp. 5-6) [Exhibit omitted].

The Policy also makes clear that the "result of the actual decision making" in the past, prior to adoption of the 1992 policy, could be demonstrated with a graph that plots combinations of LSAT scores and "UGPAs." *See* Exhibit E (Policy at p. 6) [Exhibit omitted]. This graph, attached as an exhibit to the Policy, shows that 87% of admitted applicants had index scores in 9 cells located closest to the upper right portion of the grid, which represents the highest combinations of LSAT scores and UGPAs. The grid confirms the stated policy that "[t]he further applicants are from the upper right corner the less likely they are to be offered admission." *See id.*

The Policy notes that the Law School also operates under a "constraint" because it is "part of a publicly funded university" and that "as such we feel that a reasonable proportion of our places should go to [state] residents, even if some have qualifications lower than those of some applicants from outside [state]." *See id.* (Policy at p. 2). Several Law School witnesses stated that the definition of "reasonable proportion" changed from year to year, but that generally the goal was to enroll a first-year class consisting of approximately one-third residents of the State of [state]. *See* Exhibit J ([name] depo. pp. 98-99) [Exhibit omitted]. In reference to the grid and fact that the "upper right portion" indicates the combinations of LSAT and UGPA that "characterize the overwhelming bulk of students admitted," the Policy adds the caveat that "[t]he location of out-of-state admittees as a group, would, if plotted separately, be higher and closer to the upper right corner than the location of all admittees since the group of non-resident admittees is on the whole somewhat stronger on the plotted dimensions than the group of resident admittees." *See id.* (Policy at p. 7 & n. 2).

The Policy also explains that there are "two principal reasons" why some students will qualify for admission "despite index scores that place them relatively far from the upper right corner of the grid." *See id.* (Policy at p. 8). The first reason is that files of some applicants lead to skepticism about the value of the index as predictor of law school success. The Policy provides an example of a student who had received a college UGPA of 3.57 at [name], but whose law school application was "weakened substantially" by an LSAT score at the 68th percentile, resulting in a "low index." *See id.* (Policy at p. 9). The student was admitted because standardized test scores, including the college SAT, had proven in his or her case to be a poor predictor of later academic success. *See id.*

The second type of justification for "admitting students with indices *relatively far* from the upper right corner" of the grid is to "help achieve that diversity which has the potential to enrich everyone's education and thus make a law school class stronger than the sum of its parts." *See id.* (emphasis added). The Policy gives several examples and singles out "a commitment to one particular type of diversity that the school *has long had and which should continue." See id.* (Policy at p. 12) (emphasis added). It goes on to explain that "[t]his is a commitment to *racial and ethnic diversity* with special reference to the inclusion of students from groups which have been *historically discriminated against,* like African-Americans, Hispanics, and Native Americans, who without this commitment might not be represented in our student body *in meaningful numbers." See id.* (emphasis added). The Policy notes that "[o]ver the past two decades, the law school has made special efforts to increase the numbers of such students in the school" and that by "enrolling a *'critical mass'* of minority students, we have ensured their ability to make unique contributions to the character of the Law School." *See id.* (emphasis added).

The Policy also explained that "[s]peaking generally, the faculty believes the admission process has functioned well in recent years, producing classes both diverse and academically outstanding. . . ." *See id.* It concluded, then, that "[o]ur object . . . is therefore as much to ratify what has been done and to reaffirm our goals as it is to announce new policies." *See id.* (Policy at p. 13). With respect to index scores and the distribution on the grid, the Policy stated "[w]e do expect that in the foreseeable future the proportion of students we admit from the upper right portion of the index grid will either stay constant or will increase. . . ." *See id.*

One of defendants' witnesses has described the 1992 Policy with respect to consideration of race as more "modern" than earlier policies. *See* Exhibit Q (deposition of [name], pp. 33-34 (June 2, 1998)) [Exhibit omitted]. Gone, after 1992, was any explicit reference in the Policy to a "special admissions program." With the adoption of the 1992 Policy, defendants also ceased the practice of having minority law students review some of the applications from minority applicants. *See* Exhibit J ([name] depo. p. 99) [Exhibit omitted]. In other respects, however, the 1992 Policy was not intended to change the numbers of underrepresented minorities admitted to the Law School. *See* Exhibit J ([name] depo. pp. 93-94) [Exhibit omitted].

Defendants' witnesses acknowledge that the concept of "critical mass" involves a number, although they deny that there is any one number or percentage that constitutes a critical mass. *See, e.g.,* Exhibit L ([name] depo. pp. 109-11) [Exhibit omitted]. The concept of having numbers of minorities sufficient to constitute "critical mass" or to be "meaningful" means that at some point, the number of minority students could be too low to achieve the Policy objectives with respect to underrepresented minority representation. *See, e.g.,* Exhibit K ([name] depo. pp.125-28) [Exhibit omitted].

The Law School has not changed the Policy since it became effective in the spring of 1992. See Exhibit O ([name] depo. p. 92) [Exhibit omitted]. Consequently, it governed the applications for admission for all of the years ([19___] to the present) at issue in this lawsuit.

C.   [19___] ABA/AALS Accreditation Review and the Law School's Comment on that Review

The Law School underwent a periodic accreditation review by the American Bar Association ("ABA") and Association of American Law School ("AALS") in [date]. Prior to that review, defendants submitted materials to the ABA and AALS on a number of issues considered as part of the review, including former ABA Standard 212 (and current ABA Standard 211) relating to the Law School's "commitment to providing full opportunities for the study of law and entry into the profession by qualified members of groups, notably racial and ethnic minorities, which have been victims of discrimination in various forms." *See* Exhibit R. As part of its response to the ABA inquiry on the Standard, the Law School stated:

> The Law School considers in admissions decisions the value to the educational experience of having students from a range of backgrounds and perspectives. Thus, ethnicity is one factor in making admissions selections from a pool of comparably qualified applicants. The faculty also has recognized that four specific ethnic groups have been *particularly victimized by discrimination* (African Americans, Native Americans, Mexican Americans, and Puerto Rican Americans raised on the U.S. mainland), and therefore has adopted a *special admissions program* wherein qualifications predicting success beyond the LSAT and GPA may be somewhat more emphasized in the selection process in order to yield greater numbers of members of these groups in the entering class.

See Exhibit I (Law School submission in 1991-1992 to the ABA on compliance with ABA Standard 212) (emphasis added).

As part of the 1992 accreditation review process, defendants also prepared a "self-study" that included a section on admissions. *See* Exhibit S (Law School "Self-Study" submitted in 1991-1992 to ABA, pp. 5-7) [Exhibit omitted]. That document explains the "divided" admission process that the Law School had used for years, whereby a "pool" of applicants had their applications considered largely without reference to LSAT scores and UGPA. *See id.* (Self-Study at p. 6). The self-study also lauded the "Special Admissions program [which] has achieved substantial success." *See id.* In the next sentence, the self-study cautioned and promised that "[t]here is no reason for complacency, however, and new strategies are being devised to enhance the diversity of our students in all dimensions." *See id.* A few months later, defendants adopted the 1992 Policy.

TRIAL READINESS

The ABA issued a report following its on-site evaluation of the Law School for the [19__] review. *See* Exhibit T (ABA Report on [defendant name], [date]) [Exhibit omitted]. The report included sections on the admissions process and "Programs for Promoting Opportunities for Racial and Ethnic Minorities." *See id.* (Report at pp. 37-40). The latter section again recounted the means by which the Law School promoted such opportunities:

> The faculty has targeted individuals from four groups for special admissions consideration: African Americans, Native Americans, Mexican Americans and Puerto Ricans raised on the mainland. For these applicants, factors in addition to LSAT and GPA *are reviewed more closely and given more weight* as predictors of success in law school.

See id. (Report at 37-38) (emphasis added). The report's section on "Admissions" included a similar description:

> The faculty has targeted four racial and ethnic groups for special attention in the admissions process: African Americans, Native Americans, Mexican Americans and Puerto Ricans raised on the mainland. The Special Admissions process for applications from individuals in these groups includes the reading of files by students from minority organizations, who make recommendations to the Assistant Dean, and a *deemphasis of the GPA and LSAT relative to other predictors of success as a student and attorney.*

See id. (Report at 34) (emphasis added).

The ABA's report on the [19__] accreditation review was sent to the Law School for review and comment. By letter dated [date], the Law School responded to the ABA report. *See* Exhibit U (Letter from [name], Associate Dean for Academic Affairs of the Law School to [name], dated August 14, 1992) [Exhibit omitted]. The [date] letter was written *after* the adoption of the [19__] Policy, as the letter itself makes clear. In one section of that letter, the Law School commented on and corrected certain aspects of the ABA report relating to admissions policies. The [date] letter also describes changes made in the admissions policies since the site visit in [date]. Specifically, the letter made the following points:

- *Only one fact went astray* in the [ABA report's]

  description of the admissions policies in place at the time of the team visit. . . . [I]t [the report] state[s] that the school has begun making special efforts to reach women and minority students. We have made special efforts for many years; the only recent change has been that *we have increased our efforts still further.*

- Several changes have been made in our statement of admissions policy since the time of the team visit, reflecting the review of the admissions process noted on page 34 [of the report]. . . . . *The most specific change* is that the faculty admissions policy committee will take a more active, although still rather limited, role in individual admissions decisions. . . . Student participation in reviewing the applications [*sic*] files of minority students has been ended.

*   *A more general change* has been made in the diversity component of our statement of admissions policy. In broad outline, ' '; we seek to admit students with distinctive perspectives and experiences as well as students who are particularly likely to assume the kinds of leadership roles in the bar and make the kinds of contributions to society' that have characterized our graduates who have become "esteemed legal practitioners, leaders of the American Bar. . . ." Within this broad goal, *we continue to include a specific "commitment to racial and ethnic diversity* with special reference to the inclusion of students from groups which have *historically been discriminated against,* like African Americans, Hispanics and Native Americans. . . ."

See id. ([date] letter at pp. 3-4) (emphasis added). The Law School's letter response to the ABA report offered no correction or amendment of the comments in the report, and in the earlier Law School self-study, about the deemphasis of LSAT scores and undergraduate grade point averages in the consideration of applications from minority students relative to non-minority students.

D.   Admission Decision Outcomes under the Law School's Admissions Policies

Defendants' own admission records demonstrate that race is an enormous factor in the admissions decisionmaking process. One such document is a series of "grids" or tables that plot different combinations of LSAT scores and undergraduate grade point averages for the first-year law school class that entered in the fall of 1995. *See* Exhibit V ("Admissions Grid of LSAT & GPA—1995 final grid) [Exhibit omitted]. The grids are compiled separately on the basis of a variety of categories, including by race and ethnicity, residence, and gender. In each case, the left side of the grid represents different combinations of undergraduate grade point averages (GPA), and the category along the top of the page corresponds to different ranges of LSAT scores.

Within each cell of LSAT/GPA combinations, there is a top number that represents total applications received within that combination of scores and grades, as well as a number to the left indicating the number of offers of admission, and a number on the right representing the number of deposits paid. For example, the grid indicates that for the cell represented by a GPA of 3.25 to 3.49 and LSAT scores between 156-158, there were 10 applications from African Americans and 10 offers of admission, with 3 deposits paid. In the same cell for the Caucasian applicant grid, there are 51 applications and only *one* offer of admission.

The [19___] tables can be readily examined for many similar, extraordinary differences on the basis of race/ethnicity in the rates of admission. In the case of African Americans, for example, all but one applicant with a grade point of 3.25 or above and an LSAT at or above 156 received an offer of admission (43/44) . For Caucasians, there were 1,663 applicants within those same combinations of GPA/LSAT range, of whom only 634 received offers of admission. In fact, about 90% of all offers made to

Caucasians (597/668) were made to applicants whose academic credentials met a *minimum* of both a 3.25 for GPA and 164 for LSAT score. *No offers* were made to Caucasian applicants who had both a GPA below 3.25 and an LSAT score below 156. Despite defendants' representation about admitting students whose standardized test scores have proven to be poor predictors of academic performance, *no offers* were made to Caucasians with an LSAT score below 154 (regardless of GPA); only three offers of admission (3/668) were made to Caucasians with LSAT scores beneath 156 (regardless of GPA); and only a total of 12 offers of admission (12/668) were made to Caucasians with an LSAT score below 161—the 86th percentile nationally—(regardless of GPA). For African Americans, in considerable contrast, 90% of all offers of admission (96/106) were made to applicants at or above GPA/LSAT combinations of 2.75 and 148, respectively. Slightly less than one-third of all offers (30/106) to African Americans were made to applicants whose LSAT scores were below 156, a virtual dead zone for Caucasian applications; and 15% of all offers made to African Americans were to applicants with LSAT scores beneath 154, a certain dead zone for Caucasian applications.

Asian Americans are at a systematic disadvantage similar to Caucasians. In the cell for 3.25 to 3.49 GPA and 156-158 LSAT scores, 14 Asian Americans applied, and none were offered admission. For all combination ranges at or above 3.25 GPA and LSAT score of 156, there were 292 applications from Asian Americans, with 104 offers of admission made. Only three of all offers to Asian Americans went to applicants with less than a 161 LSAT score; and 95% of offers to Asian American applicants were made to those with *minimum* LSAT scores of 164 and GPAs of 3.25.

There are also tables for "Majority" applicants and for "Selected Minorities," *i.e.* African Americans, Native Americans, Hispanics, and Puerto Ricans. In the cell for 3.25 to 3.49 GPA and LSAT score between 156 and 158, there was one offer of admission made from among 75 "majority" applicants, an acceptance rate of 1.3%. For the "Selected Minority" group, there were 15 offers made out of an applicant pool of 18, representing an acceptance rate of 83%.

Plaintiff's statistical expert, from the database supplied by defendants in discovery, constructed grids for the first-year Law School classes admitted in [19__], [19__], and [19_]. See Exhibit W (Deposition of [name], pp. 69-70 ([date])); Exhibit X (Admission Grids for years [19__-19__] as compiled from Law School database) [Exhibit omitted]. Again, much information is contained in these grids, and they can be examined in the same manner as was done above with respect to the [19__] grid. Among other things, when viewed as a whole, over the four-year period, they show that only two applicants (2/43) from a "Selected Minority" group with minimum GPA/LSAT credentials equal to plaintiff [name], *i.e.*, minimum 3.75 GPA and minimum LSAT score of 161, were denied admission. During that four-year period, the acceptance rate for "Selected Minorities" with minimum GPA/LSAT combinations of 3.25 and 156 was 84.5% (378/447). The rate at the same minimum combinations during those years for "Majority" applicants was 44.6% (3911/8767). The most striking differences, however, are evident at grade and LSAT score combinations that are at the margins for "Majority" applicants. For example, the combined acceptance rate for the four-year period for Majority applicants with GPAs of 3.25 and above and LSAT scores ranging between 156 and 163 was 8% (272/3371) compared to 80% (264/330) for "Selected Minorities."

It is undisputed, or there can be no genuine dispute, that the pool of underrepresented minority applicants to the Law School has on average generally lower LSAT scores and undergraduate grades than other groups, including Caucasians and Asian Americans. Indisputably, too, those lower scores and grades on average would make it difficult or impossible for the Law School to enroll a "critical mass" or "meaningful numbers" of underrepresented minorities *if* the importance of test scores and grades in the admissions process remained unchanged and if race and ethnicity were no longer factors. *See* Exhibit K ([name] depo. pp. 90-91, 157-158) [Exhibit omitted]. Consequently, in order to enroll a "critical mass" or "meaningful numbers" of underrepresented minorities, it is the policy and practice of the Law School to admit such minorities with generally lower test scores and grades than those of other groups. *See* Exhibit J ([name] depo. pp. 132-33); Exhibit L ([name] depo. pp. 117-18); Exhibit Y ([name] depo. pp. 83-85) [Exhibits omitted].

E.   Racial/Ethnic Composition of the Class

In the years [19__]-[19__], when [name] was Assistant Dean for admissions and the Law School had an explicit "special admissions program" benefiting underrepresented minorities, the first-year Law School class included representation of African American students in proportions of 7.8% (30/381), 9.1% (35/383), 8.4% (31/369), and 8.6% (31/358), in 1987, 1988, 1989, and 1990, respectively. *See* Exhibit Z (Descriptive Data of Entering Class [19__]-[19__]) [Exhibit omitted]. In the two years after Assistant [name] departure and before implementation of the 1992 policy, the enrollment of African Americans increased slightly. In [19__], the proportion was 9.9% (36/361), and in 1992 it was 10% (37/368). In the first class (fall 1993) enrolled under the 1992 policy, the proportion of African Americans in the class was 8.7% (33/380). In subsequent years the proportions have been 10.1% (37/363) in 1994, 8.5% (29/340) in 1995, 7.2% (23/319) in 1996, 7.3% in 1996, 7.3% in 1997, and 7% in 1998. *See* Exhibit Z [Exhibit omitted].

Similar results are shown when the numbers or proportions of total numbers of "selected minorities," *i.e.,* students who are either African Americans, Mexican Americans, Native Americans or Puerto Ricans, are considered. From 1987 to 1998, these groups were represented in the first-year class in the following proportions: 11.8% (45/381) in 1987; 13.05% (50/383) in 1988; 13.8% (51/369) in 1989; 12.8% (46/358) in 1990; 17.2 (62/361) in 1991; 18.4% (68/368) in 1992; 13.9% (53/380) in 1993; 14.3% (52/363) in 1994; 12.6% (43/340) in 1995; 13.2% (42/319) in 1996; 12.4% (42/339) in 1997; and 12.02% (41/341) in 1998. *See* Exhibit Z [Exhibit omitted].

ARGUMENT

I.   Defendants Have Violated the Equal Protection Clause and Title VI

Title VI prohibits discrimination on the basis of race or ethnicity by those receiving federal funds. *See* 42 U.S.C. § 2000d. The Supreme Court has held that Title VI prohibits the same intentional conduct as does the Equal Protection Clause. *United States v. Fordice,* 505 U.S. 717, 732 n.7 (1992); *see also Michigan Road Builders Assn v. Milliken,* 834 F.2d 583, 585 n.3 (6th Cir. 1987). The Law School is a state-operated institution which, as a recipient of federal funds, is subject to the prohibitions of Title VI. By accepting federal funds, the University has waived any defense based on sovereign immunity for claims arising under Title VI. *See* 42 U.S.C. § 2000d-7(a)(1). *Cf. Franks v. Kentucky School for the Deaf,* 142 F.3d 360, 362 (6th Cir. 1998) (Congress, through § 2000d-7(a)(1), abrogated a state's sovereign immunity for Title IX claims). Title 42 U.S.C. Section 1983 provides a remedy, including declaratory and injunctive relief, for individuals whose constitutional rights have been violated under color of state authority. *See, e.g., Will v. Michigan Department of State Police,* 491 U.S. 58, 71 n.10 (1989).

Plaintiff's motion with respect to the Equal Protection Clause and Title VI is brought on two independent grounds. First, plaintiffs seek declaratory and injunctive relief on the narrow and limited ground that the Law School's admissions policies and practices are illegal under the reasoning employed by Justice Powell in his opinion in *Bakke.* Plaintiff assumes, for the purpose of this first argument only, that Justice Powell's opinion in *Bakke* constituted the "holding" of the Court and that the opinion, notwithstanding more recent Supreme Court decisions invalidating racial preferences, retains vitality insofar as it reasoned that "diversity" is a compelling interest that universities may strive to achieve by considering race and ethnicity as "plus" factors in admissions decisionmaking. As discussed in detail below, the material facts are relatively few and undisputed and lead inescapably to the conclusion that the University has violated Title VI and the Equal Protection Clause under the rationale of Justice Powell's opinion in *Bakke.*

The second, independent argument in support of plaintiff's motion for summary judgment on the Title VI and Equal Protection claims is that Justice Powell's "diversity" or "academic freedom" rationale, as set forth in his singular opinion in *Bakke* the only basis on which defendants have justified their race-conscious decisionmaking is not a compelling interest sufficient to meet strict scrutiny. No Justice other than Justice Powell, and certainly not a majority of the Court, has ever held that "intellectual diversity" or "academic freedom" are "compelling interests" justifying use of racial classifications of any kind. Consequently, even if defendants' admissions policies and practices met the requirements of Justice Powell's "diversity" or "academic freedom" rationale, they are illegal under controlling Supreme Court cases on racial classifications.

A. Defendants' Race-Conscious Admissions Policies and Practices Are Illegal under Justice Powell's "Intellectual Diversity" and "Academic Freedom" Rationale Articulated in *Bakke*

1. The *Bakke* Case and Justice Powell's Opinion

In *Regents of University of California v. Bakke,* 438 U.S. 265 (1978), plaintiff Allan Bakke brought suit under Title VI to challenge the admissions policies of the University of California Medical School at Davis, where Bakke, a white male, had twice applied and been rejected for admission. The Davis admissions program operated on a "rolling" basis and included a "special admissions program" that provided for offers of admission to a prescribed number of economically or educationally disadvantaged applicants who were also members of specified racial minorities: "Blacks," "Chicanos," "Asians" and "American Indians." *Id.* at 275. In the years *Bakke* applied, the prescribed number of seats to be offered pursuant to the special admissions program was 16 out of 100. *Id.* at 275-76.

The Davis "special admissions program" offered seats only to "qualified" minorities; and the majority of the class was comprised of non-minorities. *Id.* at 275-76. Most minority applicants for the "special admissions" program were rejected. *Id.* at 275-76 & n.5. The program was also "flexible" insofar as there was no "floor" under or "ceiling" over the total number of minority applicants to be admitted. *Id.* at 288 n.26.

Five Justices in *Bakke* held that the Davis program unlawfully considered race in the admissions process. Four of the five concluded that the program violated Title VI and that it was unnecessary to decide whether the program was also unconstitutional. *Id.* at 410-20 (Stevens, Stewart, Rehnquist, JJ., Burger, C.J., concurring in the judgment in part and dissenting in part). The fifth vote invalidating the program came from Justice Powell, who concluded in an opinion only for himself that the Davis program violated the Equal Protection Clause of the Fourteenth Amendment and Title VI.

Justice Powell applied "strict scrutiny" to the Davis program. He rejected as "beside the point" any "semantic distinction" about whether the program amounted to "goals" or "quotas" for minority representation in the medical school, and he determined that the special admissions program was "undeniably a classification based on race and ethnic background" or a "line drawn on the basis of race and ethnic status." *Id.* at 288-89. He then considered four objectives of the program offered by Davis to justify the use of a "suspect" classification and found only one to be sufficiently compelling: "attainment of a diverse student body." *Id.* at 311. Justice Powell based his conclusion on the premises that "[a]cademic freedom, though not a specifically enumerated constitutional right, long has been viewed as a special concern of the First Amendment," *id.* at 312, and that the "freedom of a university to make its own judgments as to education includes the selection of its student body," *id.*

The constitutional interest in "diversity" that Justice Powell wrote about pertained to intellectual, viewpoint diversity: "the right to select those students who will contribute the most to the 'robust exchange of ideas'" and the "atmosphere of 'speculation, experiment and creation'—so essential to the quality of higher education." *Id.* at 312-13 (quoting *Sweezy v. New Hampshire,* 354 U.S. 234, 263 (1957)). It was in that context of discussing a state interest in an intellectually diverse student body that Powell concluded "[e]thnic diversity . . . is only one element in a range of factors a university properly may consider in attaining the goal of a heterogeneous student body," *id.* at 314, and admonished that it was "not an interest in simple ethnic diversity," *id.* at 315.

Justice Powell made clear at several points in his opinion that in assembling a diverse or heterogeneous student body, race or ethnicity was a factor that might be considered on an individualized, case-by-case basis, rather than in a systematic, generalized fashion. Thus, he reasoned that "race or ethnic background may be deemed a plus in a *particular* applicant's file. . . . The file of a *particular* black applicant may be examined for his potential contribution to diversity without the factor of race being decisive." *Id.* at 317 (emphasis added). "In short, an admissions program operated in this way is flexible enough to consider all pertinent elements of diversity in light of the *particular* qualifications of each applicant, and to place them on the same footing for consideration, although not necessarily according them the same weight." *Id.* (emphasis added). In Allan Bakke's case, it was the "denial" of his "right to *individualized* consideration without regard to his race" that Justice Powell called "the principal evil" of the Davis special admissions program. *Id.* at 318 n.52 (emphasis added).

The Davis "special admissions program," it was "evident" to Justice Powell, was guilty of a "facial intent" to discriminate. *Id.* at 318. A constitutional policy would be one, he reasoned, "where race or ethnic background is simply one element to be *weighed fairly* against other elements in the selection process." *Id.* (emphasis added). "So long as the university proceeds on an *individualized, case-by-case* basis, there is no warrant for judicial interference in the academic process." *Id.* at 319 n.53 (emphasis added). Even under a facially nondiscriminatory policy, however, an applicant could overcome a presumption of good faith on the part of the university if the "applicant can establish that the institution does not adhere to a policy of *individualized comparisons,* or can show that a *systematic exclusion* of certain groups results." *Id.* (emphasis added). It bears repeating that Justice Powell voted to invalidate the Davis program as unconstitutional even though he (alone) wrote approvingly of "diversity" as a compelling governmental interest that could justify the use of race in university admissions decisions.

2. The Law School's Admission Policies and Practices Are Unlawful under *Bakke* and Justice Powell's Opinion

The Law School's admissions policies and practices do not comply with the constitutional standard defined by Justice Powell. The reasons are several. They can be deduced from the following facts for which the record discloses there can be no genuine dispute: (1) LSAT scores and undergraduate grade point averages (together, the "index") have at all material times been important factors in the Law School's admissions process, with the general principle being that the higher an applicant's index score, the greater the chance of admission and, conversely, the lower the index score, the lower the chance of admission; (2) the LSAT scores and undergraduate grade point averages of the pool of applicants applying to the Law School who are underrepresented minorities are lower than those for other racial and ethnic groups; (3) the Law School desires to enroll a "critical mass" or "meaningful numbers" of underrepresented minorities into each year's class; and (4) in order to enroll a "critical mass" or "meaningful numbers" of minority students, it is the policy and practice of the Law School to admit underrepresented minorities whose LSAT scores and undergraduate grades are generally lower than those of other racial or ethnic groups.

Race and ethnicity are accounted for under defendants' system in a systematic manner that effectively creates a different relative importance—on the basis of race and ethnicity—for two very important variables, LSAT score and undergraduate grade point average. Both explicit policy and practice make clear and undisputed that LSAT scores and grade point averages are important generally (e.g., "[b]luntly, the higher one's score, the greater should be one's chances of being admitted, [and] [t]he lower the score, the greater the risk the candidate poses"). Acknowledging that importance, the Policy explicitly contemplates that in justification and furtherance of the commitment to "diversity," including racial and ethnic diversity, students will be admitted with "indices relatively far from the upper right corner." The clear effect, even though the policy no longer says so explicitly, is that there remains a "special admissions program" for the preferred minority groups: African Americans, Native Americans, Hispanics, and Puerto Ricans born on the U.S. mainland.

It is formally and effectively a dual system that attaches far greater importance generally to the LSAT scores and undergraduate grade point averages when comparing applicants within the majority group than when comparing an underrepresented minority applicant to members of the majority group. Moreover, what the policy contemplates, the actual admissions outcomes confirm in staggering fashion.

In the same respect (although to a much different degree) that index scores are lower for Michigan residents than non-residents (see Policy at 6, 7 & n.2), index scores are lower for the preferred minority group than for the majority group. In the case of residents, the differential treatment results from the policy decision to ensure that a "reasonable proportion" of the places in the class go to [state] residents. In the case of racial and ethnic minorities, the different treatment is designed to ensure that the preferred minorities are represented in the class in "meaningful numbers" such that they constitute a "critical mass."

The Policy does not define the meanings of either "critical mass" or "meaningful numbers" of minorities, just as it does not define what is meant by a "reasonable proportion" of residents. Undisputably, however, these concepts include reference to numbers or percentages of minority students that the Law School, as a matter of policy, admits and enrolls each year. To the extent that the Law School has committed itself to ensuring that enough seats in the class go to assembling a "critical mass" of minorities as a group or groups, the Law School is giving systematic consideration to race and ethnicity, not merely "particularized," "case-by-case" consideration to individual applicants.

Plaintiff's point is not that test scores and grades are completely unimportant for minorities. In fact, it is clear that scores and grades, which compose the "index," are generally important for everyone. *Within* the preferred racial and ethnic groups, for example, it is clear defendants follow the Policy's maxim that the "higher one's score, the greater should be one's chance of being admitted." And plaintiff assumes, at least for the purposes of this motion, that every minority admitted to the Law School meets at least the minimum qualifications set forth in the Policy: the ability to successfully complete a course of study at the Law School. *See* Exhibit E (Policy at p. 2) [Exhibit omitted]. But the fatal flaw in defendants' policies, when viewed in light of Justice Powell's rationale, is the obvious and *systematic* difference in *relative importance* of LSAT scores and grades when comparing applicants within the majority group versus comparing underrepresented minority applicants to the majority group: within the majority group, high test scores and grades relative to others in that group are obviously very important in admission outcomes generally, while it is much less important or not at all important for underrepresented minorities to have high test scores and grades when they are being compared to applicants in the majority group.

In fact, defendants' witnesses have testified that race is so important a factor in admissions that its removal from consideration would result in a "devastating " reduction in the numbers of minorities admitted to the class. See Exhibit K ([name] depo. p. 275) [Exhibit omitted]. If that is so, it is one measure of the decisive and overwhelming importance that race and ethnicity have in defendants' admissions system. Considering the overall importance in admissions decisions of LSAT scores and undergraduate grades and the observably different relative importance of those factors between the preferred racial groups and the nonpreferred groups, there is no meaningful sense in which it can be said that the two groups compete for seats in the class on "an equal footing" or that race and ethnicity are factors "weighed fairly" in the admissions process. 438 U.S. at 317-18. Defendants' admission policies are illegal, therefore, even when considered under the strictures of Justice Powell's diversity rationale.

B. Defendants' Admissions Policies and Practices Are Unlawful Because Diversity Is Not a Compelling Governmental Interest

1. Justice Powell's "Academic Freedom" or "Diversity" Rationale Was Not the "Holding" of the Court in *Bakke*

For several reasons, Justice Powell's lone opinion, with its "academic freedom" or "diversity" rationale, was not the "holding" of the Court in *Bakke*. Consequently, defendants cannot successfully defend against plaintiff's claims of constitutional and statutory civil rights violations by proving, if they could, that their race-conscious policies and practices satisfy Justice Powell's "diversity" and "academic freedom" analysis.

The four-Justice Brennan group did not adopt or endorse Powell's rationale. Nowhere in Justice Brennan's opinion does he even mention "diversity" or "academic freedom." Indeed, the Brennan group, while recognizing that "no single" opinion spoke for the Court, described the "central meaning" of all the opinions:

> [T]his should not and must not mask the *central meaning* of today's opinions: Government may take race into account when it acts not to demean or insult any racial group, but to remedy disadvantages cast on minorities by past racial prejudice, *at least when appropriate findings have been made by judicial, legislative, or administrative bodies with competence to act in this area.*

438 U.S. at 325 (emphasis added). Conspicuously, the Brennan group did *not* state that the "central meaning" of the opinions in *Bakke* was that race could be considered to achieve "intellectual diversity" or any other purported goal of a university in the pursuit or exercise of its "academic freedom." *See also Hopwood v. Texas*, 78 F.3d 932, 944 (5th Cir. 1996) (citing *Bakke*, 438 U.S. at 326 n.1, for the conclusion that the Brennan opinion "implicitly rejected Justice Powell's position").

§ 8.65   MOTION FOR SUMMARY JUDGMENT

The "diversity" rationale of Justice Powell cannot plausibly be said to represent the holding of *Bakke* when it was explicitly or implicitly rejected by eight other Justices. Justice Powell's vote was decisive of the outcome because the eight other Justices were evenly divided on the question of the lawfulness of the Davis program and the proper use of race in the admissions process. It does not follow merely from the vote alignment, however, that Justice Powell's "diversity" rationale represents some "common denominator" that commanded the assent of at least a majority of the Court. As demonstrated from the language of the other opinions, it is manifestly apparent that quite the opposite is true. There is no basis for concluding, therefore, that Justice Powell's "diversity" rationale represents the "holding" of the Court.

In *Marks v. United States*, 430 U.S. 188 (1977), the Supreme Court commented that "[w]hen a fragmented Court decides a case and no single rationale explaining the result enjoys the assent of five Justices, 'the holding of the Court may be viewed as that position taken by those Members who concurred in the judgments on the narrowest grounds.'" *Id.* at 193. An assertion that Powell's opinion represents the "holding" of the Court finds no support in an analysis to discern the "narrowest" ground on which the opinions of Powell and Brennan concurred on the permissible use of race in the admissions process. Powell approved of using race as a "plus factor" to achieve diversity in a manner that he suggested was described by the "Harvard plan" appended to his opinion. As noted, however, the Brennan opinion did not endorse Powell's justification of diversity, and Justice Brennan's reference to the "Harvard plan" contained a restriction not present in Justice Powell's analysis. Significantly, the Brennan group stated their agreement with Justice Powell that the "Harvard plan" was constitutional "under our approach, at least so long as the use of race to achieve an integrated student body is necessitated by the lingering effects of past discrimination." 438 U.S. at 326 n.1 (Brennan, J., concurring in part and dissenting in part); *id.* at 379 (asserting that "Harvard plan" allocated seats to "*disadvantaged* minority students"). Given that express limitation placed by four of the five Justices in *Bakke* who would allow some consideration of race in the admissions process, it is surely erroneous to argue that the *narrowest* ground of concurrence is found only with reference to Justice Powell's diversity rationale.

It is not at all clear that any "narrowness" analysis can or should apply to a specific proposition or mode of analysis when a majority of the Court has rejected the analysis. *See, e.g., Rutledge v. United States*, 517 U.S. 292, 298-99 (1996) (where argument that "in concert" element of crime required proof less than that needed to prove a "conspiracy" was "rejected to varying degrees, by [eight Justices]," it had not been considered precedential by lower courts). Lower courts have generally eschewed the *Marks* "narrowness" analysis when the differing opinions of the Supreme Court have no "common denominator." *See, e.g., Assn of Bituminous Contractors, Inc., v. Apfel*, 156 F.3d 1246, 1254 (D.C. Cir. 1998) (the "narrowest grounds" approach "does not apply unless the narrowest opinion represents a 'common denominator of the Court's reasoning' and 'embod[ies] *a position implicitly approved by at least five Justices who support the judgment*'") (emphasis added); *Rappa v. New Castle County,* 18 F.3d 1043, 1056-58 (3d Cir. 1994).

The judicial history following one Supreme Court opinion, *Baldasar v. Illinois,* 446 U.S. 222 (1980), *overruled in Nichols v. United States,* 511 U.S. 738 (1994), best exemplifies problems with the "narrowness" analysis in the absence of a discernible common denominator. In *Baldasar,* a plurality held that a misdemeanor conviction of an unrepresented defendant resulting in no jail time, although valid under the Sixth Amendment, could not be used to convert a subsequent misdemeanor into a felony without violating that Amendment. Justice Blackmun provided the crucial fifth vote for the holding reversing the enhancement, but concluded that the earlier conviction was invalid (and could not be used for any purpose) because the defendant was subject to more than six months jail time for the first conviction. Lower courts concluded that no rule of law at all emerged from the case because there was no "common denominator" between the opinions of the plurality and Justice Blackmun. *See, e.g., United States v. Eckford,* 910 F.2d 216, 219 & n.8 (5th Cir. 1990); *Schindler v. Clerk of Circuit Court,* 715 F.2d 341, 345 n.5 (7th Cir. 1983); *United States v. Robles-Sandoval,* 637 F.2d 692 n.1 (9th Cir. 1981) ("The Court in *Baldasar* divided in such a way that no rule can be said to have resulted."); *United States v. Castro-Vega,* 945 F.2d 496, 499-500 (2d Cir. 1991) ("[W]e find that there is no common denominator applicable to this case upon which all of the Justices in the *Baldasar* majority agreed."); *Triplett Grille, Inc. v. City of Akron,* 40 F.3d 129, 133-34 (6th Cir. 1994) ("Where a Justice or Justices concurring in the judgment in such a case articulates a legal standard which, when applied, will necessarily produce a result with which a majority of the Court from that case would agree, that standard is the law of the land.") (quoting *Planned Parenthood of Southeastern Pennsylvania v. Casey,* 947 F.2d 682, 693 (3rd Cir. 1991), *aff'd in part, rev'd in part,* 505 U.S. 833 (1992); *United States v. Nichols,* 979 F.2d 402, 416-18 (6th Cir. 1992) (stating agreement with analysis of *Baldasar* by other circuits, including opinions in *Eckford, Schindler, and Castro-Vega*), *aff'd,* 511 U.S. 738 (1994). In subsequently overruling *Baldasar,* the Supreme Court itself commented on the sometimes futility of resort to the *Marks* analysis:

> We think it not useful to pursue the *Marks* inquiry to the utmost logical possibility when it has so obviously baffled and divided the lower courts that have considered it. This degree of confusion following a splintered decision such as *Baldasar* is itself a reason for reexamining that decision.

Nichols v. United States, 511 U.S. 738, 745-46 (1994).

Although the Supreme Court has not explicitly reexamined *Bakke,* the Court has subsequently commented on its splintered nature. In *Adarand Constructors v. Pena,* 515 U.S. 200, 218 (1995), the Court noted that "*Bakke* did not produce an opinion for the Court" and that the "failure to produce a majority opinion in *Bakke* [and other cases] left unresolved the proper analysis for remedial race-based governmental action." *Id.* at 221. In *Fullilove v. Klutznick,* 448 U.S. 448 (1980), the Court made explicit that it "di[d] not adopt, either expressly or implicitly, the formulas of analysis articulated in such cases as *Bakke.*" *Id.* at 492; *see also Hopwood,* 78 F.3d at 945 ("[T]here has been no indication from the Supreme Court, other than Justice Powell's lonely opinion in *Bakke,* that the state's interest in diversity constitutes a compelling justification for governmental race-based discrimination.").

The Sixth Circuit has cited *Bakke* and its various opinions on a number of occasions, but has neither conducted any analysis under *Marks* to ascertain the "narrowest" ground joined in by the concurring judgments nor ever held that Powell's "diversity" or "academic freedom" rationale constitutes the "holding " of the Court. In a case decided shortly after *Bakke*, however, the Sixth Circuit considered the constitutionality of an affirmative action plan instituted by the Detroit Police Department. *See Detroit Police Officers' Assn v. Young*, 608 F.2d 671 (6th Cir. 1979). In *Young*, the court noted that the decision of the United States Supreme Court in *United Steelworkers of America v. Weber*, 443 U.S. 193 (1979), had addressed the lawfulness of such plans under Title VII, but that there was no "such clear authority in dealing with the constitutional issues." 608 F.2d at 694. The court then wrote that "we conclude that the opinion of Justices Brennan, White, Marshall and Blackmun in . . . *Bakke* . . . offers the most reasonable guidance," *id.*, and went on to analyze the constitutionality of the plan in question under Justice Brennan's opinion. *See also Ohio Contractors Assn v. Keip*, 713 F.2d 167, 170, 175 (6th Cir. 1983) ("Neither *Fullilove* nor *Bakke* produced a majority opinion from the Supreme Court and we depend on the several plurality opinions for guidance."); *Stotts v. Memphis Fire Department*, 679 F.2d 541, 553 (6th Cir. 1982) (citing *Bakke* for the proposition that Supreme Court approves race-conscious affirmative action "in a wide variety of situations where it is an attempt to ameliorate the effects of past discrimination"), *rev'd on other grounds*, 467 U.S. 561 (1984).

Justice Powell's "diversity" analysis and the Brennan group's remedial analysis are apples and oranges. Logic does not permit the conclusion that one always presents a narrower analysis than the other. They are just different. This remains the case even though the Brennan group purports to apply a lesser standard of review than does Justice Powell. Even when considered under the "lower" standard, the Brennan group would not accept something like the "Harvard plan" unless "necessitated by the lingering effects of past discrimination." 438 U.S. at 326 n.1. Moreover, under Justice Brennan's analysis, only members of minority groups that had been the victims of discrimination, where there was a high probability that individual beneficiaries were personally victims of societal discrimination, could receive an advantage. In voting to uphold the Davis plan, the Brennan group specifically relied on the fact that Davis looked beyond minority status to confirm disadvantage:

> [T]he Davis admissions program does not simply equate minority status with disadvantage. Rather, Davis considers on an individual basis each applicant's personal history to determine whether he or she has likely been disadvantaged by racial discrimination. The record makes clear that only minority applicants likely to have been isolated from the mainstream of American life are considered in the special program; other minority applicants are eligible only through the regular admissions program.

438 U.S. at 377 (Brennan, J., concurring in part and dissenting in part). Justice Powell's rationale based on diversity requires no such showing of disadvantage. It is meaningless and untrue, therefore, to argue that Justice Powell's vote to invalidate the Davis Program and the Brennan group's vote to sustain it proves the "narrower" scope of Justice Powell's "diversity" rationale. The facts of each case will determine which of the two rationales prove to be the "narrower" in the application. In a case of race-conscious decisionmaking that passes constitutional muster under Justice Powell's "diversity" rationale, but not under the "remedial" rationale of the Brennan group, it would be absurd to suggest that the Powell rationale is "narrower."

The only common denominator between the opinions of Justice Powell and Brennan is in their remedial analysis. *See* note 4, *supra.* The five Justices represented by Justice Powell and the Brennan group agreed that race could be taken into account in some remedial forms. And between the two opinions that expressed that view, Justice Powell's remedial analysis was clearly narrower than that of the Brennan group.

Because Justice Powell's "diversity" and "academic freedom" rationale do not constitute the "holding" of *Bakke,* defendants would find no legal refuge even if they could successfully demonstrate that their race-conscious admissions policies and practices are consistent with Justice Powell's rationale. See *Hopwood,* 78 F.3d at 944 (Justice Powell's "view [on diversity] is not binding precedent."). Defendants do not offer any ground other than diversity as a compelling interest justifying their race discrimination. Consequently, this Court should grant plaintiff's motion for partial summary judgment.

2. Supreme Court Cases Prior and Subsequent to *Bakke* Confirm that Academic Freedom or Diversity Is Not a Compelling Governmental Interest

In *Adarand Constructors v. Pena,* 515 U.S. 200 (1995), a majority of the Supreme Court held that all governmental racial classifications are reviewed under the strict scrutiny standard, which requires demonstration that the classification is justified by a compelling governmental interest and that it is narrowly tailored to achieve that interest. *Id.* at 227-35. The Court has never found a "compelling" interest other than a "remedial" one. *See Hopwood,* 78 F.3d at 944 ("No case since *Bakke* has accepted diversity as a compelling state interest under a strict scrutiny analysis."). The Court has specifically rejected non-remedial interests like an interest in providing "role models." *City of Richmond v. J.A. Croson Co.,* 488 U.S. 469, 497-98 (1989) (opinion of O'Connor, J.); *id.* at 520-21 (Scalia, J., concurring in the judgment). A majority of the Court has also rejected racial classifications as a remedy for "societal discrimination." *Shaw v. Hunt,* 517 U.S. 899, 909-10 & n.5 (1996); *Croson,* 488 U.S. at 498-99; id. at 521-22 (Scalia, J., concurring in the judgment). In *Croson,* the Court struck down racial preferences in the award of construction contracts in the City of Richmond, Virginia in part because "none of the evidence presented by the city points to any identified discrimination in the Richmond construction industry." *Id.* at 505.

Significantly, the Court has condemned *any* non-remedial interest. *Croson,* 488 U.S. at 493 ("Classifications based on race carry a danger of stigmatic harm. Unless they are *strictly reserved* for remedial settings, they may in fact promote notions of racial inferiority and lead to a politics of racial hostility.") (opinion of O'Connor, J.) (emphasis added); *id.* at 520 (Scalia, J., concurring in the judgment; *see also Hopwood,* 78 F.3d at 944 ("[T]he Court appears to have decided that there is essentially only one compelling state interest to justify racial classifications: remedying past wrongs.").

Justice Powell's assertions to the contrary notwithstanding, the Court has never accepted any "right" of the state to engage in race-conscious decisionmaking based on the First Amendment. In *Runyon v. McCrary,* 427 U. S. 160 (1976), the Court directly confronted a far more difficult issue—namely, whether private parties have the right to discriminate on the basis of the First Amendment—concluding that although "parents have a First Amendment right to send their children to educational institutions that promote the belief that racial segregation is desirable, . . . it does not follow that the *practice* of excluding racial minorities from such institutions is also protected by the same principle." *Id.* at 176 (emphasis added). If a private school's First Amendment right to express racially discriminatory views through its admissions policies and practices must yield to the equal protection claims of others, *a fortiori,* a *state's* interest in First Amendment freedoms—a far more problematic idea, since the First Amendment is usually thought of as a source of rights for people against the state, and not the other way around—should have even less weight when compared to principles of non-discrimination. In any event, the Court has never held that state entities should have *more* First Amendment protection than is afforded to private individuals and organizations. *See also Roberts v. United States Jaycees,* 468 U.S. 609, 623 (1984) (noting [t]hat "the right to associate for expressive purposes is not . . . absolute," even for a *private* entity, and holding that the State of Minnesota's interest in eradicating discrimination was sufficiently important to overcome the First Amendment interest of a private organization's right of association for expressive purposes).

Although the Court has not reexamined or overruled *Bakke,* its subsequent decisions on racial classifications are obviously highly relevant to evaluating *Bakke's* meaning. As demonstrated, Justice Powell's lonely opinion, with its non-remedial analysis, remains just that: alone. It did not command the allegiance of anyone on the Court but him, and it never has. In this case, defendants do not even purport to justify their use of racial preferences in admissions on any ground other than diversity. Defendants' broad, amorphous "diversity" justification meets neither the "societal discrimination" requirements of Justice Brennan's analysis, nor the requirement of remedying "identified" discrimination set forth by Justice Powell in *Bakke,* and confirmed by the majority in *Shaw v. Hunt and Croson. Cf. Lutheran Church-Missouri Synod v. FCC,* 141 F.3d 344, 350-56 (D.C. Cir. 1998) (FCC regulations violated Equal Protection Clause of the Fifth Amendment because stated "diversity" justification did not rise to "compelling" governmental interest, and regulations were not narrowly tailored). This Court should declare defendants' use of race-conscious admissions policies and practices illegal under the Equal Protection Clause and Title VI, and permanently enjoin defendants from engaging in those illegal practices in the future.

II.   The Same Conduct Establishes Violations of 42 U.S.C. § 1981

Title 42 Section 1981 provides that "[a]ll persons within the jurisdiction of the United States shall have the same right . . . to make and enforce contracts, to sue, be parties, give evidence, and to the full and equal benefit of all laws . . . as is enjoyed by white citizens . . . " Although its text suggests that only non-whites are the intended beneficiaries of Section 1981, the Supreme Court has held that it prohibits racial discrimination against whites to the same extent as others. *McDonald v. Santa Fe Trail Transp. Co.,* 427 U.S. 273, 295-96 (1976). A contract for educational services is a "contract" for purposes of Section 1981. See *Runyon v. McCrary,* 427 U.S. 160, 172 (1976). Section 1981(c) specifically provides that the right to contract equally without regard to race is protected from impairment under color of state authority.

141

Plaintiff may establish a violation of Section 1981 by proving that defendants engaged in intentional race discrimination. *See, e.g., Ohio Contractors Assn v. Keip,* 713 F.2d 167, 175 (6th Cir. 1975); *Watson v. Fraternal Order of Eagles,* 915 F.2d 235, 239-41 (6th Cir. 1990); *Cooper v. City of North Olmsted,* 795 F.2d 1265, 1270 (6th Cir. 1986). As demonstrated in the foregoing analysis of the Equal Protection and Title VI claims, the undisputed material facts establish that defendants have engaged in intentional race discrimination. Consequently, judgment as a matter of law is appropriate on the Section 1981 claim against defendants [name] and [name], acting in their official capacity.

III. Plaintiff and the Class Are Entitled to Partial Summary Judgment and Declaratory and Injunctive Relief

Federal Rule of Civil Procedure 56(a) permits a party seeking to recover upon a claim to move for "summary judgment in the party's favor upon all or any part thereof." Rule 56(c) permits an "interlocutory" judgment to be rendered solely on the issue of liability, and Rule 56(d) also contemplates a judgment rendered on less than the entire case. Summary judgment is appropriate under Rule 56(c) when the record demonstrates that "there is no genuine issue as to any material fact and the moving party is entitled to judgment as a matter of law." As demonstrated in the foregoing discussion, there are no genuine issues as to any facts material to plaintiff's claims that the Law School and defendants [name] and [name], in their official capacity, have violated plaintiff's rights protected by the Equal Protection Clause of the Fourteenth Amendment and by 42 U.S.C. §§ 2000d and 1981. Consequently, plaintiff and the class are entitled to partial summary judgment in their favor.

Title 42 U.S.C. § 1983 provides remedies against those who have violated the rights of others under color of state authority. Individuals who prove that their federal civil rights have been so violated may seek, among other things, a declaration that those rights have been violated and an order of the court enjoining defendants from engaging in the illegal practices in the future. *See, e.g., Will v. Michigan Department of State Police,* 491 U.S. 58, 71 n.10 (1989); *Johnson v. Railway Express Agency,* 421 U.S. 454, 460 (1975) (declaratory and injunctive relief available for violations of 42 U.S.C. § 1981). Plaintiff here seeks a declaration that the defendants' admissions policies and practices for the academic years 1995 through the present violate plaintiff's rights under the Constitution and 42 U.S.C. §§ 1981 and 2000d. Such a judicial declaration is important to vindicate plaintiff's constitutional rights and to establish an essential predicate for the individual remedial claims (*e.g.,* order of admission to the Law School or award of compensatory damages) of the plaintiff and members of the class. Plaintiff and the class also seek an order permanently enjoining defendants from engaging in the future in their illegal, racially discriminatory admissions practices. Injunctive relief is important and necessary, among other reasons, because thousands of individuals will, only a few months from now, begin filing their applications for admission to defendants' Law School. Unless enjoined from enforcing their illegal policies and practicing their illegal race discrimination, defendants will once again intentionally subject thousands of individuals to injury and indignity.

CONCLUSION

For all of the foregoing reasons, plaintiff respectfully submits she is entitled to summary judgment as follows:

1.   Finding liability against the [name], and [name] and [name] in their official capacities;

2.   Declaring that defendants have violated plaintiff's rights, and the rights of the class, under the Equal Protection Clause of the Fourteenth Amendment; Title VI of the Civil Rights Act of 1964 (42 U.S.C. § 2000d); 42 U.S.C. § 1981; and 42 U.S.C. § 1983; and

3.   Permanently enjoining defendants from applying their illegal, racially discriminatory admissions policies and practices in the future.

Dated:[date]

By [attorneys for plaintiff]

CHAPTER 10

RESOURCES ON THE INTERNET

§ 10.4 Online Sources for Locating People

Page 652, add at end of § 10.4:

http://www.teldir.com/eng/ Teldir
The Internet's most complete index of online phone books, with over 400 links to Yellow Pages, White Pages, Business Directories, Email Addresses and Fax Listings from over 170 countries all around the world.

http://www.anywho.com/ Anywho
AT&T's comprehensive listing of over 100 million listings. You can do reverse lookups, ask for a street proximity listing for a business or residential listing, use their "sounds like" match for last name lookups, and get maps of the address from MapsOnUs.

§ 10.5 Online Sources for Locating Expert Witnesses

Page 653, add at end of § 10.5:

http://www.jurispro.com/ JurisPro
JurisPro is a free online directory of expert witnesses. You can search for an expert witness by name or area of expertise. You can view the expert's qualifications, read their articles, see their photo, and contact the expert directly. JurisPro claims to be the only expert witness directory where you can hear the expert witness, and download their actual CV.

http://www.expertwitness.com/ ExpertWitness.com
Subscription service for locating Expert Witnesses.

http://www.witness.net/ Witness.Net
The mission of the Expert Witness Network is to link attorneys and expert witnesses via the World Wide Web by using online technology to reduce the time and costs associated with locating the best expert for a case.

Page 653, add new § 10.6:

§ 10.6 Online Sources for Medical Research (New)

http://www.nlm.nih.gov/ National Library of Medicine

http://www.fasthealth.com/dictionary/ Searchable medical dictionary

http://www.pharma-lexicon.com/ Medical and pharmaceutical acronyms and abbreviations and many, many Web site links

http://www.ncbi.nlm.nih.gov/entrez/query.fcgi PubMed, National Library of Medicine
PubMed, a service of the National Library of Medicine, provides access to over 11 million MEDLINE citations back to the mid-1960's and additional life science journals. PubMed includes links to many sites providing full text articles and other related resources.

http://medlineplus.nlm.nih.gov/medlineplus/medlineplus.html MEDLINEPlus
Health information from the world's largest medical library, the *National Library of Medicine*. Information that is authoritative and up to date. MEDLINEplus has extensive information from the *National Institutes of Health* and other trusted sources on over 500 diseases and conditions. There are also lists of hospitals and physicians, a medical encyclopedia and dictionaries, health information in Spanish, extensive information on prescription and nonprescription drugs, health information from the media, and links to thousands of clinical trials. MEDLINEplus is updated daily.

http://www.mayo.edu/healthinfo/resources.html Mayo Clinic
Internet resources, selected by Mayo Clinic medical librarians, which allow an individual to research medical topics. Usually, the only cost for the research is your time. This list is updated monthly.

http://www.medmatrix.org/reg/login.asp Medical Matrix
Medical Matrix is a free directory of selected medical sites on the Internet. You must register to use, but registration is free.

§ 10.5 ONLINE SOURCES FOR LOCATING EXPERT WITNESSESS

http://www.healthfinder.gov/ healthfinder®
healthfinder® is a free guide to reliable consumer health and human services information, developed by the U.S. Department of Health and Human Services. healthfinder® can lead you to selected online publications, clearinghouses, databases, Web sites, and support and self-help groups, as well as government agencies and not-for-profit organizations that produce reliable information for the public.

http://www.rxlist.com/ Medical Drug Index
A list you can search for more than 4,000 drugs.

CHAPTER 11

ALTERNATIVE DISPUTE RESOLUTION, MEDIATION AND ARBITRATION (NEW)

§ 11.1 Introduction

More and more, the rising cost of litigation and the never-ending overcrowding of the court systems are leading to more creative ways of resolving disputes between parties. There is a marked increase of contracts containing clauses requiring mandatory arbitration, for example. For years, labor contracts and the construction industry have used such clauses routinely, but their popularity is gaining among all business transaction contracts.

Alternative Dispute Resolution

Alternative Dispute Resolution is just what the name implies. You can think of it as the main concept (ADR), with Arbitration and Mediation as variations of ADR. It is faster than most litigation because the parties do not have to wait for a court date. It is less expensive, and in some respects, less stressful for the parties.

§ 11.2 Arbitration

Arbitration is probably the most common form of Alternative Dispute Resolution. Mandatory arbitration clauses may be included in any number of business contracts, thus forcing parties to such contracts to use arbitrators to resolve their differences. When contracts have mandatory arbitration clauses, the claims MAY NOT be tried in a court of law. Three examples of arbitration clauses follow:

FORM 11-1
SAMPLE FORM OF ARBITRATION CLAUSE IN AN AGREEMENT*

(i) Every dispute, difference, or question which may at any time arise between the parties hereto or any person claiming under them, touching or arising out of or in respect of this agreement (deed) or the subject matter thereof shall be referred to the arbitration of _____, etc. or if he shall be unable or unwilling to act, to another arbitrator to be agreed upon between the parties or failing agreement to be nominated by_____ or, failing agreement to two arbitrators one to be appointed by each party to the difference (whether consisting of one or more than one person) and in case of difference of opinion between them to an umpire appointed by the said two arbitrators before entering on the reference and the decision of the arbitrator (or such arbitrators, or umpire as the case may be) shall be final and binding on the parties.

OR

(ii)   In the event of any dispute, difference or question arising out of or in respect of this agreement or the commission of any breach of any terms thereof or of compensation payable thereof or in any manner whatsoever in connection with it, the same shall be referred to the Chamber of Commerce_____ (or the Association of_____) for arbitration as provided in Rules framed by the said Chamber (or Association) for the purpose. The decision or award so given shall be binding on the parties hereto.

OR

(iii) All disputes arising between the partners as to the interpretation, operation, or effect of any clause in this deed or any other difference arising between the partners, which cannot be mutually resolved, shall be referred to the arbitration of_____ failing him to any other arbitrator chosen by the partners in writing. The decision of such an arbitrator shall be binding on the partners.

---

* This form was provided courtesy of www.indyalawyer.com.

Generally, the parties agree upon an impartial third party to arbitrate the case. The *American Arbitration Association* (http://www.adr.org/index2.1.jsp) can supply arbitrators, sometimes called neutrals, or the parties may choose their own. In some instances, parties may opt for a panel of arbitrators. These panels are sometimes called tribunals. In this configuration, each party may choose one arbitrator, and then both parties must agree on the third arbitrator. Decisions of the panel would be decided by a two-thirds vote.

Usually, an arbitration is a more relaxed version of a courtroom hearing. The contract will either speak to the rules (procedure and evidence) to be used in the hearings or be silent on the matter. If the contract is silent on the matter, then the parties must either agree to invoke the *Uniform Arbitration Act*, the state adopted version thereof, or some other agreed-upon set of rules. Parties may be represented by attorneys and the procedure is similar to a court hearing. The rules for Accident Claims Arbitration of the American Arbitration Association are included here as an example.

FORM 11-2
SAMPLE RULES FOR ACCIDENT CLAIMS ARBITRATION*

Accident Claims Arbitration Rules (Including Mediation) of the American Arbitration Association

As Amended and Effective on January 1, 1994

Introduction
Mediation
The Process
The Mediator
Using the Mediation Process
Cost

Accident Claims Arbitration Rules

1. Agreement of Parties
2. Administration and Delegation of Duties
3. Panel of Arbitrators
4. Initiation under an Arbitration Provision in a Policy
5. Change of Claim
6. Initiation under a Submission
7. Fixing of Locale
8. Designation of Arbitrator
9. Qualifications of Arbitrator
10. Time and Place
11. Representation
12. Stenographic Record
13. Interpreters
14. Attendance at Hearings
15. Postponements
16. Oaths
17. Arbitration in the Absence of a Party or Counsel
18. Order of Proceedings
19. Evidence
20. Evidence by Affidavit and Posthearing Filing of Documents
21. Majority Decision
22. Closing of Hearing
23. Reopening of Hearing
24. Waiver of Rules
25. Extensions of Time
26. Serving of Notice
27. Communication with Arbitrator
28. Time of Award
29. Form of Award
30. Scope of Award
31. Award upon Settlement
32. Delivery of Award to Parties
33. Expenses

Introduction

The American Arbitration Association (AAA) is a public-service, not-for-profit organization offering a broad range of dispute resolution services to business executives, attorneys, individuals, trade associations, unions, management, consumers, families, communities, and all levels of government. Services are available through AAA headquarters in New York City and through offices located in major cities throughout the United States. Hearings may be held at locations convenient for the parties and are not limited to cities with AAA offices. In addition, the AAA serves as a center for education and training, issues specialized publications, and conducts research on all forms of out-of-court dispute settlement.

Automobile insurance policies written in every state protect an insured against personal injury caused by uninsured and hit-and-run motorists. The standard uninsured motorist endorsement is one in which the insurer promises

> to pay all sums which the insured shall be legally entitled to recover as damages from the owner or operator of an uninsured automobile because of bodily injury sustained by the insured, caused by accident and arising out of the ownership, maintenance or use of such uninsured automobile, provided determination as to whether the insured is legally entitled to recover such damages, and if so, the amount thereof, shall be made by agreement between the insured and the company or, if they fail to agree, by arbitration.

This endorsement contains a provision for arbitration, which typically reads as follows.

Arbitration
If any person making claim hereunder and the company do not agree that such person is legally entitled to recover damages from the owner or operator of an uninsured automobile because of the amount of payment which may be owing under this endorsement, then, upon written demand of either, the matter or matters upon which such person and the company do not agree shall be settled by arbitration in accordance with the rules of the American Arbitration Association, and judgment upon the award rendered by the arbitrators may be entered in any court having jurisdiction thereof. Such person and the company each agree to consider itself bound and to be bound by any award made by the arbitrators pursuant to this endorsement.

§ 11.2 ARBITRATION

In 1956, at the request of the insurance industry, the American Arbitration Association established these procedures for arbitrating such matters.

Mediation

Mediation procedures are also provided for those parties who wish to make use of them. The AAA encourages parties to submit their accident claims disputes to mediation, which has proven to be a prompt, fair, and economical method of resolving insurance claims. The mediation provisions of the AAA's Alternative Dispute Resolution Procedures for Insurance Claims will be utilized where the parties agree to mediate their dispute.

The Process

In mediation, the mediator assists the parties in reaching their own settlement, but does not have the authority to make a binding decision or award.

The Mediator

Mediators appointed under this program are experienced attorneys. They have specific training or experience in mediation and are prepared to offer prompt service. The AAA makes every effort to appoint mediators who are acceptable to both parties. Upon the objection of either party, the AAA will replace a mediator.

Using the Mediation Process

Because mediation is voluntary, all parties to the dispute must consent to participate. Upon request, a mediation submission form will be provided by the AAA, or you may indicate your willingness to mediate by placing a check mark in the appropriate box on the Demand for Arbitration form. The AAA will contact the other parties and attempt to obtain their agreement to mediate.

If there is no agreement to mediate or if mediation proves unsuccessful, the parties can continue with the arbitration.

Cost

The initial administrative fee and insurance carrier surcharge are applied to the cost of administering the mediation. In addition, there is suggested mediator compensation of $300 per case, to be paid equally by the parties. The exact compensation rate for the mediator will be agreed to by the parties in each case, with the assistance of the AAA.

Accident Claims Arbitration Rules

1. Agreement of Parties

The parties make these rules a part of their arbitration agreement whenever a policy of insurance or applicable insurance-department regulation provides; for arbitration by the American Arbitration Association (AAA) in connection with a dispute involving a motor-vehicle liability claim. These rules and any amendment of them shall apply in the form obtaining at the time the arbitration is initiated, except for any such provision that may be inconsistent with the arbitration agreement or with applicable law.

2. Administration and Delegation of Duties

When parties agree to arbitrate under these or when they provide for arbitration by the AAA and an arbitration is initiated under these rules, they thereby authorize the AAA to administer the arbitration. The duties of the AAA under these rules may be carried out through such representatives as the AAA may direct.

3. Panel of Arbitrators

The AAA shall establish and maintain an Accident Claims Panel of arbitrators made up of attorneys with negligence experience. Each of the AAA's regional offices will maintain an Advisory Committee, made up of equal numbers of at least three members of the defense bar and/or the insurance industry and three members of the plaintiff's bar, which will approve the qualifications of the members of that panel. Each committee shall meet at least once a year.

4. Initiation under an Arbitration Provision in a Policy

When the conditions precedent contained in the insurance policy or state insurance-department regulations have been complied with, arbitration shall be initiated by filing a written Demand for Arbitration. The demand shall be served by US certified mail-return receipt requested. When filed by an insured, it shall be directed to the claim, office of the insurer under whose policy arbitration, is sought, at the office where the claim has been discussed, or at the office of the insurer closest to the residence of the insured.

The demand shall set forth the following information:

(1) the name, address, and telephone number of the insured person(s) and the filing attorney;

(2) the name, address and policy number of the policyholder;

(3) the identity and location of the claims office of the insurer, if known; the claim's file number, if known; and the name of the individual with whom the claim was discussed;

(4) the date and location of the accident;

(5) nature of dispute and injuries alleged;

(6) amount of uninsured-motorist policy limits and the amount claimed thereunder; and,

(7) address of the AAA regional office at which copies of the demand are being filed.

Three copies of the demand must be filed with an AAA regional office at the same time, with a copy of the parts of the policy or regulations relating to the dispute, including the arbitration provisions together with the administrative filing fee.

The AAA will acknowledge receipt of the demand to all parties. If, within thirty calendar days after acknowledgment of the demand by the AAA, the insurer moves in court to contest coverage, applicable policy limits, or stacking of policy coverage, administration will be suspended until such issues are decided.

All issues covering compliance with conditions precedent may be decided by an arbitrator.

Issues as to applicable policy limits, or stacking of policy coverage may be referred to voluntary coverage arbitration with the agreement of all parties before an arbitrator appointed by the AAA from a panel designated to hear such issues. These issues will be submitted to the arbitrator on documents only, unless the parties agree otherwise or the arbitrator determines that an oral hearing is necessary. In the absence of an agreement to submit such issues to arbitration, accident claims arbitrators may only decide contested issues of coverage, applicable policy limits, or stacking of policy coverage where ordered to do so by a court or where so authorized by law.

Unless there is, (1) an agreement to submit such issues to voluntary coverage arbitration, (2) a motion to contest coverage, applicable policy limits, or the stacking of policy coverage made within thirty calendar days after acknowledgment of the demand by the AAA, or (3) a court order staying arbitration, the AAA will proceed with the administration of the case.

5. Change of Claim

If any party desires to make any new or different claim, same shall be made in writing and filed with the AAA and a copy thereof shall be mailed to the other party. After the arbitrator is appointed, no new or different claim may be submitted except with the arbitrator's consent.

6. Initiation under a Submission

Parties to any existing dispute may commence an arbitration under these rules by filing at any regional office of the AAA three copies of a written submission to arbitrate under these rules, setting for the information specified in Section 4.

7. Fixing of Locale

Either the county of residence of the insured or the county where the accident occurred may be designated by the insured as the locale in which the hearing is to be held. Only if all parties agree shall the hearing be held in some other locale.

8. Designation of Arbitrator

Unless applicable law or the agreement of the parties provides otherwise, the dispute shall be determined by one arbitrator, except as otherwise provided in this section.

The AAA will submit a list of nine members of the Accident Claims Panel from which each party shall have the right to strike up to two names on a peremptory basis, within twenty days of the AAA's submission of the list. The AAA will appoint the arbitrator from among the remaining names.

Where the amount claimed and available coverage limits exceed minimum statutory financial-responsibility limits, upon the request of a party made within thirty calendar days after acknowledgment of the demand by the AAA, the dispute shall be determined by three arbitrators. The AAA will submit a list of thirteen names from the Accident Claims Panel, allowing each party to strike up to three names on a peremptory basis, within twenty days of the AAA's submission of the list. The AAA will appoint three arbitrators from among the remaining names.

If the parties fail to agree on any of the persons named on the list of arbitrators, if acceptable arbitrators are unable to act, or if, for any other reason, the appointment cannot be made from the submitted lists, the AAA shall have the power to make the appointment from among other members of the panel without submitting additional lists.

9. Qualifications of Arbitrator

No person shall serve as an arbitrator in any arbitration in which that person has any financial or personal interest. An arbitrator shall disclose any circumstances likely to create a presumption of bias which might disqualify that arbitrator as an impartial arbitrator. Any party shall have the right to challenge the appointment of an arbitrator for reasonable cause. The AAA shall determine whether the arbitrator should be disqualified, and shall inform the parties of its decision, which shall be conclusive.

If for any reason an appointed arbitrator should be unable to perform the duties of the office, the AAA shall appoint a replacement from among those names remaining on the list(s) submitted to the parties. If an appointment cannot be made from the list(s), the AAA shall appoint a replacement in accordance with the provisions of Section 8.

10. Time and Place

The arbitrator shall fix the time and place for each hearing. The AAA shall mail to each party notice thereof at least twenty calendar days in advance, unless the parties by mutual agreement waive such notice or modify the terms thereof.

11. Representation

Any party may be represented by counsel or other authorized representative. A party intending to be so represented shall notify the other party and the AAA of the name and address of such representative at least three days prior to the date set for the hearing at which the representative is first to appear. When an arbitration is initiated by counsel or when an attorney replies for the other party, such notice is deemed to have been given.

12. Stenographic Record

Any party wishing a stenographic record shall make arrangements directly with a stenographer and shall notify the other party of such arrangements in advance of the hearing. The requesting party or parties shall pay the cost of the record. If such transcript is agreed by the parties to be, or determined by the arbitrator to be, the official record of the proceeding, it must be made available to the arbitrator and to the other party for inspection, at a time and place determined by the arbitrator.

13. Interpreters

Any party wishing an interpreter shall make all arrangements directly with the interpreter and shall assume the costs of such service.

14. Attendance at Hearings

The arbitrator shall maintain the privacy of the hearings unless the law provides to the contrary. Any person having a direct interest in the arbitration is entitled to attend hearings. The arbitrator shall otherwise have the power to require the exclusion of any witness, other than a party or other essential person, during the testimony of any other witness. It shall be discretionary with the arbitrator to determine the propriety of the attendance of any other person.

15. Postponements

The arbitrator may, for good cause, postpone the hearing upon the request of a party or upon the arbitrator's own initiative, and shall grant such postponement when all of the parties agree thereto.

16. Oaths

Before proceeding with the first hearing, each arbitrator may take an oath of office and, if required by law, shall do so. The arbitrator may require witnesses to testify under oath administered by any duly qualified person and, if required by law or requested by either party, shall do so.

17. Arbitration in the Absence of a Party or Counsel

Unless the law provides to the contrary, the arbitration may proceed in the absence of any party or counsel who, after due notice, fails to be present or fails to obtain an adjournment. An award shall not be made solely on the default of a party. The arbitrator shall require the party who is present to submit such evidence as is deemed necessary for the making of an award.

18. Order of Proceedings

A hearing shall be opened by the filing of the oath of the arbitrator, where required; by the recording of the place, time and date of the hearing and the presence of the arbitrator, the parties, and counsel, if any; and by the receipt by the arbitrator of the statement of the claim and answer, if any.

The arbitrator may, at the beginning the hearing, ask for statements clarifying the issues involved. The claimant shall then present its claims, proofs, and witnesses, who shall submit to questions or other examination. The respondent shall then present its defenses, proofs, and witnesses, who shall submit to questions or other examination. The arbitrator has discretion to vary this procedure but shall afford full and equal opportunity to the parties for the presentation of any material or relevant proofs.

Exhibits, when offered by either party, may be received in evidence by the arbitrator.

The names and addresses of all witnesses and exhibits in the order received shall be made a part of the record.

The Parties may, by written agreement, provide for the waiver of oral hearings. If the parties are unable to agree as to the procedure, the AAA shall specify a fair and equitable procedure.

19. Evidence

The parties may offer such evidence as is relevant and material to the dispute and shall produce such additional evidence as the arbitrator may deem necessary to an understanding and determination of the dispute. An arbitrator authorized by law to subpoena witnesses or documents may do so upon request of any party or independently.

The arbitrator shall be the judge of the relevance and materiality of evidence offered, and conformity to legal rules of evidence shall not be necessary. All evidence shall be taken in the presence of all the arbitrators and all of the parties, except where any of the parties is absent in default or waives the right to be present.

Any party intending to offer any medical report or record at the hearing must provide the other party with a copy at least twenty days in advance thereof.

20. Evidence by Affidavit and Posthearing Filing of Documents

The arbitrator may receive and consider the evidence of witnesses by affidavit, but shall give it only such weight as the arbitrator deems it entitled to after consideration of any objection made to its admission.

If the parties agree or the arbitrator directs that documents are to be submitted to the arbitrator after the hearing, they shall be filed with the AAA for transmission to the arbitrator. All parties shall be afforded an opportunity to examine such documents.

21. Majority Decision

Whenever there is more than one arbitrator, all decisions of the arbitrators must be by at least a majority. The award must also be made by at least a majority unless the concurrence of all is expressly required by the arbitration agreement or by law.

22. Closing of Hearing

The arbitrator shall specifically inquire of all parties whether they have any further proofs to offer or witnesses to be heard. Upon receiving negative replies, or if satisfied that the record is complete, the arbitrator shall declare the hearing closed and a minute thereof shall be recorded. If briefs are to be filed, the hearing shall be declared closed as of the final date set by the arbitrator for the receipt of briefs. If documents are to be filed as provided for in Section 20 and the date set for their receipt is later than that set for the receipt of briefs, the later date shall be the date of closing the hearing. The time limit within which the arbitrator is required to make the award shall commence to run, in the absence of other agreements by the parties, upon the closing of the hearing.

23. Reopening of Hearing

The hearing may be reopened by the parties at will or upon application of a party at any time before the award is made. If reopening the hearing would prevent the making of the award within the specific time agreed upon by the parties in the contract out of which the controversy has arisen, the matter may not be reopened, unless the parties agree upon an extension of time. When no specific date is fixed in the contract, the arbitrator may reopen the hearing, and the arbitrator shall have thirty days from the closing of the reopened hearing within which to make an award.

24. Waiver of Rules

Any party who proceeds with the arbitration after knowledge that any provision or requirement of these rules has not been complied with and who fails to state objection thereto in writing shall be deemed to have waived the right to object.

25. Extensions of Time

The parties may modify any period of time by mutual agreement. The AAA may for good cause extend any period of time established by these rules except the time for making the award. The AAA shall notify the parties of any such extension and its reason therefor.

26. Serving of Notice

(a) With the exception of the demand, which shall be served by US certified mail-return receipt requested, each party shall be deemed to have consented that any papers, notices, or process necessary or proper for the initiation or continuation of an arbitration under these rules; for any court action in connection therewith; or for the entry of judgment on any award made under these rules may be served upon such party by mail addressed to such party or its attorney at the last known address or by personal service, in or outside the state where the arbitration is to be held, provided that reasonable opportunity to be heard with regard thereto has been granted to such party.

(b) To facilitate communication between the parties and the AAA, the parties agree that communications received from each other or the AAA via facsimile machine, telex, telegram, or other written forms of electronic communication are valid and proper notice under these rules.

27. Communication with Arbitrator

There shall be no direct communication between the parties and an arbitrator other than at oral hearings. Any other oral or written communication from the parties to an arbitrator shall be directed to the AAA for transmission to the arbitrator.

28. Time of Award

The arbitrator shall render the award promptly and, unless otherwise agreed by the parties or specified by law, no later than thirty days from the date of closing the hearing, or, if oral hearings have been waived, from the date of transmitting the final statements and proofs to the arbitrator.

29. Form of Award

The award shall be in writing and shall be signed either by the sole arbitrator or by at least a majority if there is more than one arbitrator. It shall be executed in the manner required by law.

30. Scope of Award

The arbitrator shall render a decision determining whether the insured person has a right to receive any damages under the policy and the amount thereof, not in excess of the applicable policy limits. The award shall not contain a determination as to issues of coverage except as provided in Section 4.

31. Award upon Settlement

If the parties settle their dispute during the course of the arbitration, the arbitrator may, upon their request, set forth the terms of the agreed settlement in an award.

32. Delivery of Award to Parties

Parties shall accept as legal delivery of the award the placing of the award or a true copy thereof in the mail addressed to such party or its attorney at the last known address, personal service of the award, or the filing of the award in any other manner that may be permitted by law.

33. Expenses

The expenses of witnesses for either side shall be paid by the party producing such witnesses. All other expenses of the arbitration, including required traveling and other expenses of the arbitrator and of AAA representatives, and the expenses of any witness and the cost of any proof produced at the direct request of the arbitrator, shall be borne equally by the parties, unless they agree otherwise or unless the arbitrator in the award assesses such expenses or any part thereof against any specified party or parties.

34. Applications to Court and Exclusion of Liability

(a) No judicial proceeding by a party relating to the subject matter of the arbitration or mediation shall be deemed a waiver of the party's right to arbitrate.

(b) Neither the AAA nor any arbitrator or mediator in a proceeding under these rules is a necessary party in judicial proceedings relating to the arbitration or mediation.

(c) Parties to these rules shall be deemed to have consented that judgment upon the arbitration award may be entered in any federal or state court having jurisdiction thereof.

(d) Neither the AAA nor any arbitrator or mediator shall be liable to any party for any act or omission in connection with any arbitration or mediation conducted under these rules.

35. Release of Documents for Judicial Proceedings

The AAA shall, upon the written request of a party, furnish to such party, at its expense, certified copies of any papers in the AAA's possession that may be required in judicial proceedings relating to the arbitration.

36. Interpretation and Application of Rules

The arbitrator shall interpret and apply these rules insofar as they relate to the arbitrator's powers and duties. When there is more than one arbitrator and a difference arises among them concerning the meaning or application of these rules, it shall be decided by a majority vote. If that is unobtainable, either an arbitrator or a party may refer the question to the AAA for final decision. All other rules shall be interpreted and applied by the AAA.

Administrative Fees

An initial administrative fee in the amount of $250 shall be paid to the AAA by the party initiating the mediation or arbitration. No refund of the initial fee is made when a matter is withdrawn or settled after filing.

If the parties engage in voluntary coverage arbitration followed by arbitration of the remaining liability and damage issues, there will be an additional administrative fee of $100 per party.

Where a case is heard by three arbitrators, the party requesting three arbitrators shall pay an additional administrative fee of $300.

ALTERNATIVE DISPUTE RESOLUTION, MEDIATION AND ARBITRATION

Surcharge

The balance of the administrative costs of the AAA is covered by a $250-per-case sur-charge paid by the insurer or self insurer involved.

Arbitrator Compensation

Arbitrators from the AAA's Accident Claims Panel shall be compensated at a rate of $150 per case concluded. This fee will be paid by the AAA from the administrative fees collected in the case.

Additional-Hearing Fees

A fee of $50 is payable by each party for each hearing held after the first hearing.

Hearing Room Rental

Hearing rooms for second and subsequent hearings are available on a rental basis at AAA offices. Check with your local office for specific availability and rates.

Postponement Fees

A fee of $50 is payable by a party causing a postponement of any hearing scheduled before a single arbitrator. For second or subsequent postponements before a single arbitrator, a fee of $100 will be paid by the party causing the postponement.

A fee of $75 is payable by a party causing a postponement of any hearing scheduled before a multiarbitrator panel. For second or subsequent postponements before multi-arbitrator panel, a fee of $150 will be paid by the party causing the postponement.

---

§ 11.2   ARBITRATION

Agreements to arbitrate are necessary if the contract or document giving rise to the dispute is silent on the subject. The following agreements are examples of agreements to arbitrate when the contract or document giving rise to the dispute is silent on the subject.

FORM 11-3
SAMPLE AGREEMENT TO ARBITRATE—CONTRACTUAL ISSUE*

AGREEMENT TO ARBITRATE *(contractual issue)*

1. The parties to the dispute being, _____, Party A, and _____, Party B, entered into a contract entitled, _____, a fair and accurate copy of which is attached hereto as Exhibit A. The parties are now in conflict regarding this contract and desire to have the following issues submitted to binding and final arbitration with _____ (name arbitrator or arbitration forum):

(List issues or claims to be arbitrated):
Party A's Claims:
a)_____
b)_____
c)_____

Party B's Claims:
a)_____
b)_____
c)_____

2. The parties further agree to follow the rules and procedures for arbitration set forth by _____ *(name the arbitrator or the arbitration forum).*

3. In so agreeing the parties expressly acknowledge that the holding of the arbitrator shall be final and binding upon them, and that they are waiving any and all rights they have file their claims in court and any and all rights they may have to a jury trial on these claims.

So Agreed and Certified:
This __ day of _____ , 200__ .

_____
Party A.

_____
Party B.

_____
* Forms 11-3 and 11-4 are reprinted courtesy of www.gama.com .

ALTERNATIVE DISPUTE RESOLUTION, MEDIATION AND ARBITRATION

FORM 11-4
SAMPLE AGREEMENT TO ARBITRATE—NON-CONTRACTUAL ISSUE*

AGREEMENT TO ARBITRATE *(non-contractual issue)*

1. The parties to the dispute being,_____, Party A, and _____,
Party B, presently have a dispute falling into one of the following categories _
(check more than one if appropriate):
_____ (a) account _____ (b) note _____ (c) tort _____ (d) trover
_____ (e) personal injury _____ (f) other *(please describe)*

2. Because Party A asserts an allegedly valid claim in the amount of _____
dollars, which is denied by Party B, and Party B asserts an allegedly valid claim in the
amount of
_____ dollars, which is denied by Party A, the parties are desirous of
submitting these claims for resolution by arbitration with _____ *(name arbitrator or arbitration forum).*

Party A describes the issues surrounding its claims as being:

_____
_____
_____
_____

Party B describes the issues surrounding its claims as being:

_____
_____
_____
_____

3. The parties further agree to follow the rules and procedures for arbitration set forth
by _____
(name the arbitrator or the arbitration forum).

4. In so agreeing the parties expressly acknowledge that the holding of the arbitrator
shall be final and binding upon them, and that they are waiving any and all rights
they have file their claims in court and any and all rights they may have to a jury trial
on these claims.

So Agreed and Certified:
This __ day of _____ , 200__ .

_____

Party A.

_____

_____

* Forms 11-3 and 11-4 are reprinted courtesy of www.gama.com .

Party B.

Once the hearing has taken place and the arbitrator(s) has made a decision, an order is issued, just as in a trial. An example of such an order follows:

FORM 11-5
SAMPLE AWARD BY AN ARBITRAL TRIBUNAL

This is the award by the undersigned, made the_____ day of _____

Whereas by an agreement under the deed, dated_____ and made between (contractor) of the one part and_____ (owner of the property)of the other part (being an agreement by the said contractor) to construct certain works upon the land of the said (owner) in accordance with sanctioned plans and specifications contained therein it was agreed between the parties that if any dispute should arise in future between the parties thereto relating to or touching the said agreement or the interpretation thereof or in relation to the rights, duties or liabilities of either party the same should be referred to two arbitrators and their umpire in accordance with the provisions of _____.

And whereas disputes having arisen between the aforesaid parties relating to the said agreement the said (contractor) by writing dated_____ nominated and appointed _____ (one arbitrator) _____of etc, and the said (owner) by writing dated_____ nominated and appointed _____ (other arbitrator) _____of etc, to act as arbitrators and settle the said matters in dispute between the parties.

And whereas the said arbitrators respectively accepted the said appointments and took upon themselves to discharge the burden of the said reference and before starting the proceeding for the consideration of the disputed matter referred to them by writing under their hands dated_____ appointed me the said Presiding Arbitrator in the said arbitration.

And whereas the said arbitrators duly extended the time for making the award until the _____day of_____

And whereas the said arbitrators were unable to agree amongst themselves unanimously upon an award and under such circumstances gave me notice in writing dated_____and there upon the disputes stood referred to me.

Now be it know that, I, said Presiding Arbitrator, make my award on the following matter:

1. I find that the completion of the work although was delayed for_____ months beyond the agreed date on which it ought to have been completed but I find that such delay was caused partly by exceptionally bad weather and partly by lack of workmen caused by labor strikes and also their having taken up construction works under the Government and I find and award that the said (contractor) is not liable for any damage on that account.

2. I find that a part of the work executed by the said (contractor) was found to be defective in the following respects_____ (defects set out) and I award that the said (owner) is entitled to _____ as damages on that account.

3. I find and award that after deducting the said sum of _____ on account of the damages there is still due and owing to the said (contractor) in respect of the matters in dispute between the said parties to reference the sum of

_____

4. I direct the said (owner) shall pay the said sum of _____ to the said (contractor) on or before the_____ day of_____

5. I award and direct that the cost of the said (contractor) relating to and incidental to this arbitration reference including the costs of the arbitrators and of this award which is _____ shall be borne and paid by the said (owner) or whatever may be the award as to costs.

_____

Chief Arbiter

Once the award is written, the prevailing party may move to have a court of general jurisdiction confirm the decision and obtain a court judgment. Once this is done, the judgment may be executed and enforced with a writ of execution.

§ 11.3   Mediation

Mediation usually refers to court-ordered mediation once a lawsuit has been filed. For example, in Texas, parties in a divorce action are required to mediate once the divorce is filed. The court will appoint the mediators from a pool of qualified mediators registered with the court. The mediation process is designed to be used as a negotiating tool. It is almost never binding. The following forms are from Texas courts regarding mediation:

FORM 11-6
SAMPLE NOTICE REGARDING ALTERNATIVE DISPUTE RESOLUTION

Cause No. _____

_____
                                       IN THE DISTRICT COURT OF
Plaintiff   HARRIS COUNTY, TEXAS

vs

_____   _____ JUDICIAL DISTRICT
Defendant

NOTICE REGARDING ALTERNATIVE DISPUTE RESOLUTION

To All Counsel and Pro Se Parties:

The court has determined that, pursuant to Texas Civil Practice & Remedies Code § 154.021, this case is appropriate for alternative dispute resolution. (ADR).

By _____, the parties must either (1) file an agreement for ADR stating the form of ADR requested and the name of an agreed mediator, if applicable; or (2) set an objection to ADR. If no agreement or objection is filed, the court may sign an ADR order.

If you have any questions regarding this notice, please contact the court (clerk/co-ordinator), _____ at ( ) _____. Thank you for your prompt attention to this matter.

_____

JUDGE

_____ District Court

FORM 11-7
SAMPLE ORDER OF REFERRAL FOR MEDIATION

Cause No. _____

_____
                                       IN THE DISTRICT COURT OF
Plaintiff   HARRIS COUNTY, TEXAS

vs

_____   _____ JUDICIAL DISTRICT
Defendant

ORDER OF REFERRAL FOR MEDIATION

This case is appropriate for mediation pursuant to Tex. Civ. Prac. & Rem. Code Sec. 154.001, et seq. _____ is appointed Mediator in the above case, and all counsel are directed to contact Mediator to arrange the logistics of mediation. The Mediator's address and phone number are

_____.

Mediation is a mandatory, non-binding settlement conference, conducted with the assistance of the Mediator. Mediation is private, confidential, and privileged from process and discovery. After mediation, the Court will be advised only that the case did or did not settle. The Mediator shall not be a witness, and the Mediator's records may not be subpoenaed or used as evidence.

Fees for the mediation are to be agreed upon by the parties and the Mediator, and divided and borne equally by the parties unless agreed otherwise. Fees shall be paid by the parties directly to the Mediator, and shall be taxed as costs. Each party and counsel will be bound by the Rules for Mediation printed on the back of this order.

Named parties shall be present during the entire mediation process, and each corporate party must be represented by a person with authority to negotiate a settlement. The mediation must be completed within _____ days from the date of this Order or before the trial setting, whichever comes first. Counsel and parties shall try to agree upon a mediation date within the nest _____ days. If no agreed date can be scheduled, then the Mediator shall select a date, and all parties shall appear as directed by the Mediator.

Referral to mediation is not a substitute for trial and the case will be tried as assigned if not settled. Disputes as to fees may be submitted to the Court.

Signed _____ , 20_____.

_____

JUDGE

_____ District Court

FORM 11-8
SAMPLE RULES FOR MEDIATION (TEXAS DISTRICT COURT)

1. **Definition of Mediation.** Mediation is a process under which an impartial person, the Mediator, facilitates communication between the parties to promote reconciliation, settlement or understanding among them. The Mediator may suggest ways of resolving the dispute, but may not impose his own judgment on the issues for that of the parties.
2. **Agreement of Parties.** Whenever the parties have agreed to mediation they shall be deemed to have made these rules, as amended and in effect as of the date of the submission of the dispute, as part of their agreement to mediate.
3. **Consent to Mediator.** The parties consent to the appointment of the individual named as the Mediator in their case. The Mediator shall act as an advocate for resolution and shall use his best efforts to assist the parties in reaching a mutually acceptable settlement.

4. **Conditions Precedent to Serving as a Mediator.** The Mediator will only serve in cases in which the parties are represented by attorneys. The Mediator shall not serve as a Mediator in any dispute in which he has any financial or personal interest in the result of the mediation. Prior to accepting an appointment, the Mediator shall disclose any circumstance likely to create a presumption of bias or prevent a prompt meeting with the parties. In the event that the parties disagree as to whether the Mediator hall serve, the Mediator shall not serve.

5. **Authority of Mediator.** The Mediator does not have the authority to decide any issue for the parties, but will attempt to facilitate the voluntary resolution of the dispute by the parties. The Mediator is authorized to conduct joint and separate meetings with the parties and to offer suggestions to assist the parties achieve settlement. If necessary, the Mediator may also obtain expert advice concerning technical aspects of the dispute, provided that the parties agree and assume the expenses of obtaining such advice. Arrangements for obtaining such advice shall be made by the Mediator or the parties, as the Mediator shall determine.

6. **Mediator Cannot Impose Settlement.** The parties understand that the Mediator will not and cannot impose a settlement in their case and agree that a settlement, if any, must be voluntarily agreed to by the parties. The Mediator, as an advocate for settlement, will use every effort to facilitate the negotiations. The Mediator does not warrant or represent that settlement will result from the mediation process.

7. **Authority of Representatives.** PARTY REPRESENTATIVES MUST HAVE AUTHORITY TO SETTLE AND ALL PERSONS NECESSARY TO THE DECISION TO SETTLE SHALL BE PRESENT. The names and addresses of such persons shall be communicated in writing to all parties and to the Mediator.

8. **Time and Place of Mediation.** The Mediator shall fix the time of each mediation session. The mediation shall be held at the office of the Mediator, or at any other convenient location agreeable to the Mediator and the parties, as the Mediator shall determine.

9. **Identification of Matters in Dispute.** Prior to the first scheduled mediation session, each party shall provide the Mediator and all attorneys of record with an Information Sheet and Request for Mediation on the form provided by the Mediator setting forth its position with regard to the issues that need to be resolved.

10. **Privacy.** Mediation sessions are private. The parties and their representatives may attend mediation sessions. Other persons may attend only with the permission of the parties and with the consent of the Mediator.

11. **Confidentiality.** Confidential information disclosed to a Mediator by the parties or by witnesses in the course of mediation shall not be divulged by the Mediator. All records, reports, or other documents received by a Mediator while serving in that capacity shall be confidential. The Mediator shall not be compelled to divulge such records or to testify in regard to the mediation in any adversary proceeding or judicial forum. Any party that violates this agreement shall pay all fees and expenses of the Mediator and other parties, including reasonable attorneys' fees, incurred in opposing the efforts to compel testimony or records from the Mediator.

The parties shall maintain the confidentiality of the mediation and shall not rely on, or introduce as evidence in any arbitral, judicial or other proceeding a) views expressed or suggestions made by another party with respect to a possible settlement of the dispute b) admissions made by another party in the course of the mediation proceedings c) proposals made or views expressed by the Mediator or d) the fact that another party had or had not indicated a willingness to accept a proposal for settlement made by the Mediator.

12. **No Stenographic Record.** There shall be no stenographic record of the mediation process and no person shall tape record any portion of the mediation session.

13. **No Service of Process at or near the site of the Mediation Session.** No subpoenas, summons, complaints, citations, writs or other process may be served upon any person at or near the site of any mediation session upon any person entering, attending, or leaving the session.

14. **Termination of Mediation.** The mediation shall be terminated a) by the execution of a settlement agreement by the parties b)by declaration of the Mediator to the effect that further efforts at mediation are not longer worthwhile or c) after the completion of one full mediation session, by a written declaration of a party or parties to the effect that the mediation sessions are terminated.

15. **Exclusion of Liability.** The Mediator is not a necessary or proper party in judicial proceedings relating to the mediation. Neither Mediator nor any law firm employing Mediator shall be liable to any party for any act or omission in connection with any mediation conducted under these rules.

16. **Interpretation and Application of Rules.** The Mediator shall interpret and apply these rules.

17. **Fees and Expenses.** The Mediator's daily fee shall be agreed upon prior to mediation and shall be paid in advance of each mediation day. The expenses of witnesses for either side shall be paid by the party producing such witnesses. All other expenses of the mediation, including fees and expenses of the Mediator, shall be borne equally unless they agree otherwise.

APPENDIX D

GENERALIST FORMS AND AGREEMENTS (NEW)

The forms in this appendix are meant to help the paralegal who works in a generalist office and may be called upon to draft forms of all kinds, not just specific to civil litigation. Many paralegals work for lawyers who not only do civil litigation, but also are often called upon to take care of all their clients' legal needs. Be sure to check these forms to see if they meet the criteria for your state, and insert your state statutes where necessary.

FORM D–1
SAMPLE EMPLOYEE NON-COMPETE AGREEMENT

For good consideration and as an inducement for [Company] to employ [Employee], the undersigned Employee hereby agrees not to directly or indirectly compete with the business of the Company and its successors and assigns during the period of employment and for a period of _____ years following termination of employment and notwithstanding the cause or reason for termination.

The term "not compete" as used herein shall mean that the Employee shall not own, manage, operate, consult or to be employed in a business substantially similar to, or competitive with, the present business of the Company or such other business activity in which the Company may substantially engage during the term of employment.

The Employee acknowledges that the Company shall or may in reliance of this agreement provide Employee access to trade secrets, customers and other confidential data and good will. Employee agrees to retain said information as confidential and not to use said information on his or her own behalf or disclose same to any third party.

This non-compete agreement shall extend only for a radius of_____ miles from the present location of the Company and shall be in full force and effect for_____ years, commencing with the date of employment termination.

This agreement shall be binding upon and inure to the benefit of the parties, their successors, assigns, and personal representatives.

APPENDIX D

Signed this _____ day of _____ 20____.

_____
Company

_____
Employee

FORM D–2
SAMPLE DIRECTIVES TO PHYSICIANS
CALIFORNIA DIRECTIVE TO PHYSICIANS

Directive made this [date] day of [month] , 20[year].

I, [name], being of sound mind, willfully and voluntarily make known my desire that my life shall not be artificially prolonged under the circumstances set forth below, do hereby declare:

1. If at any time I should have an incurable injury, disease, or illness certified to be a terminal condition by two physicians, and where the application of life-sustaining procedures would serve only to artificially prolong the moment of my death and where my physician determines that my death is imminent whether or not life-sustaining procedures are utilized, I direct that such procedures be with-held or withdrawn, and that I be permitted to die naturally.

2. In the absence of my ability to give directions regarding the use of such life-sustaining procedures, it is my intention that this directive shall be honored by my family and physician(s) as the final expression of my legal right to refuse medical or surgical treatment and accept the consequences from such refusal.

3. If I have been diagnosed as pregnant and that diagnosis is known to my physician, this directive shall have no force or effect during the course of my pregnancy.

4. If I have been diagnosed and notified at least 14 days ago as having a terminal condition by [name of doctor], M.D., whose address is

    [address], and whose telephone number is
    [telephone number].

    I understand that if I have not filled in the physician's name and address, it shall be presumed that I did not have a terminal condition when I made out this directive.

5. This directive shall have no force or effect five years from the date filled in above.

6. I understand the full import of this directive and I am emotionally and mentally competent to make this directive.

Signed: _____

City, County and State of Residence: _____

The declarant has been personally known to me and I believe him or her to be of sound mind.

Witness: _____

Witness: _____

FORM D–3
TEXAS DIRECTIVE TO PHYSICIANS

Directive made this [date] day of [month], 20[year].

I, [name], being of sound mind, willfully and voluntarily make known my desire that my life shall not be artificially prolonged under the circumstances set forth in this directive.

1. If at any time I should have an incurable condition caused by injury, disease, or illness certified to be a terminal condition by two physicians, and if the application of life-sustaining procedures would serve only to artificially postpone the moment of my death, and if my attending physician determines that my death is imminent whether or not life-sustaining procedures are used, I direct that those procedures be withheld or withdrawn, and that I be permitted to die naturally.

2. In the absence of my ability to give directions regarding the use of those life-sustaining procedures, it is my intention that this directive be honored by my family and physicians as the final expression of my legal right to refuse medical or surgical treatment and accept the consequences from that refusal.

3. If I have been diagnosed as pregnant and that diagnosis is known to my physician, this directive has no effect during my pregnancy.

4. This directive is in effect until it is revoked.

5. I understand the full import of this directive and I am emotionally and mentally competent to make this directive.

6. I understand that I may revoke this directive at any time.

Signed _____

(City, County and State of Residence) _____

The declarant has been personally known to me and I believe the declarant to be of sound mind. I am not related to the declarant by blood or marriage. I would not be entitled to any portion of the declarant's estate on the declarant's death. I am not the attending physician of the declarant or an employee of the attending physician or a health facility in which the declarant is a patient. I am not a patient in the health care facility in which the declarant is a patient. I have no claim against any portion of the declarant's estate on the declarant's death.

Witness _____

Witness _____

FORM D–3
SAMPLE LEASE AGREEMENT

LEASE AGREEMENT made this _____ , _____ , between
_____ , "Landlord" and
_____ , "Tenant".

IT IS THEREFORE AGREED:

1. The Landlord shall lease to the Tenant the premises located at:
    _____

2. The term of this lease shall be for a period of (_____) year(s), commencing
    _____ , _____ , and terminating _____ ,
    _____ . The lease term can be extended only by mutual agreement of the parties.

3. The Tenant shall pay to the Landlord an annual sum of
    _____ ($_____) to lease the property. Rental payments shall be paid in monthly payments, each of which shall be in the amount of _____ ($_____), and each of which shall be paid on the _____ day of the month.

4. OPTION TO RENEW: The Tenant shall have an option to renew this lease on the premises for a (_____) year period upon the following terms and conditions:

    The Tenant's option to renew must be exercised in writing and must be received by the Landlord no less than (_____) days before the expiration of this lease or any extensions.

5. Any controversy or claim arising out of or relating to this lease agreement or the breach thereof shall be settled by arbitration in accordance with the rules then obtaining of the American Arbitration Association, and judgment upon the award rendered may be entered and enforced in any court having jurisdiction thereof.

6. The Landlord and the Tenant warrant and represent each to the other that the performance of this agreement does not violate any laws, statutes, local ordinances, state or federal regulations, regarding controlled substances, or otherwise, or any court order or administrative order or ruling, nor is such performance in violation of any loan document's conditions or restrictions in effect for financing, whether secured or unsecured.

7. This agreement shall be binding upon and inure to the benefit of the parties hereto and their legal representatives, successors and assigns.

8. Any notice required or desired to be given under this agreement shall be deemed given if in writing sent by certified mail to the addresses of the parties to this lease agreement as follows:

Landlord: _____
(Name & Address)

Tenant: _____
(Name & Address)

9. Captions are used in this agreement for convenience only and are not intended to be used in the construction or in the interpretation of this agreement.

10. In the event any provision of this agreement is held to be void, invalid or unenforceable in any respect, then the same shall not affect the remaining provisions hereof, which shall continue in full force and effect.

11. This agreement contains the entire understanding of the parties. It may not be changed orally. This agreement may be amended or modified only in writing that has been executed by both parties hereto.

12. This lease agreement shall be interpreted under the laws of the State of
_____.

_____   _____
Landlord   Date

_____   _____
Tenant   Date

FORM D–4
SAMPLE EMPLOYMENT AGREEMENT

Agreement made between [name of company] , located at [address], City of [city], County of [county] State of [state], herein referred to as "Company", and [name of employee], of [address], City of [city], County of [county], State of [state] herein referred to as "Employee."

Company hereby employs employee to perform such duties at such times and in such manner as the company may from time to time direct.

Employee agrees that he will perform those duties assigned to him to the best of his ability, to maintain a current and complete account of his work and expenses, to remit promptly to the company any monies paid to him or coming into his possession which belong to the company, to devote his full and undivided time to the transaction of company business and to refrain from being engaged in any other business during the tenure of his employment with the company.

In consideration of the foregoing, company agrees to pay to employee the amount of [amount] Dollars, ($), per [period of time] plus reasonable travel expenses incurred for the purpose of conducting company business.

This contract shall become effective on [date] and remain in effect until it is terminated by either party. Either party may terminate this agreement by providing the other party with [number] day's written notice of his or their intention. Should this agreement be terminated by either party, employee agrees that the payment in full to the date of termination shall fully satisfy all claims against the company under this agreement.

In witness whereof, the parties have executed this agreement at [place of execution], on [date]

_____
_____
_____

[Signatures]

FORM D–5
SAMPLE FORCIBLE DETAINER COMPLAINT

CASE: [case number]

	IN THE JUSTICE COURT
[name]	PRECINCT [judicial precinct]
Plaintiff	[county] COUNTY, [state]
vs.	
[name(s)]	
Defendant(s)	

GENERALIST FORMS AND AGREEMENTS

PLAINTIFF'S COMPLAINT FOR FORCIBLE DETAINER

TO THE HONORABLE JUDGE OF SAID COURT:

COMES NOW [plaintiffs name], Owner/landlord of the property, and hereinafter referred to as Plaintiff, and makes complaint against [defendant(s) names], hereinafter referred to as Defendant(s), for Forcible Detainer, and as grounds therefore would respectfully show the Court as follows:

1. Plaintiff resides at [plaintiffs address]

2. Defendant resides at [defendant(s) address(es)], a property located within the boundaries of Justice of the Peace, Precinct [judicial precinct], [county] County, [state].

3. Defendant gained possession of the premises on or about [date], through: (check one)

   ___a written lease, ___ an oral agreement, ___ forcible entry, ___ sufferance of the owner/landlord, and tenant still maintains possession of the premises.

4. Monthly rent is $ [amount] per month ($ [amount] per day when rent is divided by 30 days), and is due and payable on the [date] day of each month.

5. The Plaintiff claims that the owner/landlord should regain possession of the premises because of: (check one)

   ___non-payment of rent ___ breach of lease agreement as follows:
   _____
   _____
   _____.

6. Written notice to vacate and demand for possession of premises was given to tenant on the day of [month], 20[year], and was delivered to Defendant(s) in the following manner. (check one)

   ___ hand delivered, ___ posted to inside of door, or ___ mailed certified, return receipt requested.

7. Plaintiff seeks to regain possession of the premises and to order Defendant to: (check all that apply)

   ___ pay rent owed in the amount of $[amount], plus rent accruing through the date of judgment.

___pay reasonable attorney's fees of $[amount].

___ pay Court Costs.

_____

Plaintiff/Agent

Daytime Telephone Number

Any other known addresses of Defendant(s):_____

Or _____ None.

Sworn to and subscribed to before me this [date], day of [month], 20[year].

_____

Clerk of the Court/Notary Public

FORM D–6
SAMPLE IN FORMA PAUPERIS DECLARATION

IN THE UNITED STATES DISTRICT COURT
FOR THE [judicial district] DISTRICT OF [state]
[judicial division] DIVISION

[name]
PLAINTIFF

vs.   DECLARATION IN SUPPORT
                                             OF REQUEST TO PROCEED
                                             IN FORMA PAUPERIS

[name]
DEFENDANT

GENERALIST FORMS AND AGREEMENTS

I, [plaintiff name], declare, depose, and say that I am the plaintiff in the above entitled case; that in support of my motion to proceed without being required to prepay fees, costs or give security therefore, I state that because of my poverty, I am unable to pay the costs of said proceeding or to give security therefore, that I believe I am entitled to relief.

I further declare that the responses which I have made to questions and instructions below are true.

1. Are you presently employed? Yes____ No____

    a. If you answered YES, state the amount of your salary or wages per month, and give the name and address of your employer.

    _____

    _____

    _____

    b. If you answered NO, state the date of last employment and the amount of the salary and wages per month which you received.

    _____

    _____

    _____

2. Have you received, within the past 12 months, any money form any of the following sources?

a. Business, profession or form of self-employment?	___Yes	___No
b. Rent payments, interest or dividends?	___Yes	___No
c. Pensions, annuities or life insurance payments?	___Yes	___No
d. Gifts or inheritances?	___Yes	___No
e. Any other sources	___Yes	___No

    If you answered YES to any of the questions above describe each source of money and state the amount received from each during the past 12 months.

    _____

    _____

    _____

3. Do you own cash, or do you have money in a checking or savings account, including any funds in prison accounts?

    ___Yes ___No

    If you answered YES, state the total value of the items owned.

    _____

    _____

    _____

179

APPENDIX D

4. Do you own any real estate, stocks, bonds, notes, automobiles, or other valuable property, excluding ordinary household furnishings and clothing?

    ___ Yes ___ No

    If you answered YES, describe the property and state its approximate value.

    _____

    _____

    _____

5. List the persons who are dependent upon you for support; state your relationship to those persons (father, mother, spouse, etc.); and indicate how much you contribute toward their support.

    _____

    _____

    _____

I understand that a false statement or answer to any questions in this affidavit will subject me to penalties for perjury. I declare (or certify, verify, or state) and under penalty of perjury that the foregoing is true and correct (28 U.S.C. § 1746).

Signed this [date] day of [month] , 20[year].

_____
Signature of Plaintiff

I hereby certify that the plaintiff herein has the sum of $_____ on account to his/her credit at the _____ institution where he/she is confined.

I further certify that the plaintiff likewise has the following securities to his/her credit according to the records of said institution:_____

_____

_____

_____

_____
Authorized Officer of Institution

FORM D–7
SAMPLE IN FORMA PAUPERIS MOTION

IN THE UNITED STATES DISTRICT COURT
FOR THE [judicial district] DISTRICT OF [state]
[judicial division] DIVISION

[name]
PLAINTIFF

   VS.

                           CIVIL ACTION NO. [case number]

[name]
DEFENDANT

MOTION TO PROCEED IN FORMA PAUPERIS

I request permission to commence an action against the defendant named above without the payment of fees, costs or security. A proposed complaint is transmitted herewith.

In support of this motion I have attached the following:

1. Declaration in Support of Request to Proceed In Forma Pauperis relating to my inability to pay costs and fees.

2. Other material, if any.

_____

_____

_____

Date [date]   _____

                                 Signature

                                 [Street Address]

                                 [City, State, Zip Code]

                                 [Phone Number]

APPENDIX D

FORM D–8
PHYSICIAN'S CERTIFICATE OF MEDICAL EXAMINATION

Date:_____

Physician's Name: _____

Physician's Address: _____

_____

_____

Telephone Number: _____

RE: IN THE MATTER OF THE GUARDIANSHIP OF_____

_____, AN ALLEGED

INCAPACITATED PERSON.

1. I am a physician currently licensed in the State of Texas. I have been the doctor for _____ ("Proposed Ward") since _____, 20_____ at the following location:

___ Medical Facility _____

___ Proposed Ward's residence _____

___ Other Location_____

2. Prior to this examination, the proposed ward ( ) was ( ) was not informed that the communications with me would not be privileged.

3. Current residence of the proposed ward: (if known)

_____

4. Age of the proposed ward: _____ Sex : _____ Race: _____

FOR PURPOSES OF THIS EXAMINATION
THE FOLLOWING DEFINITION APPLIES:

An Incapacitated Person is an adult individual who, because of a physical or mental condition, is substantially unable to provide food, clothing, or shelter for himself/herself, to care for the individual's own physical health, or to manage the individual's own financial affairs.

Based on that examination and my observations, my opinion is as follows:

GENERALIST FORMS AND AGREEMENTS

I.

Physical Diagnosis:

_____
_____
_____
_____

Prognosis:

_____
_____
_____
_____

     Severity: ___ Mild ____ Moderate ____ Severe

Treatment:

_____
_____
_____
_____

Mental Diagnosis:

_____
_____
_____
_____

Prognosis:

_____
_____
_____
_____

     Severity: ___ Mild ____ Moderate ____ Severe

Treatment:

_____
_____
_____
_____

II.

Is senility a diagnosis of the proposed ward's incapacity? ___ YES ___ NO
Type of senility diagnosed:
___ Alzheimer's Disease   ___ Multi Infarct Dementia
___ Organic Brain Syndrome   ___ Other: (please describe)

_____
_____
_____

APPENDIX D

IF YES, please briefly describe the precise physical and mental conditions underlying the diagnosis of senility:

_____

_____

_____

Does any current medication affect the demeanor of the proposed ward?
___ YES ___ NO

Would this medication affect the proposed ward's ability to participate fully in a court's proceedings?   ___ YES ___ NO

Level of Adaptive Behavior?
___ Mild ___ Moderate ___ Severe ___ Profound

III.

Medical history of the proposed ward as related to incapacity:

_____

_____

_____

IV.

Is the proposed ward incapacitated according to the given definition?
___ YES ___ NO

If the proposed ward is incapacitated, then answer whether the incapacitation is PARTIAL OR TOTAL: ___ PARTIAL ___ TOTAL

If the proposed ward is incapacitated, then answer the following questions as to the proposed ward's ability to exercise these abilities:

1. ABILITY TO MAKE INFORMED JUDGMENT AS TO MARRIAGE
   ___ YES ___ NO

2. ABILITY TO MAKE INFORMED JUDGMENT AS TO VOTING
   ___ YES ___ NO

3. ABILITY TO APPLY FOR AND RECEIVE GOVERNMENTAL BENEFITS
   ___ YES ___ NO

4. ABILITY TO OPERATE A MOTOR VEHICLE
   ___ YES ___ NO

5. ABILITY TO MAKE DECISIONS REGARDING TRAVEL
   ___ YES ___ NO

6. ABILITY TO SEEK OR RETAIN EMPLOYMENT
___ YES ___ NO

7. ABILITY TO CONTRACT AND INCUR OBLIGATIONS
___ YES ___ NO

8. ABILITY TO SUE OR DEFEND LAWSUITS
___ YES ___ NO

9. ABILITY TO MANAGE PROPERTY OR TO MAKE ANY GIFT OR DISPOSITION OF PROPERTY
___ YES ___ NO

10. ABILITY TO DETERMINE RESIDENCE
___ YES ___ NO

11. ABILITY TO CONSENT TO MEDICAL, DENTAL, PSYCHOLOGICAL, AND PSYCHIATRIC TREATMENT AND TO THE DISCLOSURE OF RECORDS
___ YES ___ NO

12. ABILITY TO HANDLE A BANK ACCOUNT
___ YES ___ NO

13. ABILITY TO MAKE DECISIONS REGARDING FINANCIAL OBLIGATIONS
___ YES ___ NO

14. ABILITY TO ENTER INTO INSURANCE
___ YES ___ NO

If you have answered any of the questions in this section YES and believe the proposed ward is totally incapacitated, please explain:

_____
_____
_____
_____

If you have answered all of the questions in this section NO and believe that proposed ward is partially incapacitated, please explain:

_____
_____
_____
_____

V.

If you have any remarks concerning other sections, please explain:

_____
_____
_____
_____

_____
Physician's signature

FORM D-9
SAMPLE CONTRACT FOR PURCHASE OF RESIDENCE OR OTHER REAL ESTATE

THIS CONTRACT is made on the _____ day of _____, 20__ by and between
_____ (Seller) whose address is
_____ and
_____ (Buyer) whose address is
_____.

WHEREAS, Seller is the owner of the certain property located at

_____

and desires to sell said property to Buyer; and

WHEREAS, Buyer agrees to buy the property located at

_____;

NOW, THEREFORE, THE PARTIES AGREE AS FOLLOWS:

1. The Seller agrees to sell and the Buyer agrees to buy the property located
    at _____, and more particularly described
    as follows:

    consisting of the land and all the buildings, other improvements, and
    fixtures on the land; and all of the Seller's rights relating to the land.

2. Purchase Price. The terms upon which this offer is made are as follows:

    Purchase price : _____ dollars ($)

    Deposit upon signing of this contract: _____ dollars ($)

    Amount of mortgage: _____ dollars ($)

Balance to be paid at closing of title, by certified bank cashier's, or attorney trust check (subject to adjustment at closing): _____ dollars ($)

Total: _____ dollars ($)

3. Deposit Monies. All deposit monies will be held in a non-interest-bearing trust account by _____ until closing of Title.

4. Time and Place of Closing. Buyer and Seller agree that closing shall take place on the _____ day of _____, 20__. Buyer and Seller further agree that time is of the essence. Closing will be held at

    _____.

5. Transfer of Ownership. At the closing, the Seller will transfer ownership of the property to the Buyer. The Seller will give the Buyer a properly executed bargain and sale deed with covenants against grantors acts and an Affidavit of Title.

6. Personal Property and Fixtures. All fixtures are included in this sale unless they are listed below as being excluded.

    The following items are EXCLUDED from this sale:

7. Physical Condition of the Property. This property is being sold "as is." Seller does not make any claims or promises about the condition or value of any of the property included in this sale. Buyer makes this offer in full reliance upon his own independent investigation and judgment. There are no verbal agreements, which modify or affect this offer. The acceptance of a deed by Buyer shall be deemed to be the full performance of every obligation on the part of Seller.

8. Repair Limitation. In no event will the Seller expend more than _____ dollars ($) for repairs.

9. Condition and Use of Property. Seller makes no representation as to the condition of the property or that the premises comply with local, county, state, or federal ordinances and statues. Buyer must obtain certificates of occupancy and all other municipal certificates. Seller will not provide the buyer with a Certificate of Occupancy, Lead Paint Inspection, if applicable, or any other municipal certificate from the municipality in connection with the transfer. Buyer is advised to contact the municipality for any matters, which are of concern to him prior to signing this contract. By signing this contract, Buyer has made the necessary investigation concerning the obtainment of the Certificate of Occupancy or any other municipal certificate required by the municipality in a transfer of property within this municipality.

10. Risk of Loss. The Seller is responsible for any additional damage to the property, except for normal wear and tear, until the closing of title. If there is substantial damage, the Seller reserves the right to cancel the contract and refund Buyer's deposit monies or to negotiate the terms of the repairs with the Buyer.

11. Property Lines. The Seller does not have a survey for this premises and makes no representation that all buildings, driveways, and other improvements on the property are within its boundary lines or that no improvements on adjoining properties extend across the boundary lines of this property.

12. Ownership. The Seller agrees to transfer and the Buyer agrees to accept ownership of the property free of all claims and right of others, except for: recorded easements, _____.

13. Title Insurance. Buyer and Seller agree that Seller shall order a title binder for the subject property from a title company authorized to do business in the State of _____ in order to ensure a timely closing of subject property. Buyer shall pay for all costs associated with these title charges except as indicated below. Seller's attorney shall provide Buyer's attorney with appropriate information regarding where title has been ordered. In the event that the subject transaction does not close, through no fault of the Buyer, Seller shall be responsible for all title charges.

14. Correcting Defects. If the property does not comply with Paragraphs 12 & 13 of this contract, the Buyer must notify the Seller and the Seller will be given an additional _____ days to correct any defect. If the property still does not comply after _____ days, Buyer or Seller may cancel this contract. In the event that Seller's title is uninsurable, then Seller's only obligation will be to refund Buyer's deposit.

15. Assessments for Municipal Improvements. Seller will pay all unpaid assessments against the property for work completed before the closing. If the improvement is not completed before the closing, then Buyer will be solely responsible.

16. Adjustments at Closing. The Buyer and Seller agree to adjust the following expenses as of the date of closing: municipal water and sewer charges, real estate taxes, condominium dues, if applicable, and rents. If the property is fueled by fuel oil, the Buyer will be responsible to pay the Seller for any fuel that remains in the burner on the day of closing. The Buyer and Seller may require that any person with a claim or right affecting the property be paid off prior to closing.

17. Possession. Buyer shall receive possession at the closing of title.

18. Damages. If this offer is accepted by the Seller, and the Seller's title is insurable and Buyer neglects or refuses to complete the purchase of this property, and to execute and deliver all documents required, then the Buyer will be held liable for any and all actual damages caused to the Seller by such breach.

19. Completed Agreement. This contract is the entire and only agreement between Buyer and Seller. This contract replaces and cancels any previous agreements between the Buyer and Seller. This contract can only be changed by an agreement in writing signed by both Buyer and Seller.

20. Parties Liable. This contract is binding upon Buyer and Seller and all their heirs, successors and assigns.

21. Notices. All notices under this contract must be in writing. The notices must be delivered personally or by certified mail, return receipt requested to the other party at the address written in this contract. Service of any notices to Buyer's attorney shall be deemed as notice to Buyer.

22. Broker's Commission. The Seller agrees to pay a commission fee of ____ percent (%) of the purchase price to _____ (Broker). This commission is not earned or to be paid until the title has been transferred and the purchase price has been paid. This commission will be paid at the closing, and taken out of the Seller's proceeds. Buyer represents that he has not used the services of any other broker than above named.

23. Assignability. This agreement shall not be assignable by the Buyer without the Seller's written consent.

24. Offer to Purchase. This contract constitutes the Buyer's offer to purchase the subject property. Acceptance of the Buyer's offer is subject to Seller's review of the aforesaid document and shall be evidenced by Seller's execution of same.

25. Legal Representation. Buyer acknowledges that Buyer has the right to hire a lawyer to represent Buyer's interests in this transaction.

_____

_____

Buyer Date

I accept and agree to be bound by the above contract.

_____

_____

Seller Date

FORM D–10
SAMPLE ESCROW AGREEMENT

AGREEMENT between [name of seller] (Seller), [name of escrow agent] (Escrow Agent), and [name of buyer],(Buyer).

Seller and Buyer have simultaneously with the execution of this agreement entered into a contract (the Contract) by which Seller conveys to Buyer the following:

[list property to be conveyed]

The closing will take place [date], 19XX, at [time], at the offices of [business], located at [address], or at such place and time Seller and Buyer may jointly designate in writing. In accordance with the Contract, Buyer must deposit $[amount down]. This amount will be considered a downpayment on this account, and will be held in escrow by Escrow Agent.

The $[amount down] down payment referred to above has been paid to Escrow Agent by Buyer. Escrow Agent acknowledges receipt of $[amount down] from Buyer by check, subject to collection.

If the closing takes place under the Contract, Escrow Agent at the time of closing shall pay the amount deposited with Agent to Seller or in accordance with Seller's written instructions. Escrow Agent shall make simultaneously transfer of the said property to the Buyer.

If no closing takes place under the Contract, Escrow Agent shall continue to hold the amount deposited until receipt of written authorization for its deposition signed by both Buyer and Seller. If there is any dispute as to whom Escrow Agent is to deliver the amount deposited, Escrow Agent shall hold the sum until the parties' rights are finally determined in an appropriate action or proceeding or until a court orders Escrow Agent to deposit the down payment with it. If Escrow Agent does not receive a proper written authorization from Seller and Buyer, or if an action or proceeding to determine Seller's and Buyer's rights is not begun or diligently prosecuted, Escrow Agent is under no obligation to bring an action or proceeding in court to deposit the sum held, but may continue to hold the deposit.

Escrow Agent assumes no liability except that of a stakeholder. Escrow Agent's duties are limited to those specifically set out in this Agreement. Escrow Agent shall incur no liability to anyone except for willful misconduct or gross negligence so long as the

GENERALIST FORMS AND AGREEMENTS

Escrow Agent acts in good faith. Seller and Buyer release Escrow Agent from any act done or omitted in good faith in the performance of Escrow Agent's duties.

Special provisions:

[list any special provisions]

Whereof the parties sign their names this [day] day of   [month], 20XX

Signed in the presence of:

[witness]   [seller]
_____   _____
Witness   Seller

[witness]   [buyer]
_____   _____
Witness   Buyer

[witness]   [escrow agent]
_____   _____
Witness   Escrow Agent

FORM D–11
SAMPLE MEDICAL POWER OF ATTORNEY

DESIGNATION OF HEALTH CARE AGENT.

I,_____(insert your name) appoint:

Name:_____

Address:_____

Phone_____

as my agent to make any and all health care decisions for me, except to the extent I state otherwise in this document. This medical power of attorney takes effect if I become unable to make my own health care decisions and this fact is certified in writing by my physician.

APPENDIX D

LIMITATIONS ON THE DECISION-MAKING AUTHORITY OF MY AGENT ARE AS FOLLOWS:

_____

_____

DESIGNATION OF ALTERNATE AGENT.

(You are not required to designate an alternate agent but you may do so. An alternate agent may make the same health care decisions as the designated agent if the designated agent is unable or unwilling to act as your agent. If the agent designated is your spouse, the designation is automatically revoked by law if your marriage is dissolved.)

If the person designated as my agent is unable or unwilling to make health care decisions for me, I designate the following persons to serve as my agent to make health care decisions for me as authorized by this document, who serve in the following order:

A. First Alternate Agent

Name: _____

Address: _____

Phone _____

B. Second Alternate Agent

Name: _____

Address: _____

Phone _____

The original of this document is kept at:

_____

_____

_____

The following individuals or institutions have signed copies:

Name: _____

Address: _____

_____

GENERALIST FORMS AND AGREEMENTS

Name: _____

Address: _____

_____

DURATION.

I understand that this power of attorney exists indefinitely from the date I execute this document unless I establish a shorter time or revoke the power of attorney. If I am unable to make health care decisions for myself when this power of attorney expires, the authority I have granted my agent continues to exist until the time I become able to make health care decisions for myself.

(IF APPLICABLE) This power of attorney ends on the following date:_____

PRIOR DESIGNATIONS REVOKED.

I revoke any prior medical power of attorney.

ACKNOWLEDGMENT OF DISCLOSURE STATEMENT.

I have been provided with a disclosure statement explaining the effect of this document. I have read and understand that information contained in the disclosure statement.

(YOU MUST DATE AND SIGN THIS POWER OF ATTORNEY.)

I sign my name to this medical power of attorney on _____ day of
_____ (month, year)
at_____ (City and
State).

_____ (Signature)

_____ (Print Name)

STATEMENT OF FIRST WITNESS.

I am not the person appointed as agent by this document. I am not related to the principal by blood or marriage. I would not be entitled to any portion of the principal's estate on the principal's death. I am not the attending physician of the principal or an employee of the attending physician. I have no claim against any portion of the principal's estate on the principal's death. Furthermore, if I am an employee of a health care facility in which the principal is a patient, I am not involved in providing direct patient care to the principal and am not an officer, director, partner, or business

APPENDIX D

office employee of the health care facility or of any parent organization of the health care facility

Signature: _____

Print Name: _____Date: _____

Address: _____

SIGNATURE OF SECOND WITNESS.

Signature: _____

Print Name: _____Date: _____

Address: _____

INDEX

INDEX